Security Designs for the Cloud, Iot, and Social Networking

Scrivener Publishing
100 Cummings Center, Suite 541J
Beverly, MA 01915-6106

Publishers at Scrivener
Martin Scrivener (martin@scrivenerpublishing.com)
Phillip Carmical (pcarmical@scrivenerpublishing.com)

Security Designs for the Cloud, Iot, and Social Networking

Edited by

Dac-Nhuong Le

Haiphong University, Haiphong, Vietnam

Chintan Bhatt

U & P U Patel Department of Computer Engineering,
Charotar University of Science and Technology, Changa, Gujarat, India

Mani Madhukar

IBM Innovation Center, Block A, Embassy Golf Links, Bangalore, India

Scrivener
Publishing

This edition first published 2019 by John Wiley & Sons, Inc., 111 River Street, Hoboken, NJ 07030, USA and Scrivener Publishing LLC, 100 Cummings Center, Suite 541J, Beverly, MA 01915, USA
© 2020 Scrivener Publishing LLC
For more information about Scrivener publications please visit www.scrivenerpublishing.com.

Wiley Global Headquarters
111 River Street, Hoboken, NJ 07030, USA

For details of our global editorial offices, customer services, and more information about Wiley products visit us at www.wiley.com.

Limit of Liability/Disclaimer of Warranty
While the publisher and authors have used their best efforts in preparing this work, they make no representations or warranties with respect to the accuracy or completeness of the contents of this work and specifically disclaim all warranties, including without limitation any implied warranties of merchantability or fitness for a particular purpose. No warranty may be created or extended by sales representatives, written sales materials, or promotional statements for this work. The fact that an organization, website, or product is referred to in this work as a citation and/or potential source of further information does not mean that the publisher and authors endorse the information or services the organization, website, or product may provide or recommendations it may make. This work is sold with the understanding that the publisher is not engaged in rendering professional services. The advice and strategies contained herein may not be suitable for your situation. You should consult with a specialist where appropriate. Neither the publisher nor authors shall be liable for any loss of profit or any other commercial damages, including but not limited to special, incidental, consequential, or other damages. Further, readers should be aware that websites listed in this work may have changed or disappeared between when this work was written and when it is read.

Library of Congress Cataloging-in-Publication Data

ISBN 978-1-119-59226-6

Cover image: Pixabay.Com
Cover design by Russell Richardson

Set in size of 11pt and Minion Pro by Manila Typesetting Company, Makati, Philippines

10 9 8 7 6 5 4 3 2 1

Contents

Part I Security Designs for the Cloud Network

Part II Security Designs for the Internet of Things and Social Networks

Bright Keswan, Tarini Ch. Mishra, Ambarish G. Mohapatra, Poonam Keswani

Lalit Mohan Goyal, Mamta Mittal, Asheesh Sharma

List of Figures

List of Tables

Foreword

The distributed computing paradigm emerged as an alternative to expensive supercomputers to increase modularity and flexibility of computing infrastructures. Cloud computing represents the most consolidated distributed computing model widely adopted in private and business applications because it provides massive availability of computation and storage resources on demand. Looking at the future of Cloud computing it is easy to understand that it will be exploited in many different sectors which can benefit a lot from such a flexible and efficient technology. Indeed, the market of Cloud computing is changing.

Internet of Things (IoT) projects were still at the beginning stage in 2015, thus IoT workloads were only a small proportion of public cloud environments. There are currently 6.4 billion IoT devices in use around the world. Their number, capabilities, as well as their scope of use, keeps growing and changing rapidly. Gartner forecasts the number of IoT devices will reach 20.8 billion by 2020, and projects that by then IoT service spending will reach \$1,534 billion and hardware spending \$1,477 billion. IoT technologies are becoming strategic for the future competitiveness of enterprises that are investing in innovation and in a digital transformation. Moreover, public cloud systems offer perfect services for back-end environments for IoT services and devices.

To fit IoT requirements, new distributed computing models have been investigated in the literature (e.g., Edge Computing, Fog Computing, Servlet,...) to extend IoT resources into centralized datacenters (e.g., Cloud datacenters) or at the edge of IoT systems (e.g., Edge microdatacenters). Derived from Cloud computing, Edge computing aims to collect and process data at the edge of a digital network, close to the source of the data. Edge computing acts as an intermediate layer between IoT devices and the cloud and is able to handle some of the requests for storage and computation locally instead of remotely in the cloud. That way, Edge computing reduces the latency in resolving requests and allows real-time handling of a subset of requests.

This complex amalgamation of computing systems and networks for supporting IoT application requirements leads to a plethora of research and technological challenges which are new, especially as regards to security and privacy in IoT. Security and privacy is becoming increasingly important in IoT due to the deployment of a huge number of IoT devices (*sensors and actuators*) across various sectors, including Industry 4.0, smart cities, healthcare, homes, buildings, and smart cars. The existing literature describes many existing IoT protocols and presents the open research issues, specifically in the area of security and privacy. For example, recent IoT research conducted by the University of Graz in Austria, led to the discovery of 18 bugs in MQTT (*Message Queuing Transport Telemetry*) IoT protocol implementations, among others. Although a number of research activities have addressed securing data in the cloud, the area of securing data in the IoT (*edge datacenter,*

IoT devices, software-defined IoT networks, etc.) with tens of billions of densely deployed and often highly mobile and heterogeneous IoT nodes, has only recently begun to receive significant attention.

I would like to congratulate the editors of this volume, Dac-Nhuong Le, Chintan Bhatt and Mani Madhukar, for compiling such timely and comprehensive research contributions. The diversity of topics covered by different chapters and the profiles of contributing authors, who are internationally established researchers, is very impressive. Different chapters describe cutting edge research efforts that try to get to the depth of many of the above listed challenges, with an overall aim of providing a detailed literature review, starting from fundamental concepts to more specific technologies and application use cases. For the reasons described above, I firmly believe that this edited book will provide a comprehensive resource to students, researchers, and practitioners, and have a long-lasting impact on this important and growing research and technological field.

Rajiv Ranjan, PhD
Chair and Professor of Internet of Things, Newcastle University, UK
Chair and Professor (Visiting), Chinese University of Geosciences, Wuhan, China
Honorary Associate Professor, Australian National University, Australia
web: http://rajivranjan.net/

Preface

Due to the rapid growth of all kinds of devices currently being controlled over the Internet, the various products come with security issues. This book examines the issues and vulnerabilities inherent in these products and what can be done to solve them by investigating their roots. Programming and attention to good security practices can combat these problems, which are a result of the lax security processes of the internet of things, cloud computing and social media. This book is for those interested in understanding the vulnerabilities of the internet of things and cloud computing such as programmers who have not yet been focusing on the IoT, security professionals and a wide array of interested hackers and creators. This book assumes the reader has little experience or knowledge of the internet of things, cloud computing and social media.

Included in the 16 chapters of this book are the following studies. In Chapter 1, Anindita Desarkar and Ajanta Das present a few well-known encryption-decryption-based algorithms which are aimed at protecting cloud stored data from unauthorized access. Chapter 2 provides a detailed understanding of security issues in cloud computing. This study helps in determining and categorizing its prime security-related issues and concerns, thereby presenting an overview of the present scenario of security in the cloud computing environment. In Chapter 3, Dumka *et al.* discuss different types of security and challenges in mobile cloud computing which integrate cloud computing with mobile technology. This chapter expands the security in mobile cloud computing into three subcategories: Infrastructural or architectural issues, privacy issues and compliance issues. Chapter 4 determines the effect of security issues and conceivable arrangements, providing future security-applicable headings to those in charge of designing, developing, and maintaining fog systems. In Chapter 5, the authors examine security worries of the three cloud computing models, specifically software as a service (SaaS), platform as a service (PaaS) and infrastructure as a service (IaaS). This chapter likewise examines cloud-based security tools, cloud data encryption, homomorphic encryption and access control (identity access of the executives). A competent IoT framework is envisaged for privacy preservation and data security in Chapter 6. Chapter 7 presents an intricate movie genre recommender engine based on the K-means clustering combined with the powerful Pearson correlation similarity measure. It takes basic information from users, asks them to enter a rating for the movie and uses machine learning to give the user a recommended genre. In Chapter 8, Roy *et al.* present the various implications of SMAC (*social networks, mobiles, analytics, cloud*) for society and its possible solutions. The authors of Chapter 9 have tried to explain how we can mechanize home automation utilizing Arduino and REST engineering. The outcome likewise indicates how the utilization of Arduino and REST engineering is advantageous when contrasted with other accessible resources in the field of IoT. Chapter 10 presents a survey of the engagement of FC to unlock the potential of IoT services and also discusses the security and privacy issues of IoT. The principle of FC is discussed along with different IoT domains. Chapter 11 throws light on network-based intrusion detection systems (NIDSs) and host-based intrusion detection systems (HIDSs). Neural network, hidden Markov model and data mining techniques are mostly used in the field of database intrusion detection, which is detailed briefly in this chapter. Chapter 12 explains how to provide a solution to make healthcare more efficient in order to decrease the ratio of people with diseases like heart disease, cancer, diabetes and to manage stress. Chapter 13 introduces a holistic approach to ensure such data protection incorporating differential privacy of sensitive data in the healthcare system. The relevant algorithm for the proposed model is explained in this chapter. Chapter 14 describes different advancements and applications in fog computing. A detailed framework about CPSS (cyber-physical-social systems) in intelligent transportation is explained in Chapter 15. It characterizes the different methods and approaches required for the application of CPSS in smart transportation. Finally, the information in Chapter 16 will be useful for research scholars, industries and all working parents for handling the problem of keeping track of their toddlers with smart ways of parenting.

This book is anticipated for researchers, engineers, and developers and disseminates cutting-edge research that delivers insights into the tools, opportunities, novel strategies, techniques, and challenges for handling security issues in cloud computing, Internet of Things and social networking. As the editors of this book, we have a great appreciation for the authors' high quality of contributions as well as for the respected reviewers for their accurate, detailed and timely comments. We hope this book will stimulate further research into how to handle open security issues.

Dr. Chintan Bhatt
U & P U Patel Department of Computer Engineering
Charotar University of Science and Technology, Changa, Gujarat, India

Acknowledgments

First of all, I would like to thank the authors for contributing their excellent chapters to this book. Without their contributions, this book would not have been possible. Thanks to all my friends for sharing my happiness at the start of this project and following up with their encouragement when it seemed too difficult to complete.

I would like to acknowledge and thank the most important people in my life, my grandfather, grandmother, and finally thanks to my wife. This book has been a long-cherished dream of mine which would not have been turned into reality without the support and love of these amazing people, who encouraged me despite my not giving them the proper time and attention. I am also grateful to my best friends for their blessings and unconditional love, patience and encouragement.

Dac-Nhuong Le, PhD
Deputy-Head, Faculty of Information Technology
Haiphong University, Haiphong, Vietnam

Acronyms

API	Application Programming Interface
AES	Advanced Encryption Algorithm
ARP	Address Resolution Protocol
AP	Access Point
ABE	Attribute-Based Encryption
BLA	Bees Life Algorithm
CA	Certifying Authority
CASB	Cloud Access Security Broker
CIA	Confidentiality, Integrity, and Availability
CSP	Cloud Service Provider
CP	Clinical Pathway
CP-ABE	Ciphertext-Policy Attribute-Based Encryption
CPS	Cyber-Physical System
CPSS	Cyber-Physical-Social Systems
CPO	Clinical Pathway Ontology
CPSC	Clinical Pathway State Chart
CoF	Cloud-Based Card-on-File
CSA	Cloud Security Alliance
CS	Cuckoo Search
CoAP	Constrained Application Protocol
CTS	Cyber Transportation Systems
DBMS	Database Management System
DoS	Denial of Service
DDoS	Distributed Denial of Service
DNS	Domain Name System
DNSSEC	Domain Name System Security Extensions
D2D	Device to Device
D2S	Device to Server
DDF	Distributed Data Flow
DS-CSH	Digital Signature with a Chaotic Secure Hashing
DLP	Data Loss Prevention
EGA	Enhanced Genetic Algorithm
EGA-CA	Enhanced Genetic Algorithm-Cultural Algorithm
EGA-CS	Enhanced Genetic Algorithm-Cuckoo Search
E-PSO	Evolutionary Particle Swarm Optimization
EMG	Electromyography

EEG	Electroencephalogram
EM	Exponential Mechanism
ECG	Electrocardiograph
FC	Fog Computing
GSR	Galvanic Skin Response
GPS	Global Positioning Systems
GSM	Global System for Mobile Communications
H-SVM	Hardware-Assisted Secure Virtual Machines
HRV	Heart Rate Variability
HSPA	High Speed Packet Access
HTTPS	Hypertext Transfer Protocol Secure
HIDS	Host-Based Intrusion Detection System
ICT	Information and Communications Technology
IoT	Internet of Things
IP	Internet Protocol
IT	Information Technology
ITS	Intelligent Transportation System
ISP	Internet Service Provider
IDS	Intrusion Detection System
ISA	Instruction Set Architecture
IaaS	Infrastructure as a Service
IEEE	Institute of Electrical and Electronics Engineers
ICO	Internet Connected Object
IOP	Intraocular Pressure
IDC	International Data Corporation
LAN	Local-Area Network
LPWAN	Low Power Wide Area Network
LI	Logical Integrity
LWM2M	Lightweight Machine to Machine
LM	Laplace Mechanism
MFA	Multifactor Authentication
MITM	Man-in-the-Middle Attack
M2M	Machine to Machine
MQTT	Message Queue Telemetry Transport
MCC	Mobile Cloud Computing
MaaSP	Mobile as a Service Provider
MaaSC	Mobile as a Service Consumer
MaaSB	Mobile as a Service Broker
NIDS	Network-Based Intrusion Detection System
NIST	National Institute of Standards and Technology
NFC	Near-Field Communications
NCP	No. of Clinical Pathway Data Points
OS	Operating System
OTP	One-Time Password
OWL	Web Ontology Language
PC	Personal Computer

P2P	Peer to Peer
PaaS	Platform as a Service
PSO	Particle Swarm Optimization
PI	Physical Integrity
QoL	Quality of Life
QoS	Quality of Service
QR	Code Quick Response Code
QoE	Quality of Experience
RTT	Round-Trip Time
RFID	Radio Frequency Identification
SLA	Service Level Agreement
SDN	Software-Defined Network
SecSDN	Secure Software-Defined Network
SSL	Secure Sockets Layer
SaaS	Software as a Service
SPA	Security Program Assessment
SQL	Structured Query Language
SMS	Short Message Service
SHA	Secure Hashing Algorithm
S2S	Server to Server
SMAC	Social, Mobile, Analytics and Cloud
SE	Secure Element
SIPRNet	Secret Internet Protocol Router Network
SGD	Stochastic Gradient Descent
SSID	Service Set Identifier
TCP	Transmission Control Protocol
TLS	Transport Layer Security
TEE	Trusted Execution Environment
TPM	Trusted Platform Module
TPA	Third-Party Auditor
TP	True Positives
URL	Uniform Resource Locator
URN	Uniform Resource Name
VM	Virtual Machine
VLAN	Virtual Local Area Network
XAMP	X-Cross Platform
XSS	Cross-Site Scripting
WSN	Wireless Sensor Network
WBAN	Wireless Body Area Network

PART I

SECURITY DESIGNS FOR THE CLOUD NETWORK

CHAPTER 1

ENCRYPTION ALGORITHM FOR DATA SECURITY IN CLOUD COMPUTING

ANINDITA DESARKAR[1], AJANTA DAS[2]

[1] Department of Computer Science and Engineering, Jadavpur University, Kolkata, India
[2] Department of Computer Science and Engineering, University of Engineering & Management, Kolkata, Kolkata, India
Email: aninditadesarkar@gmail.com, cse.dr.ajantadas@gmail.com

Abstract

Cloud computing is the concept of using a virtual pool of resources to provide users with solutions to various computing problems via the internet. IT services are provided on an on-demand basis, which are accessible from anywhere, anytime through authorized users. "Storage as a Service" is one of the major services for the end users where sensitive data is stored in the cloud. As a result, data vulnerability becomes a common phenomenon where exploitation occurs through the provider or unauthorized users. So, data protection is the heart of data security where encryption algorithms play a major role. The greater complexity of these algorithms makes it more secure and safe compared to the other techniques. This chapter presents a few of the well-known encryption-decryption-based algorithms which are aimed at protecting cloud stored data from unauthorized access.

Keywords: Cloud computing, encryption algorithm, data security

1.1 Introduction

Cloud computing, which is the next-generation paradigm in computation, delivers applications and resources on an on-demand basis via the internet as services [1]. It provides an environment of hardware and software resources over the network to satisfy user requirements.

According to the National Institute of Standards and Technology (NIST) [2], cloud computing allows ubiquitous, convenient, on-demand network access to a shared pool of configurable computing resources that can be rapidly provisioned and released with minimal management effort or service provider interaction. Resources include computing applications, network resources, platforms, software services, virtual servers and computing infrastructure [3].

Computing and data storage are two basic functionalities provided by cloud computing. Cloud service consumers get the necessary access to their data and complete the computing job through the internet. They have no idea about the storage location of data and machine details which perform the computing task.

Data protection and security is the primary objective in data storage to gain the user's trust and make the implementation successful. Hence, data security is a burning issue in this domain, as data is scattered throughout various machines located in various locations. This makes it more complicated compared to the traditional systems. Though data security is the major issue, it's accompanied by several others like compliance, privacy, trust, and legal matters. Hence, adequate tools and techniques are required to be in place to make the cloud adoption initiative successful. In this chapter, various well-known techniques in cloud data security are reviewed for the purpose of achieving this goal.

Section 1.5.3 highlights existing research works in related areas. A brief overview of cloud computing is depicted in Section 1.5.4. Section 1.5.5 discusses various well-known techniques implemented in this domain. It discusses a few well-known algorithms from both domains – symmetric encryption and asymmetric encryption. Section 1.5.6 presents the comparison of these algorithms based on various parameters. Performance analysis of encryption algorithms in cloud is presented in Section 1.5.7. Section 1.5.8 contains the conclusions drawn on the basis of the above.

1.2 Related Work

Kartit *et al.* have reviewed the commonly used encryption algorithms for data security and proposed a simple, secure and privacy-preserving architecture for inter-cloud data sharing. This architecture is built on the concept of encryption and decryption algorithms, aimed at securing cloud data from unauthorized access [4]. A brief overview of various symmetric and asymmetric algorithms along with their comparison is presented by Bhardwaj *et al.* in their paper [5]. The research was enhanced by Iyer *et al.* [6], who have presented an algorithm which works towards providing a secure way to communicate and store data in cloud servers.

Conner *et al.* [7] have proposed an effective reputation management system with associated trust establishment by using multiple scoring functions and implemented the security service on a realistic application scenario in distributed environments. Friedman and West [8] and Ristenpart *et al.* [9] have presented several privacies as well as security issues that arise in a cloud computing framework. Yan *et al.* [10] described a nice scheme for handling data protection in terms of confidentiality by implementing amalgamation of identity management with hierarchical identity-based cryptography for distribution of the key as well as mutual authentication in the cloud infrastructure. The security and privacy of data stored in cloud is the challenging task. Encryption algorithms are used for data security. In each algorithm an encryption key is used that can only be accessed by the authorized user. Ukil *et al.* [11] proposed an architecture and security model towards better protection of confidentiality and privacy in a public cloud infrastructure which does not depend on the deployment of the cloud.

1.3   Cloud Computing - A Brief Overview

Cloud computing refers to the delivery of all the computing services which majorly includes servers, storage, databases, networking and software over the internet for providing resource flexibility and lowering operating cost of the users. Lower cost, speed, global scale, productivity, performance and security are the top benefits of adopting this new technique over the traditional one. It eliminates or reduces the capital expense of buying necessary hardware and software, which works towards overall cost reduction. As most of the services are provided on demand, a huge amount of computing services can be arranged within a few minutes. It is also location independent because everything is accessible online. Optimized performance is achieved as the data centers, responsible for providing secure services, are updated with the latest generation of fast and efficient computing hardware. The following subsections describe its essential characteristics, various layers and commonly available deployment models [12].

1.3.1   Essential Characteristics

Cloud computing includes various unique characteristics, of which the following five are the primary ones.

- On-Demand Self-Service: An end user can get the required services automatically without human interaction with each service provider.

- Broad Network Access: Services are available over the network and accessed through standard mechanisms which encourage the use of heterogeneous thin or thick client platforms.

- Resource Pooling: The provider's computing resources are selected across the multiple consumers through a multi-tenant model, with different physical and virtual resources dynamically assigned and reassigned according to consumer demand. The customer has no or little knowledge about the location of the resources. However, they may be able to get generic information about it like country, state or datacenter. Examples of resources include storage, processing, memory and network bandwidth.

- Elasticity: Resource allocation can be increased or decreased based on the user's need or demand. The consumer gets the feeling of unlimited availability of resources as it can be arranged in any valid quantity at any time.

- Measured Service: Cloud systems automatically control and optimize resource use by leveraging a metering capability at some level of abstraction appropriate to the type of service (e.g., storage, processing, bandwidth and active user accounts). Usage of resources is monitored, controlled and reported to provide transparency to the provider as well as the consumer.

1.3.2   Layers of Cloud Computing

Figure 1.1 below presents the three well-known layers of cloud computing: IaaS, PaaS and SaaS.

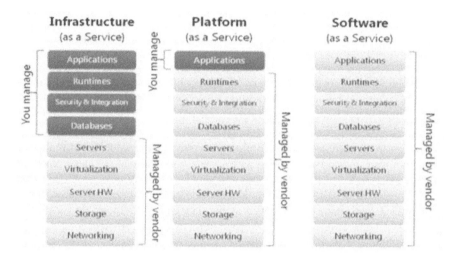

Figure 1.1   Layers of cloud computing.

Infrastructure as a Service (IaaS): IaaS is the option which provides only the base infrastructure. The end user needs to configure and manage the platform and environment and build all the required applications on top of it. Examples include AWS (EC2), GCP (CE) and Microsoft Azure (VM).

Platform as a Service (PaaS): PaaS is a cloud computing model where hardware and software tools are delivered by a third party provider. The user can build and manage applications without incurring the hazards of building and maintaining the infrastructure. Google App Engine, CloudFoundry, Heroku, and AWS (Beanstalk) are some examples of PaaS. The primary benefit of PaaS is its simplicity and convenience for users because they can access the infrastructure anywhere through a web browser. As a result, capital expenditure is removed or reduced to a great extent, which is traditionally required in the business. However, customers can face difficulties if providers experience the service outage or infrastructure disruption.

Software as a Service (SaaS): SaaS model allows providing software application as a service to the users. It basically refers to the concept of "software availability based on demand." Users generally access it through a thin client via a web browser. A few of the important characteristics include availability of software over the net, software maintenance by the vendors, subscription-based software licensing, centralized feature updating which mandates the user to download patches and upgrades. In this model, most of the services like applications, data, middleware, servers, storage and networking are maintained and managed by vendors and users only use it. Gmail is the most common example of this model.

1.3.3 Cloud Deployment Models

Following are the three majorly used deployment models which are commonly used across the world. The appropriate model should be chosen based on the organizational need.

- Private Cloud: A private cloud consists of resources which are exclusively available to a specific organization. The data center can be located on the company's onsite location or managed by third party service providers. Here all the services and infrastructure are maintained in a private network.

- Public Cloud: A public cloud is owned and maintained by third party cloud service providers where all the resources are available to multiple stakeholders or organizations. The service provider gives necessary access to the services based on the account created by the users. The user pays the cost based on the services they use.

- Hybrid Cloud: Hybrid cloud merges both the types – public and private – by the techniques which allow data and applications to be shared between them. The business receives greater flexibility, more deployment options, improvement in existing infrastructure, security and compliance by allowing the movement of data and applications between private and public clouds.

1.4 Data Security in Cloud Storage

Cloud storage is the convenient way to provide data access anytime and anywhere across the globe. Benefits brought by cloud storage majorly include scalability, accessibility and decreased IT overhead, which are also the driving factors of rapid adoption of this technology. So, there is a crying need for improved tools and techniques which keep sensitive data safe and secure in the cloud. Businesses and several enterprises have already adopted cloud services as it's able to provide cost-effective and flexible solutions as an alternative to expensive, locally implemented hardware. However, it also invites several unwanted risks as confidential files and sensitive data may be exposed to the outer world. So, enterprises always try to deploy new and improved technologies to secure cloud storage though initial measures which are implemented by cloud providers as a part of their solution. Authentication, access control and basic encryption techniques are included in the preliminary protection scheme. Subsection 1.5.5.1 of this chapter presents a few burning issues in the domain of cloud and Subsection 1.5.5.2 discusses a few such techniques which are used to increase cloud data security [13].

1.4.1 Security Issues in Cloud

Data security is a common concern for any technology, but it becomes a major challenge in the case of cloud infrastructure. Security concerns relate to risk areas such as external data storage, dependency on the "public" internet, lack of control, multi-tenancy and integration with internal security. Encryption techniques have been used for a long time to secure sensitive data. Sending or storing encrypted data in the cloud will ensure that data is secure. However, it is assumed that the encryption algorithms are strong. Following are a few common security issues faced in the cloud environment across the globe which can be overcome by deploying appropriate security algorithms.

- The physical security is lost in cloud environment as computing resources are shared with other companies. No control exists in the place where resources are running.

- Data integrity is a major issue as it changes in response to transactions like transfer, storage and retrieval. It will be a threat if it's an unauthorized transaction. So, ensuring secured data transfer is a crucial phenomenon which can be achieved by applying these security algorithms.

- Cloud service providers may break the rules by sharing personal information or sensitive data with unintended persons.

- A security issue may arise if encryption-decryption keys are not handled appropriately.

1.4.2 Symmetric Encryption Algorithms

Symmetric key algorithms are primarily meant for bulk encryption of data. This technique is very fast and consists of a big number of possible keys. The best of this set offers superb secrecy. The biggest advantage is the absence of any fast way to decrypt the data without having the same key once data is encrypted with a specific key. These types of algorithms are mainly divided into two categories: block and stream. Block algorithms are responsible for blockwise encryption of data whereas the second category does it byte by byte [14].

The strength of different encryption algorithms may differ as each of them has a specific area of expertise. Some are not very efficient in data protection, they allow decryption of encrypted information without having knowledge of a requisite key, whereas some are very competent at resisting the most obvious attack. The strength of the algorithm depends on several factors, a few of which are listed below:

- Confidentiality of the key

- Effort of guessing the key

- Difficulty in breaking the encryption algorithm

- Existence of other options to decrypt without knowing the key

- The capacity to decrypt an entire encrypted message if the logic of decryption is known for a portion.

Generally, the cryptographic strength is not established; the loopholes of the technique can be analyzed and strength can be assumed accordingly.

Key length is another vital aspect of the algorithms as security is intensely related with the key length. Though short keys compromise the security of the encrypted message, extremely long keys also don't provide the best result due to the complexity present to maintain them. If the length is increased from 80 bits to 128 bits, the effort of guessing the key also significantly increases. So, there is an increased demand for creating longer keys from a marketing perspective.

Table 1.1 below describes a few commonly used symmetric encryption algorithms along with their key length, out of which four are discussed in the subsequent section.

1.4.2.1 Advanced Encryption Standard

The advanced encryption standard (AES) is a symmetric encryption algorithm that supports a block length of 128 bits, capable of using cryptographic keys of 128, 192, and 256 bits, which was developed by two Belgian cryptographers, Joan Daemen and Vincent Rijmen. It is able to provide higher level security due to its 256-bit key length and is usually

Table 1.1   Commonly used symmetric encryption algorithms and their key length.

Algorithm	Description	Key Length
Blowfish	Block cipher developed by Schneier	1-448 bits
DES	DES adopted as a U.S. government standard in 1977	56 bits
IDEA	Block cipher developed by Massey and Xuejia	128 bits
MARS	AES finalist developed by IBM	128-256 bits
RC2	Block cipher developed by Rivest	1-2048 bits
RC4	Stream cipher developed by Rivest	1-2048 bits
RC5	Block cipher developed by Rivest and published in 1994	128-256 bits
RC6	AES finalist developed by RSA Labs	128-256 bits
Rijndael	NIST selection for AES, developed by Daemen and Rijmen	128-256 bits
Serpent	AES finalist developed by Anderson, Biham, and Knudsen	128-256 bits
Triple-DES	A three-fold application of the DES algorithm	168 bits
Twofish	AES candidate developed by Schneier	128-256 bits

suggested in several financial organizations for a secured business transaction both online or on corporate network infrastructure to protect the data of clients, staff, partners, and suppliers [15, 16]. The algorithm has the following high level steps. The subsequent Figure 1.2 represents the major steps in the algorithm.

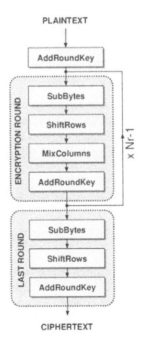

Figure 1.2   Outline of AES algorithm.

Key Expansion: Cipher key derives number of separate round keys from a short key through using Rijndael's key routine. It needs a separate 128-bit round key block for each round and one more. The key schedule builds the required round keys from the basic key.

Initial Round Key Addition: It has the AddRoundKey function where each byte of the state is combined with a block of the round key using bitwise XOR. Here, the initial round key is added with the starting state array.

Encryption Round: The encryption process needs a series of steps to modify the state array. The steps consist of four types of operations. All four of these operations are applied on the current state array and a new version is built. The details of each operation are briefly given below. An iteration of the below steps is called a round. The amount of rounds of the algorithm depends on the key size. Table 1.2 depicts the same.

Table 1.2   Key size and rounds.

Key Size (Bytes)	Block Size (Bytes)	Rounds
16	16	10
24	16	12
32	16	14

- *SubBytes*: A nonlinear substitution step where each byte is replaced with another according to a lookup table. A simple substitution occurs which converts every byte into a different value. AES builds a table containing 256 values required for substitution. For the 16 bytes of the state array, each byte is used as an index into the 256-byte substitution table and the byte is replaced by the value from the substitution table. A new version of the state array is formed because all possible 256 byte values are present in the table. The new version can be restored to its original contents using an inverse substitution table. The contents of the substitution table are not arbitrary; its entries are calculated through a mathematical formula. However, most implementations simply contain the substitution table stored in the memory as a part of the entire design.

- *ShiftRows*: A transposition step where the last three rows of the state are shifted cyclically a certain number of steps. It operates on every row of the state array. A rotation occurs to the right by a specific number of bytes as described below. The result is a new matrix consisting of the same 16 bytes but shifted with respect to each other.

  - 1st Row: Rotated by 0 bytes (no change)
  - 2nd Row: Rotated by 1 byte
  - 3rd Row: Rotated by 2 bytes
  - 4th Row: Rotated by 3 bytes

- *MixColumns*: A linear mixing operation which operates on the columns of the state, combining the four bytes in each column. Here each column of the state array is processed individually to create a new column. Processing refers matrix multiplication here. The result is another new matrix consisting of 16 new bytes.

- *AddRoundKey*: Now the 16 bytes of the matrix are considered as 128 bits and are XORed with the 128 bits of the round key. The output becomes ciphertext if this is the last round, otherwise the resulting 128 bits are interpreted as 16 bytes and another similar round started.

Final Round: In the final round, all these steps are performed except the Mix column step to make the algorithm reversible during decryption (SubBytes, ShiftRows, AddRound-Key).

1.4.2.2 3DES

Data encryption standard (DES) is a block cypher where a 56-bit key is used and consists of various operating modes; based on the purpose, they are deployed in various scenarios [17]. There is a limitation of its usage in reality due to its short key length though it's a strong algorithm. 3DES is introduced to fill this gap by using three different keys, having a total key length of 168 bits. This feature has made it extremely secure and it has been adopted by several financial institutions. Currently, two types of triple DES exist which are 3-key Triple DES (3TDES) and 2-key Triple DES (2TDES).

The outline of the 3TDES algorithm is presented in the following Figure 1.3.

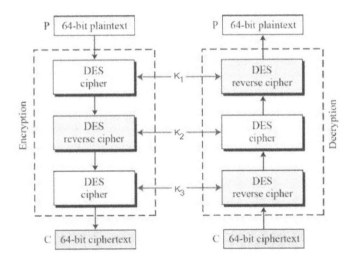

Figure 1.3   Outline of 3-key Triple DES algorithm.

Procedure:

- At first, user generates and distributes a 3TDES key which is the combination of three different keys K_1, K_2 and K_3. So the actual 3TDES key length comes to $3 \times 56 = 168$ bits.

- The plaintext blocks are encrypted by single DES having key K_1.

- The output of the previous step is decrypted using single DES having key K_2.

- In the next step, the output of previous step is encrypted by single DES with key K_3.

- The current output is ciphertext.

- Decrypting the ciphertext is just opposite of the previous one. First, it is decrypted using K_3, encrypted with K_2 and finally decrypted with K_1.

1.4.2.3 Blowfish

Blowfish is a fast, compact, and simple block encryption algorithm which works very efficiently against hackers and cyber-criminals [18]. It supports a wide array of products like secure E-mail encryption tools, backup software, password management tools and TiVo. It allows a variable-length key, up to 448 bits, and is optimized for execution on 32-bit or 64-bit processors. Several famous applications exist which use Blowfish encryption, a few of which include AEDIT (a free Windows word processor incorporating text encryption), Coolfish (an encrypting text editor for Windows) and FoopChat (encrypted chat and advanced file sharing using a client/server architecture).

The algorithm has two major parts: a key expansion part and a data encryption part.

Key Expansion Part or Subkey Generation: Original key is broken by key expansion into a bundle of subkeys:

Algorithm 1.1 Key Expansion Part or Subkey Generation

Begin

---

1. Key Size is variable but it generates very large subkeys. The key size lies between 32 bits to 448 bits.

2. Concept of P-array consists of 18, 32-bit subkeys.

3. There are 4 S-boxes containing 256 entries of 32 bits.

4. P-array is initialized first then four s boxes with fixed string.

5. P-arrays are XORed with subkeys, i.e., from P_1 to P_{18}.

6. Once the subkeys are generated the encryption process begins.

end

Data Encryption Part: This process involves 16 times iteration of a simple function. Each round contains a key-dependent permutation and key and data substitution.

1.4.2.4 RC6

Rivest Cipher 6 (RC6), an improved version of the basic Rivest Cipher RC algorithm, uses 128-bit block size and supports key sizes of 128, 192 and 256 bits and was developed by Ron Rivest, Matt Robshaw, Ray Sidney, and Yiqun Lisa Yin to meet the requirements of an advanced encryption standard (AES) competition. It may be parameterized to support a wide variety of word lengths, key sizes and number of rounds. Considering the structure, RC6 and RC5 are similar; they use data-dependent rotations, modular addition, and XOR operations. Being a secure, compact and simple block cipher, good performance and flexibility are offered [13, 19].

New features of RC6 include using four working registers instead of two and the presence of integer multiplication as an additional primitive operation. Using multiplication greatly increases the diffusion achieved per round, allowing for greater security, fewer rounds and increased throughput.

1.4.3 Asymmetric Encryption Algorithms

Asymmetric encryption refers to public key cryptography which is a new method compared to symmetric encryption. Here two keys are used for a plain text encryption. Secret keys are exchanged over the network which ensures that malicious persons cannot misuse the keys. The message can be decrypted by a person having the secret key and that is the reason for using two related keys for boosting security. A public key is made freely accessible to everybody who wants to send a message whereas a private key is kept secret. A message encrypted by a public key can only be decrypted by the private key. However, a message encrypted by a private key can be decrypted by a public key. A public key need not be secured as it's available to everybody; hence, it can be passed through the internet. The technique offers better security than symmetric encryption during message transmission as it uses two keys, though it takes a longer time than the other one. A few well-known techniques are described below which follow asymmetric encryption principles [16].

1.4.3.1 RSA

The RSA[1] algorithm was developed by Ron Rivest, Adi Shamir and Len Adleman in 1977 and was named after the inventors [14, 19]. This is the most widely used public key cryptography algorithm across the globe. It has the capability to encrypt a message without exchanging the secret key separately. It can be applied in both public key encryption and digital signatures. Security level depends on the difficulty of factoring large integers. For example, an encrypted message can be sent to B from A without any previous communication of secret keys. A applies B's public key for message encryption whereas B uses the private key for decryption. Similarly, the technique is applicable to sign a message where it can be signed by A with its private key and can be verified by B using A's public key.

The basic version of the algorithm is depicted as follows:

Algorithm 1.2 RSA

Begin

1. Produce p and q, two large random primes, having approximately equal size, and their product $n = p \times q$, which should be the required bit length.

2. Calculate n and φ such that $n = p \times q$ and $\varphi = (p - 1) \times (q - 1)$.

3. Select an integer e where $1 < e < \varphi$ and $gcd(e, \varphi) = 1$.

4. Calculate the secret exponent d where $1 < d < \varphi$ such that $ed \equiv 1 \bmod \varphi$.

5. The public key is (n, e) and private key is (d, p, q).

end

Note:

- n is commonly called the modulus.

- e is called the public exponent/encryption exponent.

- d is called the secret exponent/encryption exponent.

After generation of the public key and private keys from the above steps, Encryption, Decryption, Digital signing and Signature verification occurs in the following ways.

Similarly, it works for the domain of Digital Signing.

---

[1] https://www.rsa.com/

Algorithm 1.3 RSA Encryption (Performed by Sender A)

Begin

1. Obtains the receiver B's public key (n, e).

2. Designate the plain text message as a positive integer m where $1 < m < n$.

3. Calculates the cipher text $c = m^e \bmod n$.

4. Transmit the cipher text c to B.

end

Algorithm 1.4 RSA Decryption (Performed by Receiver B)

Begin

1. Applies his private key (n, d) to calculate $m = c^d \bmod n$.

2. Plain text is pulled out from the message representative m.

end

Algorithm 1.5 RSA Digital Signing (Performed by Sender A)

Begin

1. A message digest, the information needed to be sent, is built.

2. The digest is represented as an integer m, which lies between 1 and $n - 1$.

3. The private key (n, d) is used to generate the signature $s = m^d \bmod n$.

4. The signature s is sent to the receiver B.

end

Algorithm 1.6 RSA Digital Verification (Performed by Receiver B)

Begin

1. The public key (n, e) of sender A is used to compute integer $v = s^e \bmod n$.

2. The message digest H is extracted from the integer.

3. The message digest H' of the information that has been signed is calculated separately.

4. Check whether $H = H'$.

5. The signature is valid if $H = H'$ is true.

end

Summary of RSA:

1. $n = p \times q$ where p, q are distinct primes

2. $\varphi = (p-1)(q-1)$

3. $e < n$ so that $gcd(e, \varphi) = 1$

4. $d = e^{-1} \bmod \varphi$

5. $c = m^e \bmod n, 1 < m < n$

6. $m = c^d \bmod n$

1.4.3.2 Diffie-Hellman Key Exchange

The Diffie-Hellman key exchange protocol was invented in 1976, and was the first technique to establish a shared secret over an unsecured communication channel. The concept of key exchange was one of the first problems addressed by cryptography. The main idea is to use a key which can be used by two parties for encryption in such a way that an eavesdropper cannot get the key [20]. The outline of the algorithm is presented below.

Assumption:

- Here, four variables are considered to keep it simple and for practical implementation. Variables include prime p, g (a primitive root of p), two private values a and b. Both p and g are publicly available numbers.

- Users (consider Alice and Bob) choose private values a and b. A key is also generated and exchanged publicly. Another person receives the key and generates a secret key so that they both have the common secret key to encrypt.

Algorithm 1.7 Diffie-Hellman Key Exchange

Begin

1. Alice and Bob both decide on a prime number p and a base g.

2. Alice selects a secret number a, computes ($x = g^a \bmod p$) and sends Bob x.

3. Bob selects a secret number b, computes ($y = g^b \bmod p$) and sends Alice y.

4. Alice calculates ($y^a \bmod p$).

5. Bob calculates ($y^a \bmod p$).

6. By the laws of algebra, Alice's key is the same as Bob's key.

end

Both Bob and Alice can use this number as their key. However, p and g need not be protected.

1.4.4   Security Enhancement in Cloud Using Encryption Algorithms: Observations

Research work has been carried out to find the utility of deploying the security algorithms in cloud. A few of these observations are listed below [19, 21].

- Data security in cloud-based applications can be enhanced to a great extent by applying RSA and AES algorithms.

- Private key determination is not feasible for hackers (*even if they have the public keys generated*) if RSA uses 1024-bit keys and AES uses 128-bit keys.

- In a scenario where the user forgets to log out from the cloud web portal after using it and an attacker breaks into the user system, it will not be possible to access or download data without entering the private key in the system.

- However, if the attacker is successful in breaking into the user's system and guesses the private key, it may be possible to download the encrypted data but accessing the original data still remains a hurdle.

1.5   Comparison of Encryption Algorithms

The following Table 1.3 presents a comparison of the encryption algorithms discussed above based on various parameters.

Table 1.3   Comparison of encryption algorithms.

Algorithm / Parameter	3DES	AES	Blowfish	RSA	Diffie-Hellman
Encryption Technique	Symmetric key	Symmetric key	Symmetric key	Asymmetric key	Asymmetric key
Used Keys	Same key in Encryption and Decryption	Same key in Encryption and Decryption	Same key in Encryption and Decryption	Different key in Encryption and Decryption	Key Exchange
Throughput	Lower than DES	Lower than blowfish	Very High	High	Low
Key Lengths	112 - 168 bits	128,192 or 256 bits	32 - 448 bits	>1024 bits	Key Exchange Management
Rounds	48	10,12,14	16	1	56
Security Against	Brute Force, Chosen-plain text, Known plain text	Chosen-plain text, Known plain text	Dictionary Attacks	Timing Attacks	EavesDropping
Modification	The key size is increased from 56 to 168 bits	128, 192 or 256. Its structure was flexible to multiples of 64	Key length in blowfish should be multiples of 32	Key length in RSA algorithm can be 256 ,512,1024,2048, 4096 bit	No modification in key length
Created by	IBM	Vincent Rijmen , Joan daeman	Bruce Schiener	Ron Rivest,Shamir & leonard Adleman	Whitfield diffie, Martin Hellman
Year	1978	1978	1993	1978	2002
Algorithm Structure	Feistal Structure	Feistal Structure	Feistal Structure	Feistal Structure	Tree Based
Cloud Compatibility	Yes	Yes	Yes	Yes	Yes
Algorithm used in Cloud	Not used in Cloud	Google Drive, OneDrive, Dropbox	Mozy Backup, Foopchat, GigaTribe	Amazon web Services, RSAWeb	CurveCP
Application	Microsoft OneNote,Outlook 2007	Password Manager	IDS Server,Sql Server 2000	Online Credit Card Security System,RSA Signature Verification	Protocols like SSL,SSH,IPSec

1.6   Performance Analysis of Encryption Algorithms in Cloud

The encryption algorithms discussed above are analyzed in terms of mean processing time in local system as well as cloud network. The mean time refers to the difference between the start and end time of encryption taken by a particular algorithm, which is calculated in milliseconds. The following Table 1.4 presents the comparison details. It is evident from the table that each algorithm takes much less time in cloud compared to its non-cloud environment, which again proves the suitability of implementing these algorithms in cloud.

Table 1.4 Comparison performance of encryption algorithms.

Input	AES	AES Cloud	DES	DES Cloud	Blowfish	Blowfish Cloud
10 KB	11.5	1.5	7.5	2	4	2
13 KB	14.7	2	10	2.5	4.7	2
39 KB	21	3	3.15	6.5	8.25	2.75
56 KB	24.5	3.75	50.25	9.25	15.7	3

1.7 Conclusion

Moving to cloud is the ultimate objective for most of the industries and organizations as it involves multiple benefits like using software which is not present in the computer or accessing data from anywhere in the world. However, security, privacy and data theft are the challenges of this platform, which demand the appropriate deployment of security algorithms in cloud to ensure end-user security. The cloud providers generally use a set of tools and techniques to ascertain this. But implementing the encryption algorithms discussed in this chapter definitely makes the platform more secure and reliable for its users. As a result, the usage of cloud computing will be enhanced and will become more popular among its users.

REFERENCES

1. Lee, G. (2010). *Cloud Computing: Principles, Systems and Applications*/Nick Antonopoulos, Lee Gillam. L.: Springer.
2. Mell, P., & Grance, T. (2011). The NIST definition of cloud computing.
3. Hfer, C. N., & Karagiannis, G. (2011). Cloud computing services: taxonomy and comparison. *Journal of Internet Services and Applications*, 2(2), 81-94.
4. Kartit, Z., Azougaghe, A., Idrissi, H. K., El Marraki, M., Hedabou, M., Belkasmi, M., & Kartit, A. (2016). Applying Encryption Algorithm for Data Security in Cloud Storage. In *Advances in Ubiquitous Networking* (pp. 141-154). Springer, Singapore.
5. Bhardwaj, A., Subrahmanyam, G. V. B., Avasthi, V., & Sastry, H. (2016). Security algorithms for cloud computing. *Procedia Computer Science*, 85, 535-542.
6. Iyer, S. S., Dand, H., & Patil, R. (2017). *An Algorithm for Encrypted Cloud Communication.*
7. Conner, W., Iyengar, A., Mikalsen, T., Rouvellou, I., & Nahrstedt, K. (2009, April). A trust management framework for service-oriented environments. In Proceedings of the 18th international conference on World wide web (pp. 891-900). ACM.
8. Friedman, A. A., & West, D. M. (2010). Privacy and security in cloud computing. Center for Technology Innovation at Brookings.
9. Ristenpart, T., Tromer, E., Shacham, H., & Savage, S. (2009, November). Hey, you, get off of my cloud: exploring information leakage in third-party compute clouds. In Proceedings of the 16th ACM conference on Computer and communications security (pp. 199-212). ACM.
10. Yan, L., Rong, C., & Zhao, G. (2009, December). Strengthen cloud computing security with federal identity management using hierarchical identity-based cryptography. In IEEE International Conference on Cloud Computing (pp. 167-177). Springer, Berlin, Heidelberg.

11. Ukil, A., De Sarkar, A., Jana, D., & Wyld, D. C. (2013). Security policy enforcement in cloud infrastructure. In ICCSEA, SPPR, CSIA, WimoA-2013 (pp. 01-09).

12. Le, D. N., Kumar, R., Nguyen, G. N., & Chatterjee, J. M. (2018). *Cloud Computing and Virtualization*. John Wiley & Sons.

13. Le, D. N., Kumar, R., Mishra, B. K., Chatterjee, J. M., & Khari, M. (Eds.). (2019). *Cyber Security in Parallel and Distributed Computing: Concepts, Techniques, Applications and Case Studies*. John Wiley & Sons.

14. Shaik, K., Rao, N., & Venkat, T. (2017). Implementation of Encryption Algorithm for Data Security in Cloud Computing. *International Journal of Advanced Research in Computer Science*, 8(3).

15. Shinde, M. R., & Taur, R. D. (2015). Encryption Algorithm for Data Security and Privacy in Cloud Storage. *American Journal of Computer Science and Engineering Science*.

16. e-tutorials accessed at http://etutorials.org/Linux+systems/unix+internet+security/Part+II+Security+Building+Blocks/Chapter+7.+Cryptography+Basics/7.2+Symmetric+Key+Algorithms/

17. Jain, N., & Kaur, G. (2012). Implementing DES algorithm in cloud for data security. VSRD *International Journal of Computer Science & Information Technology*, 2(4), 316-321.

18. Iyer, S. S., Dand, H., & Patil, R. (2017). *An Algorithm for Encrypted Cloud Communication*.

19. Mewada, S., Shrivastava, A., Sharma, P., Purohit, N., & Gautam, S. S. (2015). Performance Analysis of Encryption Algorithm in Cloud Computing. *International Journal of Computer Sciences and Engineering*, 3, 83-89.

20. Ahmed, M., Sanjabi, B., Aldiaz, D., Rezaei, A., & Omotunde, H. (2012). Diffie-Hellman and its application in security protocols. *International Journal of Engineering Science and Innovative Technology* (IJESIT), 1, 69-73.

21. Le, D. N., Seth, B., & Dalal, S. (2018). A Hybrid Approach of Secret Sharing with Fragmentation and Encryption in Cloud Environment for Securing Outsourced Medical Database: A Revolutionary Approach. *Journal of Cyber Security and Mobility*, 7(4), 379-408.

CHAPTER 2

ANALYSIS OF SECURITY ISSUES IN CLOUD ENVIRONMENT

Sushruta Mishra[1], Nitin Tripathy[1], Brojo Kishore Mishra[2], Chandrakanta Mahanty[3]

[1] School of Computer Engineering, KIIT University, India
[2] Department of CS&IT, CVRCE, India
[3] Department of CSE, GIET, India
Email: mishra.sushruta@gmail.com, diabloz197@gmail.com, brojokishoremishra@gmail.com, chandra.mahanty@gmail.com

Abstract

The rapid growth and outreach of cloud computing technology enables various organizations to outsource their computational tasks or helps to sell their computational entities which are idle. At present, cloud computing appears to be a very promising trend, which has tempted several firms to adopt this technology. However, there are still other aspects that a firm must take care of before entering into the cloud computing zone. Among these aspects, security is the most crucial attribute that must be taken care of smoothly and efficiently. Security in cloud computing acts as a very technically feasible yet robust characteristic feature that is capable of providing multipurpose alternative solutions to problems. In the absence of effective security being put in place, the credibility and benefits of cloud computing services are of very little use. The main objective of this chapter is to provide a detailed understanding of this security issue in cloud computing. This study helps in determining and categorizing its prime security-related issues and concerns, thereby presenting an overview of the present scenario of security in cloud computing environment. Later in this chapter, a secure software-defined network (SDN) based architecture, which includes proper authentication of user, efficient routing, resistance to various attacks and third-party coordination, is also described in detail. The basic aim of highlighting this architecture is to analyze a SDN-cloud environment with embedded security features that can be helpful in resisting various types of attacks like flow table overloading, Byzantine attacks and control plane saturation.

Keywords: Cloud computing, software-defined networks, security, Byzantine attacks, control plane saturation, genetic algorithm

2.1 An Insight into Cloud Computing

Cloud computing is a model in which a shared pool of resources is provided for various use cases through the integration of a network of servers. The adoption of this technology has brought forth large-scale cost reductions in many areas which include storage, computation and content hosting. These cost benefits are experienced through practical implementations of the cloud model such that a variable pricing setup is achieved. Cloud computing offers various architectural models which are utilized by various industries through the modification of their applications [1]. Certain merits of cloud computing are listed below.

- *Cost Reduction*: Cloud computing is based on a utility model of pricing, i.e., pay-per-use, for resources that are owned, operated and maintained by third-party cloud vendors. This means that users of cloud do not pay for idle resources or maintenance. As a result, cloud computing has lower costs as compared to traditional computing.

- *Increased Storage*: Cloud service providers maintain hardware and other resources at a large scale, including storage services. Furthermore, the maintenance of such resources/services is carried out by the cloud providers. These factors combine with efficient variable workload management to provide massive scalable storage.

- *Flexibility*: Rapidly changing and evolving market/business environments require companies to adapt and deliver at a fast pace. Cloud computing accommodates such fast paced delivery of products, services and organizational changes by providing and utilizing the necessary components for deployment.

Cloud computing consists of various deployment models which vary in their accessibility, thereby catering to different sets of requirements:

a) Public Cloud: Accessible by anybody with an Internet connection and proper credentials. Most suitable for personal or small scale business use.

b) Private Cloud: Only the members of the group/organization using the private cloud can access it.

c) Community Cloud: Multiple organizations working together access a common cloud.

d) Hybrid Cloud: A cloud solution that integrates multiple cloud deployment platforms.

A common cloud architecture setup is shown below in Figure 2.1. This simple depiction of a cloud system consists of the cloud service providers and users, without showing any complicated components (*e.g., geographic dispersion of cloud network, redundancy*) of cloud computing, serving to illustrate the concept of cloud computing in a comprehensible manner, whilst also being a self-explanatory depiction of the network model with the cloud users. While the cloud users are properly identified in the architecture in terms of their remote location and access, a point to note is that the admin users that manage the cloud resources are not considered as cloud users in the architecture of the cloud service provider. Furthermore, as cloud computing is a concept rather than jargon, it can be put to consideration as to whether or not the LAN users in Figure 2.1 should be classified as cloud users. The LAN users may not be considered cloud users if the definition of cloud computing is applied, which states that the implementation of the architecture is for the remote access of shared resources. On the contrary, cloud computing architecture is based on the technology of grid computing and distributed computing, implementations of which lead to cloud infrastructure. LAN users, therefore, are seen as cloud users when they use the cloud services from the servers by accessing them when needed.

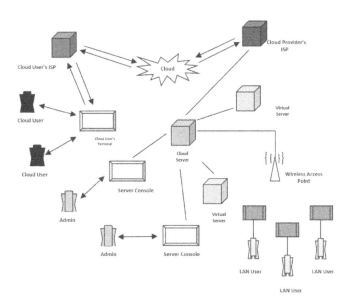

Figure 2.1   Cloud architecture.

2.2   Critical Challenges Concerning Cloud Computing

Cloud computing presents many benefits for users. While these benefits compensate for the issues with the cloud, the challenges faced still need to be addressed and are presented below [2].

2.2.1   Data Protection

Security of data is of paramount significance to enterprises. These enterprises are faced with the problem of data leakage whether it is business data to competitors or the private data of customers. As such, data security guarantees of cloud vendors are heavily scrutinized by enterprises that are often unaware of the infrastructure location and security arrangements. Enterprises that own datacenters use firewalls for security as part of the current model. On the other hand, enterprises would have to be dependent on the cloud service providers for security in the cloud computing model.

2.2.2 Data Recovery and Availability

Enterprise applications strictly adhere to service level agreements which are managed by operational teams. Operational teams also perform other tasks, including in production environments:

- Clustering and failover data replication system monitoring (transaction, logs, etc.).

- Maintenance and runtime administration.

- Calamity recovery and performance management.

2.2.3 Management Capacities

Management of cloud platform and infrastructure is a key element of cloud computing and involves features such as load balancing, redundancy and replication. These features present many benefits and as such the currently lackluster management options must be improved.

2.2.4 Regulatory and Compliance Restrictions

Cloud infrastructure setup is faced with many challenges concerning governmental regulations. For example, the private and sensitive data of customers is required to be located within the country in certain European nations. This presents issues regarding the feasibility of cloud providers to be in compliance with such regulations, which would require cloud infrastructure to be deployed in those nations.

2.3 Basic Models Governing Cloud Computing

Cloud computing includes three essential service models which are offered by cloud suppliers, which are shown in Figure 2.2.

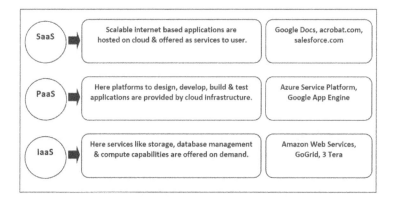

Figure 2.2 Cloud computing models.

2.3.1   Cloud Computing Models

2.3.1.1   *Software as a Service (SaaS)*
This model consists of consumers being offered a fully integrated application that they can access through the Internet. In the cloud, a single application is deployed and services various customers on demand. As a result, customers do not pay for the infrastructure or application, but only for their usage, and cloud providers only need to maintain the single deployment, lowering their costs as well. Google, Salesforce and Microsoft are some of the top SaaS providers in the cloud market.

2.3.1.2   *Platform as a Service (PaaS)*
In this model, customers focus on building their own applications on top of an underlying platform which is managed by the cloud vendor. The provider predefines the infrastructure and software to offer combinations that can be used for faster, more efficient and scalable application development. Combinations that are commonly used include the LAMP stack (Linux, Apache, MySQL and PHP) and restricted J2EE. Popular PaaS providers are Amazon with Elastic Beanstalk and Google with their App Engine.

2.3.1.3   *Infrastructure as a Service (IaaS)*
Compute instances on servers, block storage, and network infrastructure are some of the basic resources that are provided as shared and distributed resources in cloud computing. The IaaS model consists of the provision of these basic components as infrastructure on which cloud users deploy complete systems. Amazon and Microsoft are the top two IaaS providers in the cloud market.

2.3.2   Security Concerns of Cloud Computing

Security is seen as a vital part for the consolidation of cloud computing as an efficient and viable multifunctional alternative [3]. This perspective has been agreed upon by numerous different teams like academicians [4], business decision teams [5] as well as government associations [6, 7]. Numerous resemblances in such points of view present a serious issue about the critical privacy as well as legal concerns of cloud computation which include service availability, lock-in provider, information privacy and reputation exchange of fate [8]. Such issues incorporate not just current concerns, specifically acquired from the embraced innovations, but also noble problems arising due to the formation of key cloud characteristics such as sharing of resources, scalability and virtual reality (such as hypervisor liabilities and data leakage) [9]. The refinement among such categories is more effectively recognizable by evaluating cloud computing definition developed by the NIST in [10], which likewise presents ideas of service models (SaaS, PaaS and IaaS) as well as implementation models (public, community, private and hybrid clouds). Because of the consistently developing enthusiasm for cloud computing, continuous efforts are being made to determine the present security issues for such methodology, taking into account identified problem domains as well as feasible alternatives. In the planning to sort out the data identified with security over cloud to further encourage investigations the main concerns are identified and a model is prepared consisting of seven classes: network security, information security, virtualization, interfaces, governance, legal concerns and compliance.

Every classification includes some of the likely security threats, leading to categorization with subcategories that present the vital concerns distinguished through the mentioned references. Some vital security concerns are depicted in Figure 2.3.

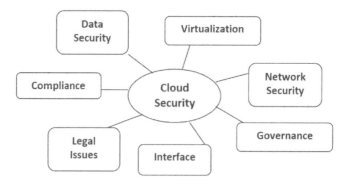

Figure 2.3   Cloud computing security issues.

2.3.2.1 *Network security*

Network security deals with the issues related to network communications and setups in regard to cloud frameworks. Extending from the user's existing cloud network to provide cloud service is the preferred method for network security, thereby implementing local security measures and strategies for resources that are remotely situated.

  a. *Transfer Security*: Gigantic resource sharing, distributed systems and synchronization of virtual machines mean increased information moving through the cloud, which requires VPN techniques to protect the system from sniffing, side-channel, spoofing and man-in-the-middle attacks.

  b. *Security Configuration*: Setting up of high performing and efficient security and privacy protocols and systems that meet the required standards.

  c. *Firewalling*: Firewalls help in protecting internal cloud framework of the provider against internal and external threats and enable virtual machine isolation, address and report fine-grained filtering, denial-of-service (DoS) prevention and finding of external security evaluation methods. Efforts to develop reliable firewalls and other cloud-specific security measures reveal the need to adapt existing solutions to this new computing paradigm.

2.3.2.2 *Interfaces*

Concentrates all user, administration and programming interface problems for the use and control of clouds.

  a. *API*: Interfaces for programming, interacting with virtual systems and resources (crucial for IaaS and PaaS) should be given protection to avoid misuse.

  b. *User Interface*: End-user interface to explore resources and tools that implies the need to adopt environmental protection measures [11, 12].

  c. *Administrative Interface*: Enables remote IaaS resource management, PaaS development (coding, deployment and test case handling) and SaaS application entities (access to user, coordination and management).

  d. *Authentication*: Some operations are necessary to allow cloud access. Many services depend upon normal operation and are therefore susceptible to a plethora of attacks [13-16]. Multi-tenancy and resource sharing enhance the consequences.

2.3.2.3 Data Security

Data security concerns protecting data with respect to privacy, integrity and availability (which are not only applied to cloud systems but also to any systems which require fundamental security).

a. *Cryptography*: Most practices have been used to protect critical data, which is strictly necessary for industry, government and federal legislation.

b. *Redundancy*: Vital for prevention of loss of data. Many businesses depend on IT for their vital operations and processing, therefore, availability and reliability of real-time operational specific information need to be guaranteed.

c. *Disposal*: Fundamental methods for disposing of data are deficient and usually called deletion. An important requirement in cloud is the complete removal of information, which also includes log backup and covered data repositories.

2.3.2.4 Virtualization

Hypervisor vulnerabilities, separation of virtual machines and other issues related to the usage of virtual entities techniques.

a. *Hypervisor Vulnerabilities*: The hypervisor forms the core virtualization software constituent. Although the security issues of hypervisors are known, the unavailability of solutions or the solutions being proprietary leads to the need for further research to enhance these security features.

b. *Isolation*: The same resources and hardware are shared by multiple virtual machines such that data leaks and cross-virtual-machine attacks can be exploited. The concept of isolation can also be applied to finer resources such as storage, memory and computation.

2.3.2.5 Governance

Issues in cloud computing solutions that relate to loss of control over security and administration.

a. *Security Control*: Governance over security mechanisms and policies are lost due to prohibition of vulnerability assessment and penetration tests on the customer side by terms of use, while insufficient service level agreements lead to vulnerabilities in security.

b. *Data Control*: Implications regarding loss of control over various aspects of data management such as redundancy and location due to migration of data to cloud.

c. *Lock-in*: As a result of the lack of proper uniform standards (protocols and formats), users are faced with issues in migration and service termination due to possible dependency on a specific cloud service provider.

2.3.2.6 Compliance

This category includes availability of service and audit processing requirements.

a. *Service Level Agreement* (SLA): Contractual agreement between the cloud service provider and consumer regarding safety and reliability of service and the associated techniques to enforce it.

b. *Audit*: Enables consumers, providers and third parties to assess safety and availability. Continuous analysis of service conditions requires transparent and efficient methodologies and is usually recommended under contracts or legal rules and regulations. Solutions to deal with this problem are being developed by providing an API that enables users to automatically audit and avail other suitable features in an open manner.

c. *Loss of Service*: Service blackouts may not be related to the cloud but, rather, are more genuine for such a case because of interactions among services (an SaaS using virtual resources provided by an IaaS), as is the case in numerous examples. Suitable disaster recovery regulations and methods are therefore required to incorporate customer redundancy (if possible).

2.3.2.7   Legal Issues

Legal issues are those relating to novel cloud computing concepts, like various sites of information and privilege monitoring.

a. *Data Location*: Consumer-related data is stored in several regions which are dependent on the geographical location are interrelated by the law.

b. *Provider Privilege*: Possible dangers to accessibility, privacy and veracity of customer files and processes are malicious insiders of the provider.

c. *E-discovery*: As a direct consequence of law administration, hardware may be confiscated for investigations involving customers; this affects all consumers whose information is situated on identical physical devices. In this scenario, secrecy of data is of critical concern.

2.4   Security Countermeasures in Cloud Computing

2.4.1   Countermeasures for Communication Issues

The CSA provides a set of guidelines and recommendations for communication and network security which are as follows:

- Combining virtual LANs, IDS, IPS and firewalls for data protection.

- Use of strict access management policies to counter customer data leakage in VLAN and common infrastructure.

- For virtual network traffic monitoring and visibility, virtual and standard physical devices with tight integration with the hypervisor should be used.

2.4.2   Countermeasures for Architecture Security

A security test should be done to practically counter the security issues in cloud computing. Various publications define theoretical approaches for secure cloud computing and consider the various security components which include multifactor authentication (MFA), API level security, storage encryption, and identity and access management. Secure cloud architecture is achieved by the integration of these components with the cloud.

2.4.3 Countermeasures for Challenges Inherited from Network Concepts

- *SQL Injection Attacks*: SQL injection attacks are checked by cleaning user input through filtration and other methods. One such method which has been recommended by various researchers is the use of a proxy-based architecture which detects and removes users' input that may contain SQL instruction patterns.

- *Cross-Site Scripting (XSS) Attacks*: Techniques that use many methods of detecting security problems and repairing them include content-based data leakage prevention, active content filtering and detection of web applications vulnerability detection have been offered as counters against XSS attacks. Identification of malicious content in a network as a way to reduce workload on web browsers is an approach put forward in research papers as well.

- *Man-in-the-Middle Attacks (MITM)*: SaaS security, endpoint and server security process and endpoint virtualization are certain factors that must be analyzed to prevent such an attack. Security regulations and considerations in private networks at enterprise levels also apply to private clouds as well. Public clouds, on the other hand, require infrastructure modifications to be made, particularly at the network level, so as to accommodate the implementation of security techniques.

- *DNS Attacks*: Even though they reduce the impact of DNS security issues, the interception and alteration of the route between the sender and receiver by a hostile entity has made security technologies such as DNSSEC (domain name system security extensions) insufficient. This has sparked the need for more advanced security measures.

- *Sniffer Attacks*: On the basis of address resolution protocol (ARP) and round-trip time (RTT), sniffing systems deployed on a network can be spotted by a hostile sniffer detector. Alterations to guest operating systems and control over every data flowing through a hypervisor can be achieved by a hacker, should they gain authority of the hypervisor. It is, therefore, imperative that the behavior of the components of a hypervisor system be analyzed so as to build a better cloud security system through observation of guest virtual machines' processes and interactions between the infrastructure modules.

- *Denial-of-Service Attacks*: Intrusion detection system (IDS) and defense federation are two of the methods of defending again such attacks. Multiple IDSs operate through message passing on various clouds, generating an alert for attacks on any cloud. This alert is followed by a vote to decide on the reliability of the attacked cloud, thereby preventing the performance from being adversely affected.

- *Cookie Poisoning*: Sanitization of cookies and implementation of encryption techniques for the cookie data are methods to avoid cookie poisoning. The encryption method is supported by certain proposed schemes that handle cookie poisoning attacks sufficiently.

- *Distributed Denial-of-Service Attacks*: DDoS attacks are a serious security threat to cloud computing, especially when considering the large-scale network of a cloud infrastructure. As such, various methods have been proposed to fight against the attacks:

    - Swarm-based logic for protection.

- Integration of IDS in the virtual machines, such as SNORT for tracking all incoming and outgoing traffic.

- Integration of IDSs on the physical machines as well, which have proven to be effective on the Eucalyptus cloud.

2.4.4 Countermeasures for CAS Proposed Threats

The Cloud Security Alliance identifies and documents various threats to cloud security, some of which were previously discussed. Certain tools and techniques are provided to handle these threats and are as follows:

- *Confronting Abuse and Nefarious Use of Cloud Computing*: Initial sign-up and verification systems must be strict as a means to counter this issue. Other methods that are known to work are as follows:

  - Thorough evaluation and testing of customer networks.
  - Rejecting traffic from sources that are publicly blacklisted for a personal network.

- *Confronting Insecure Application Programming Interfaces*: Cloud provider interfaces' security architecture need to be properly evaluated as part of preventing this threat. Additionally, the dependency chain of an API needs to be understood through the integration of encryption techniques with authentication and access control.

- *Confronting Malicious Insiders*: This is a threat that involves a hostile current or former employee of a cloud provider with access to the cloud network obtaining sensitive data or making unauthorized changes in the network. As such, the methods for tackling such a threat are as follows:

  - Strict legal compliance in human resource management and contracts.
  - Encryption of data transmissions and passwords as well.
  - Access control and monitoring across the cloud with the purpose of transparency across the network. This should be aided by an intrusion alert system.

- *Confronting Shared Technology Vulnerabilities*: This issue occurs in the case of improper configuration of software security and weak access control mechanisms. These lead to the vulnerabilities which are exploited by hackers carrying out malicious activities on the affected systems. As such, security best practices should be employed when setting up the cloud servers and network, followed by regular security checks for weaknesses or unauthorized alterations to the configuration. Furthermore, strict authorization and access management systems should be deployed and monitored, with SLAs being followed strictly for administrative authority and management.

- *Confronting Data Loss/Leakage*: Implementation of strict API access management is a method of dealing with this issue. Data protection considerations during the development phase and the production environment should be evaluated as well. A key part of data protection is secure transmission of the data over the cloud network, which entails encryption techniques aided by proper key creation, storage and access control. Furthermore, backups, recovery strategies, distributed storage and data availability from the provider's side may be implemented.

- *Confronting Account, Service and Traffic Hijacking*: This threat occurs due to unauthorized access via stolen credentials or exploitation of weak security measures. Therefore, proactive security measures should be applied to the user access control system. One such measure is the use of MFA (multifactor authentication) at various stages along with monitoring systems. Another approach is to analyze and adhere to strict cloud security policies and SLAs set by the relevant authority. Techniques of limited effectiveness are often applied by cloud providers in the real world due to various factors which include feasibility of security countermeasures and availability of the required technology and infrastructure to accommodate those security measures.

2.5 Discussion of an Implemented SDN Security Framework

There are several security-based issues discussed in the previous studies of several researchers. In [17], the authors present an insight into the security challenges faced by cloud environment. Several cyber attacks faced by cloud platforms are also discussed. In another profound study [18], the prime focus of the study was to present a detailed analysis of security aspects of both IoT and cloud computing. Also, the integration of IoT with cloud computing is highlighted. At the end it was realized that cloud computing can provide a fog environment model for various scenarios. In [19], the authors developed and implemented an adaptive attribute optimization technique to optimize the efficiency of prediction of dengue fever risk disorders. The result indicated that the classification with the proposed algorithm yielded positive and optimum results with various parameters. In [20], the authors have implemented some vital biologically inspired computation techniques to classify various types of tumors. Multilayer perceptron was used for classification process. The important characteristics of cloud computing are analyzed in detail in [21] along with various security threats and their solutions. At the end, some vital research challenges concerning cloud computing are also highlighted. A multilevel categorization framework of various security vulnerabilities across cloud applications are presented in [22]. Several types of attacks are detected and their associated risk levels.

2.5.1 System Design

Issues which are associated with network vulnerability attacks can be solved by the SecSDN system presented. The proposed system contains multiple controllers which are present in the control plane. It also includes multiple data plane switches, cloud monitoring server to reduce flow table overload attacks, plane saturation attacks and Byzantine attacks. The proposed SecSDN-cloud framework is illustrated in Figure 2.4. Three different use-initiated attack types are handled by SecSDN-cloud framework. Furthermore, it provides superior communication. SecSDN-cloud includes three phases (user authentication, control assignment and communication) to defend against attackers. It also contains a cloud monitoring server, i.e., third-party software is enabled in SecSDN-cloud architecture [23].

Five different predefined policies and seven important package features are used for analyzing the traffic flows of clients. The five actions made are Alert (used for inspecting the new flow), Move (used for installing the flow after analysis), Quarantine (used for isolating the new flow), Block (used for obstructing the flow) and Discard (used for removing the new flow).The seven important packet features are the port number, source TCP port, destination TCP port, source IP, destination IP and source Ethernet and destination Ethernet. Malicious flows are separated from legitimate flows on the basis of the switch control policy. All incoming packet information is also updated on the monitoring server. The cloud monitoring server provides switches which take part in the SDN network with policies and trust values whereby switches can approve the authenticity of one another. Traffic flows are responsible for evaluating switch trust values. The trust appreciation of a switch is characterized by the probability of unused flow table passages and the probability of complete transfer of packets. Using the traffic flows the above probabilities are computed based on a specific time.

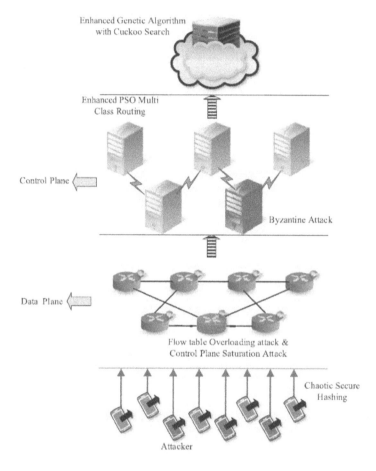

Figure 2.4   SecSDN-cloud environment.

2.5.2   Phase 1: User Authentication Phase

To be part of an SecSDN-cloud network, an authentication phase is required for authentication of every user. For this purpose it uses an algorithm called as DS-CSH algorithm. DS-CSH algorithm verifies the users according to their digital signatures. For security purposes, secure hashing algorithm (SHA) produces hash functions. It accomplishes authentication, digital signature and integrity. This research utilizes SHA3-384, in which the "384" means number of bits of the process.

Confused hash functions utilize mapping plans to decide the trajectory and select usable introductory conditions. By using Lyapunov exponents we can define the chaotic behavior. If a system is recognized as chaotic, then the difference in trajectory increases in relation to the initial condition and depends on the amount of time expended. The difference in trajectory relative to the initial condition increases depending on the period of time spent. The difference between them is expressed in the equation below.

$$d_t = d_0 2^{\lambda t} \tag{2.1}$$

Here, d_0 = initial distance, d_t = distance at time t and λ = Lyapunov exponents, which are calculated by averaging points in the equation below.

$$\lambda = \frac{1}{t_N - t_0} \sum_{k=1}^{N} log_2 \frac{d(t_k)}{d(t_k - 1)} \tag{2.2}$$

Here,

- N = number of points,

- t_0 = initial time,

- t_N = time at point,

- N, $d(t_k)$ = distances at point k, and

- $d(t_k - 1)$ = distances at point $k - 1$.

A system is considered to be chaotic or nonchaotic by analyzing the λ value from Equation (1.2). A system becomes chaotic if $\lambda > 0$. In sponge structure, message blocks are XORed and converted to the permutation function f, and input string (IS) is padded and converted to f. The above structure is used by SHA3 algorithm. This algorithm performs over bits of width b, rate r and output length d. The formulated sponge is represented in the equation below.

$$Z = Sponge[f, pad, r](N, d) \tag{2.3}$$

Here, hash function is generated having length 384 from the sponge bit string. The length of a message is not limited by the use of SHA3-384. The generated hashed function is sent to authentication switches. The packets of valid users will be verified according to predefined policy. An attacker can be identified with hash functions prior to the entry of the associated packets in the SecSDN-cloud network.

2.5.3   Phase 2: Controller Assignment Phase

In this phase we discuss how the control plane saturation attack is resolved by allocating controllers to switches utilizing the improved genetic algorithm merged with cuckoo search (EGA-CS) algorithm. Latency and load of the controller are treated as important metrics in this hybrid algorithm. The EGA classifies the chromosomes, and the CS then assigns controls [23].

Two key features of the hybrid algorithm are to produce optimum results globally and use minimal computing power. Selection, crossover and mutation are among the genetic operators. The aim of the CS algorithm is to select the best "eggs," where "eggs" indicate the quantity of controllers involved in the network. The EGA-CA hybrid 1 algorithm pseudo code is presented below.

2.5.3.1 Genetic Algorithm

A genetic algorithm is developed for natural biological assessment processes. This genetic algorithm begins with the number of chromosomes. Here we have to have more focus on fitness functions. Based upon this function the most appropriate individual is chosen from a set of individuals. Individuals with a better fitness value are considered superior solutions when compared to individuals with lower fitness values. When the most appropriate individuals have been selected the new population is generated through the application of mutation and crossover techniques to the original population. The chromosomes are ordered to determine the ongoing top chromosome with the best fitness value. After that, ordered chromosomes are handled using EGA-CS algorithm to diagnose the controller, which finds a perfect match with a switch. The best control unit identified is assigned to the switches to reduce the control plane saturation attack. These attacks are harmful because they overload the controllers and also reduce the network performance. The main aim of EGA-CA algorithm 1 is controller load allocation [24, 25]. This aim is achieved by selecting the best controller. The algorithm runs until it gets all the important features of the controllers. This study estimates latency and controller load fitness in the genetic algorithm, which approves high quality controllers and removes low quality controllers. The controllers present in SDN network are treated as chromosomes.

2.5.3.2 CS Algorithm

The CS algorithm was derived by studying a bird species (*specifically, the cuckoo*). This CS algorithm is a population-based meta-heuristic algorithm. The principles behind it are as follows:

- An egg is laid by the female cuckoo in a nest arbitrarily selected from the accessible nests.

- Future generations follow the top nest with superior eggs.

- An alien egg with a static number of nests at a probability of $P_a[0, 1]$ can be identified by a bird. As a result, the bird either discards the egg or builds a new nest in a new place.

As per the discussed EGA-CS hybrid model indicated in Figure 2.5, the outcomes generated by genetic algorithm are successful in generating a new solution which anticipates the Lévy flight, as stated in the following equation:

$$x_i^{t+1} = x_i^t + \alpha \oplus Levy(\lambda) \tag{2.4}$$

Here, α is represented as step size for upgrading a new solution and the value should be greater than 0. Now we have to estimate the Lévy flight. We use Lévy flight for determining the fitness from the node links. The best value is selected from the assessed fitness value based on the top control device allocated to a switch. These values are classified based on the optimum value of fitness function previously bestowed. By utilizing the EGA-CS algorithm all packets among the switches are assigned to controllers. Processing does not have to be delayed for packets. Here, the network has a dynamic environment so that controllers change dynamically according to the incoming packets. The number of initialized chromosomes varies with respect to time; therefore, the fitness value is generated every time. All fitness values are ordered and a single random fitness value is selected to run the CS algorithm. Here, the arbitrarily chosen fitness value will dependably be a standout amongst other best values acquired. In this task, controllers that are marginally loaded are chosen for the processing of packets that arrive from the switches. The controller task strategy is intended to fight control plane saturation attacks.

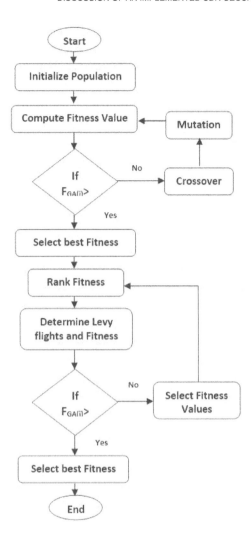

Figure 2.5   Proposed EGA-CS algorithm.

2.5.4   Phase 3: Communication Phase

This phase is used for transmitting data through a nodal route. By applying multiclass PSO [24] routing this proposed routing protocol is designed. PSO multiclass routing is carried out by means of traffic flow communication between controllers. This protocol is used for discovering the link module and gathers information from the network nodes. It then selects the route, where a node controls the QoS of other nodes. If another node has a higher QoS value than the current node, the other node is chosen for transmission as the only hop neighbor. If any change is required then the QoS of all nodes is regularly upgraded with the current status. Here E-PSO routing protocol uses a data traffic classifier for each node to classify them. To separate QoS classes with traffic flows the above-mentioned classifier is used.

The congestion of the node, the connection congestion and the node delay are achieved by the objective function of the individual controller. The task of the individual controller is to classify all the inward network flows into several categories. The equation below represents the objective function.

$$OF_n^i = Cn_n^{QoS_i} + \alpha(Nc^i + Pd^i) + \beta_n Lc^i + 1 \qquad (2.5)$$

Here,

- $Cn_n^{QoS_i}$ = the QoS of a controller,

- Nc^i = congestion at a controller,

- Pd^i = propagation delay, and

- Lc^i = link congestion of a controller.

Here, α_n and β_n are treated as weighted parameters. The node congestion is calculated by the following equation:

$$Nc^i(t_c) = Tl^i \times Bo^i \qquad (2.6)$$

The current congestion on the controller $Nc^i(tc)$ is formulated in terms of ρ_i = traffic load and ω_i = buffer occupancy. These metrics are calculated as follows:

$$Tl^i = \frac{\lambda^i}{\mu^i} \qquad (2.7)$$

$$Bo^i = \frac{Q^i}{L^i} \qquad (2.8)$$

Here,

- μ^i = service rate of controller i,

- λ^i = arrival rate of controller i,

- Q^i = queue length, and

- L^i = buffer length of controller I.

Then, Pd^i of the ith controller is calculated using the following equation:

$$Pd^i = \frac{D^{ij}}{Tx_{rt}^{ij}} \qquad (2.9)$$

Here,

- D^{ij} = distance between controllers I and j, and

- Tx_{Sd} = rate of transmission from one controller to another. For increasing QoS we have to minimize Nc^i, Lc^i and Pd^i.

Subsequently, the general work flow and design of the proposed secure SDN-cloud framework is resistant to three distinct kinds of attacks. Several switches, several controls along with monitoring unit are included in mitigating the damage caused by the activities of an attacker.

2.6   Result Analysis

In this segment, new security algorithms are used in proposed SecSDN-cloud environment. It requires the three phases that are mentioned below.

2.6.1   Simulation Environment

For implementing the developed secure SDN-cloud model, OMNeT++ simulation environment is used. For implementing the SecSDN-cloud model, OMNeT++ simulation environment supports OpenFlow INET files in different libraries. Simulation metrics are depicted in Table 2.1. The metrics which are included in the table are utilized by the proposed algorithm. Network performance analysis depends upon the number of OpenFlow switches, hosts, controllers and other parameters.

Table 2.1   Simulation parameters.

Specifications	Values
Number of hosts	16
Number of controllers	3
Number of switches	4
Queue type	Drop tail queue
Buffer capacity	10
Data rate	100 Mbps
Send interval	2 sec
Simulation time	30 sec

2.6.2   Analysis of Different Attacks

The main aim of SecSDN-cloud environment is to fight the different attacks described below.

2.6.2.1   Byzantine Attack

The main objective of Byzantine attacks is to delay the transmission and processing of packets. This delay is achieved due to the control failures in the network. To overcome these attacks the proposed SecSDN-cloud framework allocates controllers to different switches. It also uses a cloud monitoring server to run the EGA-CS algorithm.

2.6.2.2   Flow Table Overloading Attack

In SDN network, flow table size is linked to an individual switch. But the problem is the size of the flow table is limited. If switches are susceptible to attacks then they are trying to overload the flow table. Overloading of flow table occurs due to the longer processing time of an individual packet. This type of attack is somehow related to DDoS attack. To overcome this issue, SecSDN-cloud uses different policies which are applicable to different switches. These policies are helpful in avoiding the bad flows. For implementing these policies in individual switches a third party monitoring server is required. Therefore, even if the flow table of a switch is fully engaged, the flows are reduced based on the confidence values. In SecSDN-cloud framework, the monitoring unit has guidelines for individual switches in order to overcome the flow table overloading attack.

2.6.2.3   Control Plane Saturation Attack

These attacks are also called buffer saturation attacks. In SDN network, the loads on the controllers are increased due to the engagement gap created by communication between decoupling control and data planes. SYN flooding attacks are responsible for the above attacks. To overcome these attacks, SecSDN-cloud architecture uses multiple controllers so that no individual controller is fully loaded. By implementing multiple controllers the proposed framework minimizes loads by dividing the load among different controllers.

2.6.3   Comparative Analysis

Seven comparative plots are shown in this subsection to examine the capacity of the proposed system to fight different attacks. The seven parameters are bandwidth consumption, saturation time, loss of connectivity, loss of packets, holding time, throughput and end-to-end delay. Loss of packets, end-to-end delay and throughput parameters provide the QoS support in the proposed framework during data transmission.

2.6.3.1   Average Buffer Saturation Time

Due to the overloading of the controller buffer, control plane saturation attacks happen. Faster-filling buffer is responsible for more intense attack. The presented SecSDN-cloud contains multiple controllers in such a way that buffers are filled slowly. The buffers in the controllers are filled faster in LineSwitch as compared to SecSDN. Here we can conclude that the size of a buffer plays a main role in the above-mentioned attacks. If buffer size increases then intensity of attacks also increases.

Figure 2.6 portrays the outcomes obtained from developed simulation for the presented SecSDN-cloud framework by designing the graph between the mean buffer overload saturation times with respect to the bandwidth of the attacker. The performance of the presented SecSDN-cloud framework is 10% higher than LineSwitch regarding the saturation time.

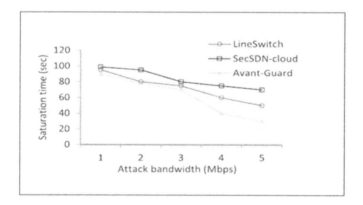

Figure 2.6   Comparison between LineSwitch, SecSDN-cloud and AvantGuard.

2.6.3.2   Network Connectivity Loss

The loss of connectivity is also an important parameter for the security of SecSDN-cloud. Network performance depends on the connectivity between the nodes. If the connectivity between two nodes decreases then network performance is also reduced.

The loss of connectivity on the basis of the security level during the Byzantine attack is shown in Figure 2.7. Connectivity of data and control planes are supported by the switches present in the controller. SecSDN-cloud provides fewer connectivity issues as compared to BFT.

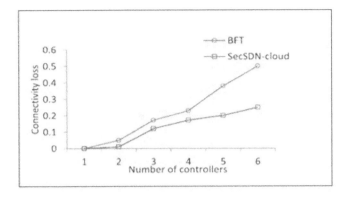

Figure 2.7   Comparison between BFT and SecSDN-cloud in response to a Byzantine attack.

2.6.3.3 Holding Time

Holding time is a significant metric in the presented SecSDN-cloud. If the holding time decreases, the chances of an attack are higher. Holding time is used to overcome the overloading of flow table attack. So, we can conclude that an SDN framework is more secure if it has longer hold times at higher attack rates.

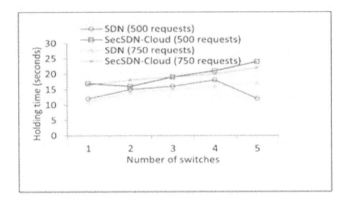

Figure 2.8   Flow table overloading attacks against robustness.

The effectiveness of attacks overloading the flow table is shown in Figure 2.8. The attackers aim for a single switch for entities to reside in and obstruct the entry of legitimate packets. A flow table with inadequate resource support has trouble with an overloading attack on the flow table. The presented SecSDN-cloud analyzes incoming packets in terms of server policies. This blocks all malicious traffic and increases the holding time.

2.6.3.4 Bandwidth Consumption

Bandwidth consumption is related to the number of attackers participating in the network. During the process the flow controllers should utilize least bandwidth in SDN network. Figure 2.9 shows the comparison of bandwidth between present and presented

SecSDN-cloud. For maintenance purposes a centralized controller requires more band-width, so SecSDN-cloud involves several controllers distributed at random. It also fights attackers by only permitting genuine network flows. To overcome these attacks legitimate traffic uses less bandwidth for processing.

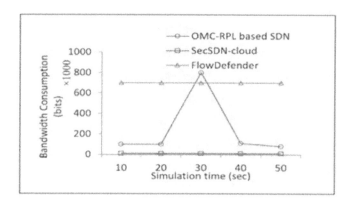

Figure 2.9   Comparison of bandwidth consumption of different frameworks with respect to simulation time.

2.6.3.5 Effectiveness of the QoS

The QoS provides high quality services to individual users in the network. This measure-ment is measured against different parameters such as throughput, bit rate, delay and loss of packets. Here, the efficiency of QoS is defined by three important parameter throughputs, end-to-end delay and loss of packets.

The amount of data transmitted within a specified time period from one entity to another is called network throughput. Tp (throughput) is formulated as follows:

$$T_p = \frac{NP_s}{T} \tag{2.10}$$

Here NP_s = number of packets transferred and T = time interval of transmission.

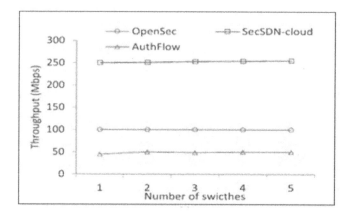

Figure 2.10   Comparison of throughput of different frameworks with respect to switches count.

Figure 2.10 displays performance enhancements in relation to the presented SecSDN-cloud architecture. If we want to increase the performance of throughput then we have to protect the network from the attackers. End-to-end latency analysis is depicted in Figure 2.11.

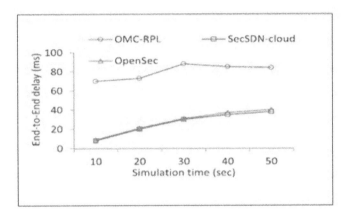

Figure 2.11   Comparison of end-to-end delay of different frameworks with respect to simulation time.

The definition of end-to-end latency states the interval needed in transmitting data from sender to receiver within a network. If the number of incoming packets increases then the simulation time also increases, subsequently increasing the delay in SecSDN-cloud. Delay in network happens due to the failure of a node or due to the connectivity issues between two nodes. Presented SecSDN-cloud overcomes the above issues. We focus more on the parameters which are used to reduce the end-to-end delay metric. Presented SecSDN-cloud improves QoS. Loss of packets arises due to the packets discarded by an overloaded packet device. Due to limitations in the size of buffers and queues, only a limited number of packets can be accepted by a device. Network attack packets can lead to loss of packets for genuine users.

Figure 2.12 depicts that the SecSDN-cloud reduces packet losses, as harmful attacks can be mitigated.

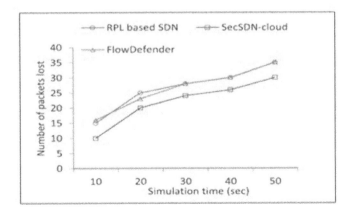

Figure 2.12   Comparison of packet loss of different frameworks with respect to simulation time.

2.7   Conclusion

Security plays an integral part in determining the efficiency of cloud computing framework. The credibility and effectiveness of cloud computing models are reduced in the absence of proper security measures being in place. The primary focus of this chapter was to discuss security issues concerning cloud computing. Various security issues were presented and classified in our study and countermeasures were highlighted. Also, a secure software-defined network (SDN) based framework was discussed in detail along with its implementation. This model framework can help in resisting various types of vulnerabilities like flow table overloading, Byzantine attacks and control plane saturation in the network.

REFERENCES

1. Le, D. N., Kumar, R., Nguyen, G. N., & Chatterjee, J. M. (2018). *Cloud Computing and Virtualization*. John Wiley & Sons.

2. Le, D. N., Kumar, R., Mishra, B. K., Chatterjee, J. M., & Khari, M. (Eds.). (2019). *Cyber Security in Parallel and Distributed Computing: Concepts, Techniques, Applications and Case Studies*. John Wiley & Sons.

3. Feuerlicht, G., Burkon, L., & Sebesta, M. (2011). Cloud computing adoption: what are the issues. *System Integration*, 18(2), 187-192.

4. Fox, A., Griffith, R., Joseph, A., Katz, R., Konwinski, A., Lee, G., ... & Stoica, I. (2009). Above the clouds: A Berkeley view of cloud computing. Dept. *Electrical Eng. and Comput. Sciences*, University of California, Berkeley, Rep. UCB/EECS, 28(13), 2009.

5. Shankland, S. (2009). HP's Hurd dings cloud computing, IBM. CNET News.

6. ENISA, C. C. (2009). Benefits, risks and recommendations for information security. *European Network and Information Security*.

7. Carroll, M., Van Der Merwe, A., & Kotze, P. (2011, August). Secure cloud computing: Benefits, risks and controls. In 2011 Information Security for South Africa (pp. 1-9). IEEE.

8. Mather, T., Kumaraswamy, S., & Latif, S. (2009). *Cloud security and privacy: an enterprise perspective on risks and compliance*. O'Reilly Media, Inc.

9. Chen, Y., Paxson, V., & Katz, R. H. (2010). What's new about cloud computing security. University of California, Berkeley Report No. UCB/EECS-2010-5 January, 20(2010), 2010-5.

10. Chen, Y., Paxson, V., & Katz, R. H. (2010). What's new about cloud computing security. University of California, Berkeley Report No. UCB/EECS-2010-5 January, 20(2010), 2010-5.

11. Salesforce, Salesforce security statement, salesforce.com/company/privacy/security.jsp, 2011.

12. Espiner, T. (2007). Salesforce tight-lipped after phishing attack. zdnet. co. uk/news/security-threats/2007/11/07/salesforce-tight-lippedafter-phishing-attack-39290616.

13. McMillan, R. (2010). Google attack part of widespread spying effort. Computerworld, 13, 5.

14. E. Mills, Behind the china attacks on google, CNET News, January 2010.

15. J. Bosch, Google accounts attacked by phishing scam, BrickHouse Security Blog, October 2009.

16. T. Telegraph, Facebook users targeted by phishing attack, The Telegraph, May 2009.

17. Subramanian, N., & Jeyaraj, A. (2018). Recent security challenges in cloud computing. *Computers & Electrical Engineering*, 71, 28-42.

18. Stergiou, C., Psannis, K. E., Gupta, B. B., & Ishibashi, Y. (2018). Security, privacy & efficiency of sustainable Cloud Computing for Big Data & IoT. *Sustainable Computing: Informatics and Systems*, 19, 174-184.

19. Sushruta Mishra, Hrudaya Kumar Tripathy, Amiya Ranjan Panda (2018), An Improved and Adaptive Attribute Selection Technique to Optimize Dengue Fever Prediction, *International Journal of Engineering & Technology*, Vol.7, pp: 480-486.

20. Mishra, S., Tripathy, H. K., & Mishra, B. K. (2018). Implementation of biologically motivated optimisation approach for tumour categorisation. *International Journal of Computer Aided Engineering and Technology*, 10(3), 244-256.

21. Singh, A., & Chatterjee, K. (2017). Cloud security issues and challenges: A survey. *Journal of Network and Computer Applications*, 79, 88-115.

22. Hussain, S. A., Fatima, M., Saeed, A., Raza, I., & Shahzad, R. K. (2017). Multilevel classification of security concerns in cloud computing. *Applied Computing and Informatics*, 13(1), 57-65.

23. Abdulqadder, I. H., Zou, D., Aziz, I. T., Yuan, B., & Li, W. (2018). SecSDN-cloud: Defeating vulnerable attacks through secure software-defined networks. *IEEE Access*, 6, 8292-8301.

24. Nayyar, A., Le, D. N., & Nguyen, N. G. (Eds.). (2018). *Advances in Swarm Intelligence for Optimizing Problems in Computer Science*. CRC Press.

25. Chatterjee, S., Sarkar, S., Hore, S., Dey, N., Ashour, A. S., Shi, F., & Le, D. N. (2017). Structural failure classification for reinforced concrete buildings using trained neural network based multi-objective genetic algorithm. *Structural Engineering and Mechanics*, 63(4), 429-438.

CHAPTER 3

SECURITY AND CHALLENGES IN MOBILE CLOUD COMPUTING

ANKUR DUMKA[1], MINAKSHI MEMORIA[2], ALAKNANDA ASHOK[2]

[1]Graphic Era Deemed to be University, Dehradun, India
[2]Tula Institute, Dehradun, India
[3] Women Institute of Technology, Dehradun, India
 Email: ankurdumka2@gmail.com

Abstract

Cloud computing is an emerging field in which security is one of the major concerns. Integrating mobile technology with cloud technology is a demanding task these days. This chapter discusses different security issues and challenges in mobile cloud computing when integrating cloud computing with mobile technology. To this end a discussion of various security protocols and solutions provided by different researchers is presented in an organized manner, thereby paving the way for future directions in this area. This chapter extends the discussion to the three subcategories of security issues in mobile cloud computing–infrastructural or architectural issues, privacy issues and compliance issues–and the challenges in these security parameters.

Keywords: Mobile cloud computing, IoT, SaaS, PaaS, IaaS, security, virtualization

3.1   Introduction

In order to increase the computational resource for mobile users, network operators and providers of cloud computing the term mobile cloud computing came into existence. Mobile cloud computing (MCC) is used for execution of rich mobile applications with a wide range of user experiences. Thus, it integrates mobile technology with cloud technology for integrating and improving the functioning of the internet of things (IoT) [1, 2]. Integration of these features all together helps in generating a new generation of phones which are better than existing phones in terms of speed, size and computational speed along with the ability to handle a wide range of applications. With the growth of communication and technologies, access to technologies is become easier but security of these devices is always a challenge. This chapter focuses on security issues related to mobile cloud computing integrated with IoT.

Integration of the mobile environment with cloud computing has also emerged which has several challenges that effect the performance of devices. Some of the challenges are life of battery, storage, bandwidth, heterogeneity, scalability and availability. Some of the essential features of MCC are as follows:

1. On-demand self-service,

2. Wider network access,

3. Rapid elasticity, and

4. Resource pooling.

On-demand self-service delivers computational resources, such as storage, software, etc., automatically as and when needed by the client without the use of any human interaction. Wider network access provides resources over a wider range that can be used by many client applications without a heterogeneous platform across the network. The rapid elasticity feature of MCC provides the functionality of service in an elastic manner that can be extended to a range. Resource pooling is the pooling of resources of the service provider in order to serve multiple clients by means of virtualization or multi-tenant model [3, 4].

The MCC model can be deployed as private cloud, public cloud, hybrid cloud or community cloud, with private cloud being operated within a particular organization. Public cloud is deployed in the public cloud domain which can be used by general public clients, with the cloud service provider having full ownership of public cloud. Hybrid cloud infrastructure is a combination of two or more clouds, including private and public clouds with unique entities bound together by standardized or propriety technology that enable data and application portability. Community cloud is set up by many organizations that share the same cloud infrastructure, policies, requirements, values, etc.

3.1.1   Mobile Cloud Computing

With the advancement of the use of the internet within mobile devices, the scope and usage of mobile cloud computing has also increased manyfold. Thus, mobile cloud computing is defined as a system which stores and processes data outside the mobile environment [5, 6]. Mobile cloud computing provides a convenient and easy way to use internet services by mobile users and also provides extensive computation and storage in the cloud environment, thus overcoming the problem of limited memory and computation processing limitation of mobiles.

Mobile applications use cloud services like SaaS, PaaS and IaaS which are linked to servers operating within the cloud and thus support a large number of mobile clients. The mobile cloud architecture can be categorized into three components: mobile clients, middleware and cloud services. They all are related in a manner such that each client is connected with cloud services managed by middleware. This middleware is used to push the updates to services by means of hypertext transfer protocol (HTTP).

Models for mobile cloud computing can be categorized as Mobile as a Service Consumer (MaaSC), Mobile as a Service Provider (MaaSP), and Mobile as a Service Broker (MaaSB). The most commonly used mobile cloud computing model is the MaaSC model, which provides higher throughput and uses outsourced computation and storage for a wider range of applications. The MaaSP-cloud model provides the capability of the service provider to each client. The service provided by each client is based on sensing and processing capabilities of the connecting mobile devices with application data ranging from GPS, camera, and other device-related data. Other devices use this data for improving performance and accuracy of various applications. The MaaSB model is useful for those mobile devices which are limited in their capacity. This model uses mobile devices as a gateway for providing network services by means of Bluetooth, WiFi or cell phone provider network for communicating and sending data to cloud resources. These mobile devices also provide security for sensor networks [7, 8].

Figure 3.1 Mobile as a service consumer model.

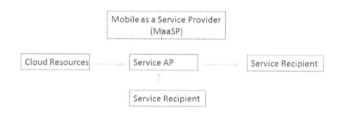

Figure 3.2 Mobile as a service provider service model.

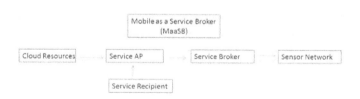

Figure 3.3 Mobile as a service broker service model.

Figures 3.1, 3.2 and 3.3 represent the model for the service consumer model, and service provider service model, service broker service model for mobile cloud computing. For mobile cloud computing, there are many issues like security, limited battery and computational power due to the small size of mobile phones. Also, issues like varying signals and mobile network problems may lead to degradation in the performance of operation which may lead to inefficient connectivity with cloud environment due to limited internet connections.

3.1.2   Internet of Things and Cloud Computing

The internet of things (IoT) is one of the emerging technologies used for capturing the environmental parameters by means of sensors and can help in accessing and processing the data anytime and everywhere by using the internet. Integration of cloud computing with IoT brings a revolution to the technology. The issue of limited power and storage capacity of IoT is being resolved by integrating cloud computing with IoT. Thus, integrating cloud computing with IoT makes the processing of large data captured by IoT devices more cost-effective and convenient. The sensors used in IoT are limited, with low processing power and limited resources and integration of cloud with IoT also helping to overcome this problem by sending and processing the data in cloud computing [9].

3.2   Literature Review

Dinh *et al.* [7] and Rahimi *et al.* [10] propose the architecture of mobile cloud computing, whereas Fernando *et al.* [8] and Alizadeh and Hassan [11] discuss the challenges within the mobile cloud computing model, and Ra *et al.* [12], Kovachev *et al.* [13], and Guan *et al.* [14] propose different types of application models for mobile cloud computing. Suo *et al.* [15] and Shahzad *et al.* [16] discuss different security issues within the mobile cloud computing model. Different researchers discuss the concept of an energy saving and computational overloading model of mobile cloud computing. Yang *et al.* [27], Xiao and Xiao [18] and Gonzalez *et al.* [19] discuss data security within cloud computing and how to set up thrust between consumers and cloud service providers for efficient working of cloud computing. In their paper, Kumar and Rajalakshmi [20] discuss and analyze the issues concerning mobile cloud security and vulnerabilities related to mobile cloud computing. They also discuss the use of smart card web services (SCWS), which provide suitable security solutions for mobile cloud computing. Khan *et al.* [21] discuss light data security and application security framework within mobile cloud computing which proposes cryptography techniques. Alizadeh *et al.* [22] discuss the authentication method for the user side and cloud side in mobile cloud computing and propose a solution for usability, security, efficiency and privacy as measuring parameters.

3.3   Architecture of Integration of Mobile Cloud Computing with IoT

In mobile cloud computing with IoT mobile networks, cloud computing and IoT are combined. This is useful in providing services for things using mobile devices. Cloud computing exists when a lot of data exists in different places and tasks are performed in another place. The applications run on remote server using mobile devices and the results are shown on things connected to it through IoT. There is a base station to connect mobile devices with mobile networks and then both establish connection and control interface between each other. The user of mobile devices send a request and it is transmitted to the central processor using cloud through a web browser application. Mobile networks provide services to mobile users, such as authentication, authorization and accounting, based on home agent and subscriber's data stored in their databases. After that the request is transmitted to cloud using the internet. Then the cloud controller processes these requests and provides services such as utility computing and virtualization. Through the internet these services can be used to process IoT as per their requirement of application [23, 24].

By integration of IoT and mobile cloud computing we have the opportunity to expand the use of available technology that is provided in the cloud environment. Now the application and information that use IoT can be integrated with the use of cloud storage. The cloud offers mobile users and wireless users access to all the information and applications anywhere, anytime they are needed for IoT connectivity. Figure 3.4 represents the architecture for integration of mobile cloud computing with IoT [25-27].

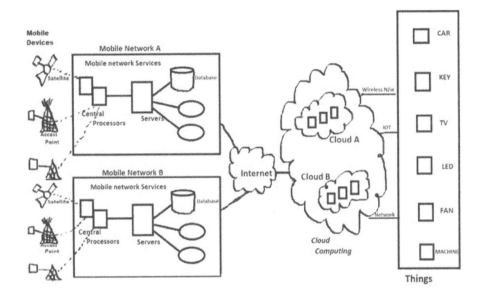

Figure 3.4   Architecture of integration of mobile cloud computing with IoT.

The details of cloud computing can be specified by four layer architecture. There are four layers which describe the cloud services. These are described as follows:

- Software as a Service: SaaS supports software as per requirement. In this layer the user can access information and application and pay for only that usage. Today SaaS is offered by companies such as Google, Salesforce, Microsoft and Zoho. They provide the services and allow sharing and accessing of files from different resources simultaneously.

- Platform as a Service: PaaS provides a platform and solution stack as a service. It also offers an integrated environment for building, testing and deploying remote application. The end users do not manage and control cloud infrastructure using operating system, storage, servers and network. It provides a predefined combination of operating system and application servers such as XAMP[1] (X-cross platform) limited to J2EE (Java 2 Platform, Enterprise Edition), LAMP (Linux, Apache, MySQL and

---

[1]https://www.apachefriends.org/

PHP), WAMP platform (Windows, Apache, MySQL and PHP) and Ruby.[2]   These services are provided by Salesforce,[3] App Engine,[4] Google, etc.

- Infrastructure as a Service: IaaS provides processing, storage, network and other computing resources so that end users are able to run their application using software and pay-per-use resources. Infrastructure can be expanded and shrunk as per their requirement. The end users do not manage and control cloud infrastructure but it has control over storage, operating system, applications and possibly limited control of networking components. Examples of IaaS are 3Tera, GoGrid, Amazon Elastic Compute Cloud[5] and S3.

- Data Center Layer: This layer provides the infrastructure and hardware facility for clouds. It provides high speed networking services for customers by connecting a number of servers. Basically this layer can be placed at low populated places and can provide high power stability and low risk of disaster.

Figure 3.5 represents the architecture for a cloud computing model which includes SaaS, IaaS and PaaS integrated with data center layer.

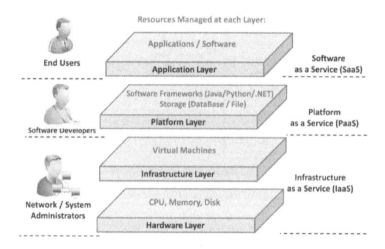

Figure 3.5   Cloud computing architecture.

The security issues in mobile cloud computing can be categorized into the following types:

1. Infrastructural or architectural issues

2. Privacy issue

3. Compliance issue

[2]https://www.ruby-lang.org/en/
[3]https://www.salesforce.com/
[4]https://cloud.google.com/appengine/
[5]https://aws.amazon.com/ec2/

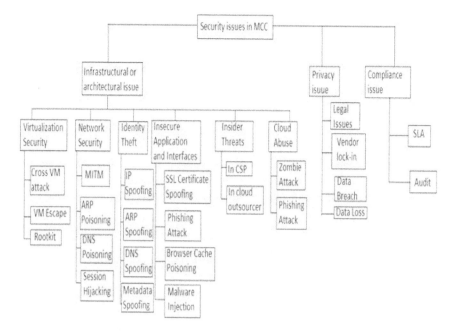

Figure 3.6   Classification of security issues in mobile cloud computing.

3.3.1   Infrastructural or Architectural Issues

Infrastructural and architectural issues cover issues related to virtualization security, network security, issues with data segregation, insider attacks or issues related to administrative interference [28-31], which are classified as follows:

1. Virtualization Security: Virtualization allows a service provider to support multiple users for storing of data by using the concept of SaaS services and also supports on-demand services. This feature poses a security issue and challenge if the data is not segregated in a proper manner at physical or application level. Some of the issues related to this are isolation of multiple virtual machines running on the same physical machine, cross-VM attack, injection of malicious code within the application or hypervisor vulnerability. Virtualization security can be of the following types:

   - Cross-VM Attack: A cross-VM attack positions a malicious VM into the same physical hypervisor platform and thus access shared hardware and cache location in order to perform a variety of side-channel attacks. Some of these attacks are denial-of-service (DoS) attack, detection of utilization of hardware, and monitoring of remote keystroke by means of timing interference.

   - VM Escape: VM escape bypasses the isolation of hosts and VMs by running malware within the VM and thus makes direct communication with hypervisor which causes a threat to the security of cloud environment. Thus, in this attack, the attackers access privileges to the hypervisor can result in them accessing the host operating system, thus allowing them to get full control over the environment.

   - Rootkits: VM-based rootkits are a type of malware that take control of the operating system, thus taking control of the hypervisor.

2. Network Security: Network security is related to security issues in networking communications and configurations. There are many networking protocols like ARP, RARP, HTTP, SMTP, etc., which are more prone to attack in the cloud system where they are implemented or used. There are many attacks like DNS poisoning, ARP poisoning, DoS, etc., which can hamper the working of the network. Various encryption techniques like SSL, TLS, etc., can be used to prevent such attacks. Network security can be categorized as:

   ▪ MITM: A man-in-the-middle (MITM) attack can occur due to improper configuration of SSL security encryption technique. An MITM attack can enable an attacker to access the communication between data centers and virtual machines and thus can cause a threat to the security of the network.

   ▪ ARP Poisoning: ARP poisoning is used by attackers for redirecting all inbound and outbound traffic from other virtual machines (VMs) to its virtual machines. It is based on the fact that ARP doesn't require proof of origin.

   ▪ DNS Poisoning: DNS poisoning is used for tricking the domain name server (DNS) in order to send the traffic in the wrong direction by modifying DNS cache.

   ▪ Session Hijacking: Session hijacking allows the attacker to assume the user's identity by exploiting improper implementation of session id in HTTP protocol, where the user accesses the information from a remote server using this protocol, thus allowing anonymous authentication and encrypted traffic to thwart such attack.

3. Identity Theft: Identity theft is a type of security breach where an entity wants to hide his identity by pretending he is part of the network in order to consume resources of the network and extract crucial information from it. Various forms of identity theft are IP spoofing, ARP spoofing, DNS spoofing and metadata spoofing, which are discussed below.

   ▪ IP Spoofing: In IP spoofing, the attacker sends the packet with the header by changing the source address to the destination system and the system treats this packet as its own packet coming from a legal sender and accepts this packet. The destination system is not able to find any changes in the packet as this spoofing is carried at network level.

   ▪ ARP Spoofing: In ARP spoofing, the attacker sends an updated ARP message on local area network. The attacker links the MAC address with IP address and can receive any kind of data that belongs to only the actual IP address. ARP spoofing can modify data and stop any transmission that should not be done with that IP address.

   ▪ DNS Spoofing: DNS spoofing is a type of attack which is applied on actual websites and creates a fake website navigated by the user through the internet and looks like the real one having the stolen credentials of users and traffic diversion. It can go on for a long time before being detected as a serious security issue.

   ▪ Metadata Spoofing: A metadata spoofing attack allows the attacker to modify the service's WSDL file at service delivery time, which will enable the attacker to enter into the network and steal valuable information or inject malicious code within the network.

- Phishing Attack: A phishing attack allows the attacker to fool the user by setting up a fake URL similar to the real web application in order to get the credentials and certificates of the user.

4. Insecure Application and Interfaces: This security issue is due to the fact that cloud environment uses application and interfaces for exploration of resources and tools from virtualized environment. There is a chance that this application and these interfaces can be attacked if they are not managed properly. Somorovsky *et al.* [33] have discussed security analysis of control interfaces of Amazon and Eucalyptus by taking examples of signature wrapping and XSS techniques. Insecure application and interfaces can be of the following types:

   - SSL Certificate Spoofing: SSL protocol is a security protocol which enables a secure and safe communication from the user's browser to the server by means of an SSL certificate which can be verified by the user's browser. Any breach of the SSL certificate will lead to a warning alert at the user's side. The breach of the SSL certificate can be done by impersonating a legitimate server through an SSL certificate poisoning attack to intercept sensitive information.

   - Phishing Attack: Phishing attacks are well known for arranging the weblink as per requirement and switching a user to a false link to get sensitive data. In a phishing attack, an attacker can use the cloud service to host the phishing attack website to expropriate accounts and services of other users in the cloud.

   - Browser Cache Poisoning: This cache poisoning, which is also called DNS poisoning or DNS cache poisoning, is applied to corrupt the internet's domain name server by changing the internet address with some other address or savage address. When a web user requests that address, the request is redirected by the savaged entry in the table to a different address. At that point another hijacking program can be downloaded by savage location to the user's location.

   - Malware Injection: In this type of attack the attacker tries to inject hostile service or virtual machine on cloud. The attacker tries to create his own hostile services implementation module or virtual machine instance and tries to add it to the cloud system. Then the attacker tries to act as though this service is a valid service to the cloud system that is some new service implementation instance among the valid instances. If he succeeds, there can be an easy redirection of the request of the legal user to the hostile service implementation and the attacker can easily enter a code to execute and transfer the hostile service instance into cloud.

5. Insider Threats: An insider threat is a threat from a malicious person within the organization. Since these persons are familiar with the network and the authorized person for the network they can cause great harm to the cloud environment. These attacks can be prevented by applying coherent demarcation of duties or transparent management of policies for the employees.

6. Cloud Abuse: Cloud abuse harms the services of cloud by means of breaking of encryption keys, sharing of pirated software or DDoS attack or phishing attack. This attack can be avoided by proper validation and verification checks at the initial registration phase and also by constant monitoring of the network traffic. Cloud abuse can be of the following types:

- Zombie Attack: In a zombie attack the attacker tries to exploit the victim through the internet by sending some requests from noble hosts in the existing network. These types of hosts affected by an attacker are called zombies. The request for virtual machine is accessible by each user by using the network. An attacker exploits a large number of requests through zombies. Such an attack changes the actual behavior of cloud and also affects the availability of cloud service. A large number of requests can occur that overload the cloud, which can result in unavailability of service or denial of service or distributed denial of service to the servers. In the presence of the attacker's exploited requests, cloud is not able to take real or genuine user's request.

- Phishing Attack: Phishing attacks are well known for arranging the weblink as per requirement and switching a user to a false link to get sensitive data. In a phishing attack, an attacker can use the cloud service to host the phishing attack website to expropriate accounts and services of other users in the cloud.

3.3.2 Privacy Issues

There are several advantages in mobile cloud computing but there are some privacy issues. Some of them are as follows:

1. Legal issues

2. Vendor lock-in

3. Data breach

4. Data loss

Cloud computing provides the facility to store a large amount of personal data and purchased media data such as audio, video and image files. For a user, there is the possibility of losing access to some amount of purchased data. To remove these types of risks, the user should be aware of the rights of data ownership. Mobile cloud computing utilizes the required information about users such as profiles, locations and capability of devices, which can be used by the cloud controller server to achieve local access optimization.

The hosting is done at different places for customers and service providers. There can be many law enforcement measures used directly or indirectly in between that access of data through cloud. Due to dissimilar cloud architecture and loss of administrative control of the customer on the actual cloud, some governance issues like vendor/data lock-in arise. The availability of a large number of cloud servers and mobile devices on one hand but fewer uniform standards and APIs on the other hand has emerged as a vendor lock-in issue. As demanded by the court of law for a particular customer, law enforcement results in disclosure of hardware devices but it will also affect all customers whose data were stored on these devices. So, a breaching issue arises here, as this breaching onto cloud that stores data of various users and organizations can attack data of all other users who need confidentiality, authenticity and integrity. The major challenges are remote integrity check, data control, identity management, key management and data ownership.

In mobile cloud computing, privacy is also one of the biggest issues. Some other issues are data confidentiality, data authenticity, data integrity, availability, non-repudiation and access control. Data confidentiality is a concept that refers to only the sender and receiver having access to the message. A third party will not be able to access that data.

But this is the biggest challenge because the cloud controller has to provide the access control for authentic users only. For authenticity, establishing proof of identities that can communicate only with those nodes that have been claimed is required. Data integration is performed when data from different resources is required. But if data from one location belongs to only a particular user and data from another location do not have these features and standards, it is not possible to provide privacy at that time. Integrity also prevents undetected modification of data by any unauthorized user, which is not feasible with the type of system discussed above. Access control ensures that the use of network services and resources is done between only authorized users. It also acts as a frame to provide data authenticity, confidentiality and integrity. It actually starts with authentication, which finalizes the authentic user for particular data where access of data comprises reading of data (data confidentiality) and writing of data (data integrity). Availability ensures that data can be accessed by the authorized user when needed. Data loss consists of data unavailability in the event of carelessness, power outage, malicious attacks and natural disasters such as floods, earthquakes, etc. It can turn into a problematic situation when the data to be used is very important such as data related to health, forces, etc. The efforts are required to minimize these losses but it can spoil the data breach and vice versa. We can provide encryption to minimize data breach but if that encryption key is lost the the complete data is lost. Contrarily, if offline backup is used to prevent loss of valuable data there is a high potential of exposure to data breaches. Therefore, it is required that there also be strong encryption techniques, security of encryption keys, data integrity checks and efficient data backup strategies.

3.3.3 Compliance Issues

Compliance issues can be categorized into two types as follows:

1. SLA (service level agreement)

2. Audit

Compliance consists of principles that enforce rules that implement the policies or parts of regulations. In order to achieve environmental and health benefits, a large degree of compliance is required. There are different types of regulations, such as government and state regulations, but some are suggestions like those used for organizations. Software architecture can serve as a reference to indicate where the compliance policies should be applied in the architecture. This reference architecture does not have any platform dependencies. Pattern consists of a specific context in which a solution is provided to a surveying problem. It helps improve software equality by promoting data scalability, reusability and consistency. This pattern can be segregated into various categories such as security, analysis, architecture and design pattern. SLA ensures that services and procedures are adopted to guarantee a certain level of security. SaaS (security as a service) provides delivery of security services to the users through cloud using the internet as the other cloud service. This model provides the continuous monitoring of data and its related transactions mainly on the receiver side and decreases the parameters required for security on the provider side. This service includes some services and tools such as identity and access management, data loss prevention, web security, email security, security assessment, business continuity and disaster recovery, intrusion management, encryption and network security. If these kinds of services are used then it gives benefit in cost, scalability, expertise, continuous update and ease of management.

3.4 Proposed Preventive Measure for Security in MCC

Security is always one of the major issues in cloud computing. Many security schemes already exist for securing mobile cloud computing. A discussion of some of those proposed by researchers follow.

- H. Liang & C. Han proposed a novel approach for preventing issues of virtualization security which is achieved by deployment of virtual machine. This technique uses mandatory access control techniques for controlling resources and thus help in isolating guest virtual machines [32].

- Z. Hao & Y. Tang worked on the issue of virtualization security by proposing a new technique termed as SMOC which gives permission to make a copy of the operating system and mobile application to virtual machine on cloud for data security [33].

- S. Jin & J. Ahn proposed a newly developed technique called H-SVM which also focuses on virtualization security. This technique secures guest virtual machine from infected hypervisor by means of memory virtualization. The technique proposed was highly vulnerable in nature [34].

- M. B. Mollah proposed a solution for data security, which entails sharing and searching of data from mobile devices for sharing and searching data in cloud in a secure manner by making use of public and private key encryption and digital signature [35].

- V. Odelu proposed a solution for data security in mobile cloud computing by using two novel schemes: Secure and lightweight CP-ABE (SL-CP-ABE) and CP-ABE Constant-size type text and secret key (CP-ABE-CSCTSK). These techniques are used to access control and outsource computational process from cloud to mobile [36].

- Y. Duan & M. Zhang focused their research approach towards offloading security issues where users keep their private information in a phone while offloading is being performed. This offloading will be used to avoid the problem of unauthorized access or the security problem of integrity [37].

- S. A. Saab & F. Saab also restricted their research area to the field of offloading security issues where they proposed a mobile application offloading technique that consists of profiling, decision making and offloading engine. This profiling and decision making are used by dynamic partitioning in order to reduce power consumption and decrease security issues. An offloading engine is used to offload an app to cloud for processing [38].

- S.L. Tang & L. Ouyang had focused their research on issues related to mobile cloud computing application where they proposed an application program interface (API) model which further categorizes factors into three subfactors: 1) authentication of user registration with strong password, 2) using security mechanism of encryption, decryption or digital signature and 3) API with backend service [39].

- Z. Sitova & J. Sedenka confined their research to security issues in mobile devices where they proposed a biometric technique for authentication of user within mobile device. This biometric technique uses the hand movement of the user who is grasping the mobile phone, thus generating patterns which are used for identification for authorized and unauthorized users [40].

3.5 Conclusion

This chapter discussed cloud computing and mobile cloud computing and integration of cloud computing with IoT, and how the integration of cloud computing is beneficial to the mobile-based application. The integration of cloud computing with mobile-based application and IoT leads to many security loopholes as far as terms of security and breach of security is concerned. This chapter primarily focused on security issues related to mobile cloud computing integration with IoT and the different factors that affect the normal working of security of mobile cloud computing with IoT. Also discussed were the different security issues in this field and the different factors affecting security in this area and how they can be treated in order to provide an efficient and normal working of mobile cloud computing with IoT-enabled service.

This chapter categorized security issues into three types: Infrastructural or architectural issues, privacy issues and compliance issues. These three categories were studied in detail and various issues related to them were discussed. This chapter also discussed some of the preventive measures proposed by different research scholars for mobile cloud computing based on different areas of mobile cloud computing.

REFERENCES

1. Padma, M., & Neelima, M. L. (2014). Mobile Cloud Computing: Issues from a Security Perspective. *International Journal of Computer Science and Mobile Computing*, 3(5), 972-977.

2. Grozev, N., & Buyya, R. (2014). InterCloud architectures and application brokering: taxonomy and survey. *Software: Practice and Experience*, 44(3), 369-390.

3. He, W., Yan, G., & Da Xu, L. (2014). Developing vehicular data cloud services in the IoT environment. *IEEE Transactions on Industrial Informatics*, 10(2), 1587-1595.

4. Jeffery, K. (2014). Keynote: CLOUDs: A large virtualisation of small things. In The 2nd International Conference on Future Internet of Things and Cloud (FiCloud-2014).

5. Huang, D., Xing, T., & Wu, H. (2013). Mobile cloud computing service models: a user-centric approach. *IEEE network*, 27(5), 6-11.

6. Mollah, M. B., Azad, M. A. K., & Vasilakos, A. (2017). Security and privacy challenges in mobile cloud computing: Survey and way ahead. *Journal of Network and Computer Applications*, 84, 38-54.

7. Dinh, H. T., Lee, C., Niyato, D., & Wang, P. (2013). A survey of mobile cloud computing: architecture, applications, and approaches. *Wireless communications and mobile computing*, 13(18), 1587-1611.

8. Fernando, N., Loke, S. W., & Rahayu, W. (2013). Mobile cloud computing: A survey. *Future generation computer systems*, 29(1), 84-106.

9. Rahimi, M. R., Ren, J., Liu, C. H., Vasilakos, A. V., & Venkatasubramanian, N. (2014). Mobile cloud computing: A survey, state of art and future directions. *Mobile Networks and Applications*, 19(2), 133-143.

10. Rahimi, M. R., Venkatasubramanian, N., & Vasilakos, A. V. (2013, June). MuSIC: Mobility-aware optimal service allocation in mobile cloud computing. In 2013 IEEE Sixth International Conference on Cloud Computing (pp. 75-82). IEEE.

11. Alizadeh, M., & Hassan, W. H. (2013, July). Challenges and opportunities of mobile cloud computing. In 2013 9th International Wireless Communications and Mobile Computing Conference (IWCMC) (pp. 660-666). ieee.

12. Ra, M. R., Sheth, A., Mummert, L., Pillai, P., Wetherall, D., & Govindan, R. (2011, June). Odessa: enabling interactive perception applications on mobile devices. In Proceedings of the 9th international conference on Mobile systems, applications, and services (pp. 43-56). ACM.

13. Kovachev, D., Cao, Y., & Klamma, R. (2011). Mobile cloud computing: a comparison of application models. arXiv preprint arXiv:1107.4940.

14. Guan, L., Ke, X., Song, M., & Song, J. (2011, May). A survey of research on mobile cloud computing. In 2011 10th IEEE/ACIS International Conference on Computer and Information Science (pp. 387-392). IEEE.

15. Suo, H., Liu, Z., Wan, J., & Zhou, K. (2013, July). Security and privacy in mobile cloud computing. In 2013 9th International Wireless Communications and Mobile Computing Conference (IWCMC) (pp. 655-659). IEEE.

16. Shahzad, A., & Hussain, M. (2013). Security issues and challenges of mobile cloud computing. *International Journal of Grid and Distributed Computing*, 6(6), 37-50.

17. Yang, S., Kwon, D., Yi, H., Cho, Y., Kwon, Y., & Paek, Y. (2014). Techniques to minimize state transfer costs for dynamic execution offloading in mobile cloud computing. *IEEE Transactions on Mobile Computing*, 13(11), 2648-2660.

18. Xiao, Z., & Xiao, Y. (2013). Security and privacy in cloud computing. *IEEE Communications Surveys & Tutorials*, 15(2), 843-859.

19. Gonzalez, N., Miers, C., Redigolo, F., Simplicio, M., Carvalho, T., Nslund, M., & Pourzandi, M. (2012). A quantitative analysis of current security concerns and solutions for cloud computing. *Journal of Cloud Computing: Advances, Systems and Applications*, 1(1), 11.

20. Kumar, R., & Rajalakshmi, S. (2013, December). Mobile cloud computing: Standard approach to protecting and securing of mobile cloud ecosystems. In 2013 International Conference on Computer Sciences and Applications (pp. 663-669). IEEE.

21. Khan, A. N., Kiah, M. M., Khan, S. U., & Madani, S. A. (2013). Towards secure mobile cloud computing: A survey. *Future Generation Computer Systems*, 29(5), 1278-1299.

22. Alizadeh, M., Abolfazli, S., Zamani, M., Baharun, S., & Sakurai, K. (2016). Authentication in mobile cloud computing: A survey. *Journal of Network and Computer Applications*, 61, 59-80.

23. Kumar, K., Liu, J., Lu, Y. H., & Bhargava, B. (2013). A survey of computation offloading for mobile systems. *Mobile Networks and Applications*, 18(1), 129-140.

24. Lei, L., Zhong, Z., Zheng, K., Chen, J., & Meng, H. (2013). Challenges on wireless heterogeneous networks for mobile cloud computing. *IEEE Wireless Communications,* 20(3), 34-44.

25. Xia, F., Ding, F., Li, J., Kong, X., Yang, L. T., & Ma, J. (2014). Phone2Cloud: Exploiting computation offloading for energy saving on smartphones in mobile cloud computing. *Information Systems Frontiers*, 16(1), 95-111.

26. Yang, S., Kwon, Y., Cho, Y., Yi, H., Kwon, D., Youn, J., & Paek, Y. (2013, March). Fast dynamic execution offloading for efficient mobile cloud computing. In 2013 IEEE International Conference on Pervasive Computing and Communications (PerCom) (pp. 20-28). IEEE.

27. Aceto, G., Botta, A., De Donato, W., & Pescap, A. (2013). Cloud monitoring: A survey. *Computer Networks*, 57(9), 2093-2115.

28. Dobre, C., & Xhafa, F. (2014). Intelligent services for big data science. *Future Generation Computer Systems*, 37, 267-281.

29. Brodkin, Jon. "Gartner: Seven cloud-computing security risks." Infoworld 2008 (2008): 1-3.

30. Sun, Y., Zhang, J., Xiong, Y., & Zhu, G. (2014). Data security and privacy in cloud computing. *International Journal of Distributed Sensor Networks*, 10(7), 190903.

31. Le, D. N., Kumar, R., Mishra, B. K., Chatterjee, J. M., & Khari, M. (Eds.). (2019). *Cyber Security in Parallel and Distributed Computing: Concepts, Techniques, Applications and Case Studies*. John Wiley & Sons.

32. Liang, H., Han, C., Zhang, D., & Wu, D. (2014, December). A lightweight security isolation approach for virtual machines deployment. In International Conference on Information Security and Cryptology (pp. 516-529). Springer, Cham.

33. Somorovsky, J., Heiderich, M., Jensen, M., Schwenk, J., Gruschka, N., & Lo Iacono, L. (2011, October). All your clouds are belong to us: security analysis of cloud management interfaces. In Proceedings of the 3rd ACM workshop on Cloud computing security workshop (pp. 3-14). ACM.

34. Jin, S., Ahn, J., Seol, J., Cha, S., Huh, J., & Maeng, S. (2015). H-svm: Hardware-assisted secure virtual machines under a vulnerable hypervisor. *IEEE Transactions on Computers*, 64(10), 2833-2846.

35. Mollah, M. B., Azad, M. A. K., & Vasilakos, A. (2017). Secure data sharing and searching at the edge of cloud-assisted internet of things. *IEEE Cloud Computing*, 4(1), 34-42.

36. Odelu, V., Das, A. K., Rao, Y. S., Kumari, S., Khan, M. K., & Choo, K. K. R. (2017). Pairing-based CP-ABE with constant-size ciphertexts and secret keys for cloud environment. *Computer Standards & Interfaces*, 54, 3-9.

37. Duan, Y., Zhang, M., Yin, H., & Tang, Y. (2015). Privacy-preserving offloading of mobile app to the public cloud. In 7th USENIX Workshop on Hot Topics in Cloud Computing (HotCloud 15).

38. Saab, S. A., Saab, F., Kayssi, A., Chehab, A., & Elhajj, I. H. (2015). Partial mobile application offloading to the cloud for energy-efficiency with security measures. *Sustainable Computing: Informatics and Systems*, 8, 38-46.

39. Tang, L., Ouyang, L., & Tsai, W. T. (2015, August). Multi-factor web API security for securing Mobile Cloud. In 2015 12th International Conference on Fuzzy Systems and Knowledge Discovery (FSKD) (pp. 2163-2168). IEEE.

40. Sitov, Z., ednka, J., Yang, Q., Peng, G., Zhou, G., Gasti, P., & Balagani, K. S. (2016). HMOG: New behavioral biometric features for continuous authentication of smartphone users. *IEEE Transactions on Information Forensics and Security*, 11(5), 877-892.

CHAPTER 4

FOG COMPUTING AND ITS SECURITY ISSUES

Jyotir Moy Chatterjee[1], Ishaani Priyadarshini[2], Shankeys[3], and Dac-Nhuong Le[4]

[1]Department of IT, LBEF, Kathmandu, Nepal
[2]Ishaani Priyadarshini, Newark
[3] National Institute of Technology, Raipur
[4] Haiphong University, Haiphong, Vietnam
 Email: {jyotirm4, ishaanidisha, shankeygarg1793}@gmail.com, nhuongld@dhhp.edu.vn

Abstract

Fog computing is architecture that expands the cloud framework by providing computing utilities on the edges of a system. It very well may be portrayed as a cloud-like architecture having comparable information, calculation, archives and application administrations, however is generally diverse in that it's distributed. Likewise, fog systems (fit for processing a lot of information locally) are completely compact, and can be installed on heterogeneous equipment. These highlights make the fog framework profoundly appropriate for time and area delicate applications. For instance, Internet of Things gadgets are required to rapidly process a lot of information. This extensive variety of usefulness-driven applications intensifies numerous security issues regarding information, virtualization, isolation, organization, malware and monitoring. Like Cloud, Fog gives information, process, archiving and application administrations to end clients. In this chapter, we expand the inspiration and points of interest of fog computing and examine its applications in a progression of genuine situations, such as smart grid, smart traffic lights in vehicular networks and software-defined networks, and attempt to distinguish normal security problems. Comparable advancements like edge computing, cloudlets and micro data centers have likewise been included to give a comprehensive audit process. The dominant part of fog applications is persuaded by the craving for usefulness and end-client prerequisites, while the security viewpoints are regularly overlooked or considered as an untimely idea. This chapter likewise determines the effect of those security issues and conceivable arrangements, providing future security-applicable headings to those in charge of designing, developing, and maintaining fog systems.

Keywords: Fog computing, cloud computing, internet of things (IoT), edge computing, cloudlets, micro data centers, software-defined networks, smart grid

4.1 Introduction

Fog computing is a decentralized computing design whereby information is prepared and stored between the wellspring of origin and a cloud infrastructure. This results in the minimization of information transmission overheads, and along these lines, enhances the execution of computing in cloud platforms by reducing the necessity to process and store extensive volumes of pointless information. The fog computing worldview is generally propelled by a continuous increase in IoT gadgets, where a consistently increasing measure of information (concerning volume, assortment, and speed [1]) is created from a regularly expanding cluster of gadgets.

IoT gadgets give rich usefulness, for example, availability, and the improvement of new usefulness is often information roused. These gadgets require computing assets to process the procured information; be that as it may, quick choice procedures are likewise required to maintain an abnormal state of usefulness. This can exhibit adaptability and unwavering quality issues while utilizing a standard customer server engineering, where information is detected by the customer and handled by the server. In the event that a server was to end up overburdened in a customary customer server design, at that point numerous gadgets could be rendered unusable. The Fog worldview plans to give an adaptable decentralized answer for this issue. This is accomplished by creating another progressively dispersed neighborhood platform between the cloud system and end-client gadgets [2], as shown in Figure 4.1.

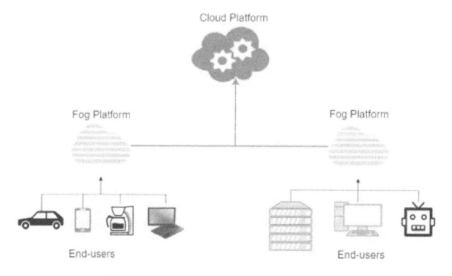

Figure 4.1   Fog computing architecture by Cisco.

This platform is equipped for filtering, aggregating, processing, analyzing and transmitting information, and will bring about saving time and correspondence assets. This new worldview is named fog computing, initially and formally introduced by Cisco [3].

Cloud computing gives numerous advantages to individuals and associations through offering exceptionally accessible and proficient computing assets at a moderate cost [4]. Many cloud services are accessible in current business arrangements; however they are not reasonable for idleness, compactness and area-sensitive applications such as IoT, wearable computing, smart grids, connected vehicles [5] and SDNs [6]. Idleness relies upon the speed of Internet association, asset conflict among visitor virtual machines (VM) and has been shown to increase with removal [7]. Besides, such applications create substantial volumes of different information at a high speed, and when information achieves a cloud system for examination, the opportunity to inform the IoT gadget to make a receptive move might be gone. For instance, consider IoT gadgets in the medicinal domain where the inactivity of acting on the detected information could be life-saving. Cisco spearheaded the conveyance of the fog computing model that expands and brings the cloud platform closer to the end-client's gadget to determine previously mentioned issues.

According to [8], a fog system has the following attributes:

- It will be situated at the edge of system with rich and heterogeneous end-client bolster;

- It provides support to a wide scope of industrial applications because of instant reaction ability;

- It has its own particular computing, storage, and networking services;

- It will work locally (single jump from gadget to fog node);

- It is exceedingly a virtualized platform; and

- It offers inexpensive, adaptable and convenient sending as far as both equipment and software.

Other than having these attributes, a fog system is not the same as cloud computing in different aspects and represents its own particular favorable circumstances and hindrances. Some of the more prominent attributes are listed below [9-12]:

- A fog system will generally have little computing assets (memory, processing and storage) when contrasted with a cloud system, however, the assets can be increased upon request;

- It can process information created from a different arrangement of gadgets;

- It can be both thick and inadequately appropriated in view of topographical area;

- It bolsters machine-to-machine (M2M) correspondence and wireless availability;

- It is feasible for a fog system to be installed on small particular gadgets like switches and IP cameras;

- As of now, one of its main uses is for versatile and compact gadgets.

The information benefit chooses the appropriate place (Cloud or Fog) for information examination, distinguishes which information requires activity and increases security by making information unknown. Numerous scientists and business infrastructure designers trust that fog platforms will be produced and discharged later on to give an improved and more solid infrastructure to deal with the regularly increasing extension of associated computational gadgets. Be that as it may, similar to every dispersed system, the introduction to digital dangers is likewise common and often uplifted by the engineer's craving to give practical systems first, and afterward include safety efforts a while later. Numerous scientists are adopting a security-driven or secure by outline [13] rationality for producing such dispersed systems. Be that as it may, this viewpoint is still in its infancy and needs a far-reaching understanding of the security dangers and difficulties facing a fog infrastructure.

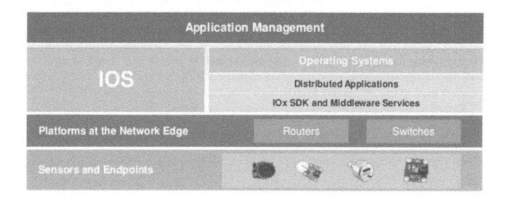

Figure 4.2 Cisco IOx enables fog computing.

4.2 Current Fog Applications

The Cisco Fog worldview can be seen in a wide and integrative way as an empowering agent of many trendsetting innovations. It can include, multiply and affect a few upgraded highlights, for example, quick investigation, interoperability among gadgets, increased reaction time, incorporated or M2M administration, low transfer speed utilization, productive power utilization, gadget deliberation and numerous others. Comparative methodologies like fog computing have now been taken to increase the convenience and capability of cloud platform [14]. With the coming of such wide relevance, the Fog and its comparative platforms like edge computing, cloudlets and micro-server farms are inclined to attacks that can trade off confidentiality, integrity, and availability (CIA) [15, 16].

4.2.1 Why Do We Need Fog?

In the previous couple of years, cloud computing has given numerous opportunities for endeavors that offer customers a range of computing services. Current "pay-as-you-go" cloud computing model turns into a proficient other option to owning and managing private server farms for customers facing web applications and clump processing [17]. Cloud computing liberates the undertakings and their end clients from numerous points of particular interest, for example, storage assets, calculation confinement and system correspondence cost. In any case, this ecstasy turns into an issue for inert delicate applications, which require nodes in the vicinity to meet them to defer necessities [8]. Whenever systems and gadgets of IoT are getting more involved in individuals' life, current cloud computing worldview can barely fulfill their prerequisites of portability bolster, area mindfulness and low dormancy.

Fog computing is suggested to address the above issue [18]. As fog computing is executed at the edge of the system, it gives low dormancy, area mindfulness, and enhances quality of service (QoS) for streaming and ongoing applications. Common illustrations include industrial automation, transportation, and networks of sensors and actuators. Besides, this new infrastructure underpins heterogeneity as fog gadgets include end-client gadgets, access points, edge switches and routers. The Fog worldview is very much situated for continuous enormous information investigation, underpins thickly appropriated information gathering points, and gives favorable circumstances in entertainment, advertising, individualized computing and different applications.

4.2.2 What Can We Do with Fog?

We expound on part of fog computing in the following six motivating situations. The upsides of fog computing fulfill the prerequisites of utilizations in these situations.

Smart Grid: Vitality stack balancing applications may keep running on organized edge gadgets such as smart meters and microgrids [19]. In view of vitality request, accessibility and the most minimal value, these gadgets automatically change elective energies like sun oriented and wind.

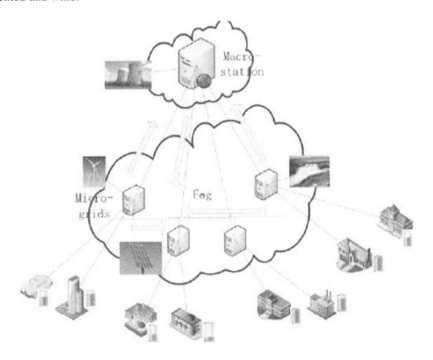

Figure 4.3   Fog computing in smart grid.

As shown in Figure 4.3, fog collectors at the edge process the information produced by grid sensors and gadgets, and issue control orders to the actuators [8]. They likewise channel the information to be devoured locally, and send the rest to the higher levels for representation, constant reports and value-based investigation. Fog bolsters transient storage at the most minimal level to semi-lasting storage at the most elevated level. Worldwide scope is given by the Cloud business intelligence examination.

Smart Traffic Lights and Connected Vehicles: A camcorder that detects ambulance vehicle flashing lights can automatically change road lights to open paths for the vehicle to go through traffic. Smart road lights interact locally with sensors and recognize the nearness of walkers and bikers, and measure the separation and speed of approaching vehicles. As shown in Figure 4.4, intelligent lighting turns on once a sensor recognizes a development and switches off as traffic passes. Neighboring smart lights serving as fog gadgets coordinate to make green traffic wave and send warning signs to approaching vehicles [8]. Wireless access points like Wi-Fi, 3G, street side units and smart traffic lights are conveyed along the streets. Vehicle-to-vehicle, vehicle-to-access point, and access point-to-access point interactions improve this situation.

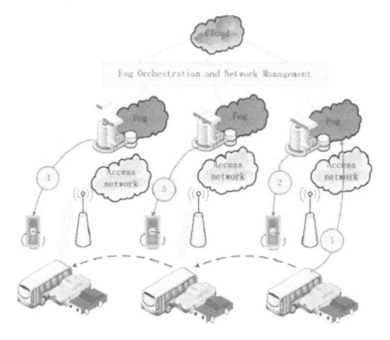

Figure 4.4 Fog computing in smart traffic lights and connected vehicles.

Wireless Sensor and Actuator Networks: Customary wireless sensor networks (WSNs) miss the mark in applications that go past sensing and tracking; however, expect actuators to apply physical activities like opening, closing or notwithstanding carrying sensors [8]. In this situation, actuators serving as fog gadgets can control the estimation procedure itself, the dependability and the oscillatory practices by creating a shut circle system. For instance, in the situation of self-maintaining trains, sensor monitoring of a train's metal roller can distinguish warm levels, allowing applications to send an automatic alarm to the train operator to stop the train at the next station for crisis maintenance, preventing a potential crash. In life-saving air vent situations, sensors on vents monitor air flowing in and out of mines and automatically change the windstream if conditions end up being risky to miners.

Decentralized Smart Building Control: The utilization of this situation is encouraged by wireless sensors sent to quantify temperature, stickiness, or levels of different gases in the building environment. For this situation, information can be traded among all sensors in a story, and their readings can be combined to frame solid estimations. Sensors will utilize conveyed basic leadership and initiation in fog gadgets to respond to information.

The system segments may then cooperate to bring down the temperature, inject natural air or open windows. Forced air systems can expel dampness from the air or increase the moistness. Sensors can likewise follow and respond to developments (e.g., by turning light on or off). Fog gadgets could be allotted at each floor and could team up on more elevated amount of incitation. With fog computing connected in this situation, smart buildings can maintain their texture, outer and internal environments to save energy, water and different assets.

IoT and Cyber-Physical Systems (CPSs): Fog computing-based systems enhance a critical class of IoT and CPSs. In light of the customary information transporters including internet and telecommunication systems, IoT is a system that can interconnect ordinary physical articles with distinguished locations [20]. CPSs highlight a tight combination of the system's computational and physical elements. CPSs likewise coordinate the integration of PC- and information-driven physical and engineered systems. IoT and CPSs guarantee to change our reality with new connections between PC-based control and correspondence systems, engineered systems and physical reality. Fog computing in this situation is based on the ideas of installed systems in which software projects and PCs are implanted in gadgets for reasons other than calculation alone. Cases of the gadgets include toys, autos, therapeutic gadgets and machinery. The objective is to integrate the reflections and accuracy of software and networking with the elements, uncertainty and clamor in the physical environment. Using the emerging knowledge, principles and techniques for CPSs, we will have the capacity to grow new generations of intelligent medicinal gadgets and systems, "smart" roadways, buildings, factories, rural and robotic systems.

SDN: As shown in Figure 4.5, fog computing structure can be connected to execute the SDN idea for vehicular networks. SDN is a developing computing and networking system and has ended up being a standout among the most mainstream topics in the IT industry [21].

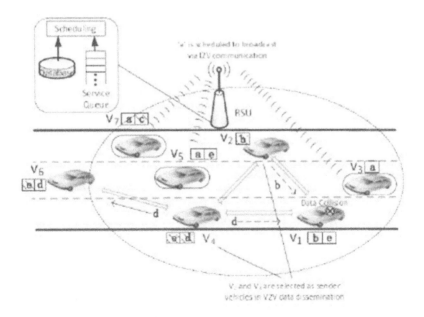

Figure 4.5   Fog computing in SDN in vehicular networks.

It isolates control and information correspondence layers. The central server may require circulated usage. SDN ideas were considered in WLAN, wireless sensor and mesh topology, yet they don't involve multi-hop wireless correspondence, multi-hop routing. Also, there is no correspondence between peers in this situation. SDN ideas together with fog computing will resolve the main issues in vehicular networks, intermittent availability, crashes and high packet misfortune rate, by augmenting vehicle-to-vehicle with vehicle-to-infrastructure interchanges and brought together control. SDN ideas for vehicular networks was first suggested in [22, 23].

4.3 Security and Privacy in Fog Computing

We concede that security and protection ought to be tended to in each layer in planning fog computing framework. In this section we present some information about fog computing security and protection. Because of the attributes of fog calculation, more work may be required in the future to handle these issues.

4.3.1 Trust and Authentication

In cloud computing architecture, data centers are normally possessed by cloud service providers (CSP). Be that as it may, fog specialist organizations can be distinctive parties because of the following various sending decisions:

1. Internet service providers or wireless bearers, who have control of gateways or cellular base stations, may construct fog with their existing infrastructures;

2. Cloud specialist co-ops, who need to extend their cloud administrations to the edge of the system, may likewise configure fog infrastructures;

3. End clients, who possess a nearby private cloud and need to decrease the cost of proprietorship, might want to transform the neighborhood private cloud into fog and rent save assets on the neighborhood private cloud. This editability confounds the trust circumstance of fog.

A reputation-based trust model [24] has been effective in eCommerce, peer-to-peer (P2P), client audits and online social media. In [25] a powerful reputation-based system for asset choice in P2P networks is suggested which uses an appropriated polling calculation to survey the unwavering quality of an asset before downloading. In designing a fog computing reputation-based trust system, we may need to handle issues such as 1) how to accomplish tireless, one of a kind, and distinct personality, 2) how to treat intentional and incidental rowdiness, 3) how to direct discipline and reclamation of reputation. Likewise, there are trusting models in view of extraordinary equipment, such as secure element (SE), trusted execution environment (TEE) or trusted platform module (TPM), which can give trust utility in fog computing applications [26].

4.3.2 Man-in-the-Middle Attacks (MITM)

Man-in-the-middle attacks can possibly turn into a run of the mill attack in fog computing. In this subsection, we use MITM attacks, for instance, to uncover the security issues in fog computing. In this attack, gateways serving as fog gadgets might be imperiled or supplanted by counterfeit ones [27]. Some examples are KFC or Star Bar customers connecting to noxious access points which give misleading SSID as open honest-to-goodness ones. Private correspondence of casualties will be captured once the aggressors take control of gateways [6].

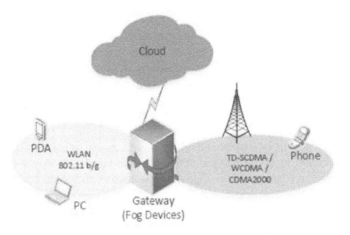

Figure 4.6   Scenario for a man-in-the-middle attack against Fog.

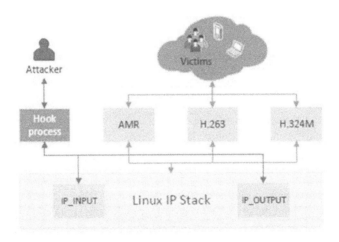

Figure 4.7   System design of man-in-the-middle-attack in Fog.

A rogue fog node is a fog gadget or fog instance that pretends to be real and urges end clients to associate with it. For instance, in an insider attack, a fog administrator might be approved to oversee fog instances, yet may instantiate a rogue fog instance instead of a genuine one. Stojmenovic and Wen showed the achievability of a man-in-the-middle attack in fog computing, before which the portal ought to be either exchanged or supplanted by a phony one [6]. Once associated, the foe can control the incoming and outgoing solicitations from end clients or cloud, gather or alter client information stealthily, and effortlessly dispatch additional attacks. The existence of a phony fog node will be a major risk to client information security and protection. This issue is difficult to address in fog computing for a few reasons: 1) complex trust circumstance calls for various trust administration plans, and 2) dynamic creating, deleting of virtual machine instance make it difficult to maintain a boycott of rogue nodes. Han *et al.* have suggested an estimation-based technique which empowers a customer to abstain from connecting rogue access points (AP) [28]. Their approach uses the round-trip time between end clients and the DNS server to distinguish rogue AP at the customer side.

Authorization is a vital issue for the security of fog computing since administrations are offered to enormous scale end clients by front fog nodes. The authors in [6] have considered the main security issue of fog computing as the authorization at various levels of fog nodes. Customary PKI-based validation isn't productive and has poor adaptability. Balfanz *et al.* have suggested a modest, secure and easy to use answer for the authorization issue in a nearby specially appointed remote system, relying on a physical contact for pre-confirmation in an area restricted channel [29]. Correspondingly, NFC can likewise be utilized to improve the authorization method for the situation of cloudlet [30]. As the use of biometric verification, such as fingerprint authorization, facial authorization, touch-based or keystroke-based authorization, etc., in mobile computing and cloud computing rises, it will be helpful to apply biometric-based authorization in fog computing.

4.3.3   Network Security

Because of the preponderance of wireless connections in fog networking, wireless system security is an enormous worry to fog networking. Some examples of this are jamming attacks, sniffing attacks and so on. Ordinarily, in order to organize, we need to trust the arrangements physically produced by a system administrator and disengage arranged administration traffic from customary information traffic [31]. Notwithstanding, since fog nodes are sent to the edge of the internet, which definitely brings overwhelming weight to the system administration, we can imagine the cost of maintaining enormous scale cloud servers which are disseminated everywhere throughout the system edge without simple access for maintenance. The work of SDN can facilitate the execution and administration, and increase organizational versatility and lessen costs, in numerous parts of fog computing. We additionally contend that applying SDN strategy in fog computing will bring fog networking security new difficulties and openings.

In what manner can SDN enable the fog to arrange security?

1. Network Monitoring and Intrusion Detection System (IDS): CloudWatch [32] can use OpenFLow [33] to course traffic for security monitoring applications or IDS.

2. Traffic Isolation and Prioritization: Traffic separation and prioritization can be utilized to keep an attack from congesting the system or dominating shared assets, for example, CPU or circle I/O. Without much of a stretch, SDN can utilize VLAN ID/tag to seclude traffic in VLAN gathering and isolate pernicious traffic.

3. Network Resource Access Control: Klaedtke *et al.* suggested an access control scheme on a SDN controller in light of OpenFlow [34].

4. Network Sharing: Fog-upgraded switch in home system can be opened to visitors, if the system shared with visitors is painstakingly planned with security concerns in mind. Yap *et al.* suggested OpenWiFi, in which the visitor Wi-Fi validation is moved to the cloud to set up visitor personality; access independently accommodates visitors; and accounting is implemented to designate obligation of visitors [35].

4.3.4 Secure Data Storage

In fog computing, client information is outsourced and client's control over information is given over to fog node, which introduces the same security dangers as in cloud computing. In the first place, it is difficult to guarantee information integrity, since the outsourced information could be lost or incorrectly adjusted. Second, the transferred information could be mishandled by unapproved parties for different interests. To address these dangers, auditable information storage benefit has been suggested with regards to cloud computing to secure the information. Methods, such as homomorphic encryption and accessible encryption, are combined to give integrity, secrecy and unquestionable status for cloud storage system to enable customers to check their information stored on untrusted servers. Wang *et al.* have suggested privacy-preserving public auditing for information stored in cloud, which depends on a third-party auditor (TPA), using homomorphic authenticator and arbitrary veil strategy to secure privacy against TPA [36]. To guarantee the unwavering quality of information storage, earlier storage systems utilized eradication codes or system coding to manage information defilement identification and information repair, while Cao *et al.* have suggested a plan using LT code, which gives less storage cost, considerably quicker information recovery, and practically identical correspondence cost [37]. Yang and Jia have given a decent diagram of existing work towards information storage auditing administration in cloud computing. In fog computing, there are new difficulties in designing a secure storage system to accomplish low-dormancy, bolster dynamic task and manage interplay between fog and cloud [38].

4.4 Secure and Private Data Computation

Another vital issue in fog computing is to accomplish secure and privacy-preserving calculation outsourced to fog nodes.

Verifiable computing empowers a computing gadget to offload the calculation of a capacity to different possibly untrusted servers, while maintaining evident outcomes. Alternate servers assess the capacity and restore the outcome with proof that the calculation of the capacity was completed effectively. The term verifiable computing was formalized in [39]. In fog computing, to instill trust in the calculation offloaded to the fog node, the fog client ought to have the capacity to check the rightness of the calculation. The following are some existing techniques to satisfy verifiable computing. Gennaro *et al.* have suggested a verifiable computing protocol that enables the server to restore a computationally stable, non-interactive confirmation that can be checked by the customer [39]. The protocol can give (at no extra cost) input and yield privacy for the customer to such an extent that the server does not take in any information about the input and yield. Parno *et al.* have fabricated a system, called Pinocchio, with the end goal that the customer can confirm general calculations done by a server while relying just on cryptographic suspicions [40]. With Pinocchio, customers make a public assessment key to portray their calculation, and the server at that point assesses the calculation and utilizes the assessment key to create a proof of rightness.

Data Search secures information privacy. Sensitive information from end clients must be encoded before being outsourced to the fog node, making compelling information use administrations challenging. A standout among the most critical administrations is watchword search, i.e., catchphrase sought among encoded information documents. Scientists have built up a few accessible encryption plots that enable a client to securely look over scrambled information through catchphrases without unscrambling. Song *et al.* were the first to suggest schemes for searching encrypted data, which give provable mystery to encryption, inquiry disengagement, controlled searching, and support of concealed question [41]. Afterwards, many different plans were created, some of which are given in [42].

4.4.1 Privacy

The leaking of personal information, such as area or utilization, is the focus of increased attention when end clients use administrations like cloud computing, wireless system, and IoT. There are additional challenges for preserving such privacy in fog computing, since fog nodes are in the vicinity of end clients and can gather more sensitive information than the remote cloud lying in the center system. Privacy-preserving procedures have been suggested in numerous situations, including cloud [43], smart grid [44], wireless system [45], and social network [46].

For Data Privacy in the fog system, privacy-preserving calculations can be run in the middle of the fog and cloud, while those calculations are generally asset-restricted toward the end gadgets. Fog node at the edge for the most part gathers sensitive information produced by sensors and end gadgets. Methods such as homomorphic encryption can be used to permit privacy-preserving accumulation at the nearby gateways without unscrambling [47]. Differential privacy [48] can be used to guarantee non-exposure of privacy of a self-assertive single passage in the informational index if there should arise an occurrence of factual questions.

Usage Privacy is also a privacy issue which uses design with which a fog customer uses the fog administrations. For instance, in smart grid, the reading of the smart meter will reveal heaps of information about a family, for example, the times when nobody is at home and when the TV is turned on, which totally invades the client's privacy. In spite of the fact that privacy-preserving systems have been suggested in smart metering [49], they can't be connected in fog computing straightforwardly, because of the absence of a TTP (i.e., a smart meter in smart grid) or partner gadget like a battery. Without much of a stretch, the fog node can gather insights into end client use. One conceivable innocent arrangement is that the fog customer makes sham errands and offloads them to various fog nodes, hiding genuine assignments among the fake ones. Be that as it may, this arrangement will increase the fog customer's installment and waste assets and vitality. Another arrangement would outline a smart method for partitioning the application to ensure that the offloaded asset uses don't reveal privacy information.

Location Privacy mainly alludes to the area privacy of fog customers. For the most part, a fog customer offloads its errands to the closest fog node; the fog node on which the assignments are offloaded can infer that the fog customer is close by and more distant from different nodes. Besides, if a fog customer uses numerous fog administrations at various areas, it might reveal its trajectory to the fog nodes, assuming the fog nodes conspire. For whatever length of time that such a fog customer is appended onto an individual or a vital question, the area privacy of the individual or the protest is in danger. In the event that a fog customer in every case entirely picks its closest fog server, the fog node can definitely realize that the fog customer that is utilizing its computing assets is adjacent. The best way to safeguard the area privacy is through character obscurity with the end goal that despite the fact that the fog node knows a fog customer is close by it can't recognize the fog customer. There are numerous strategies for character obscurity; for instance, in [50], the creators utilize a trusted third party to produce a counterfeit ID for each end client. As a general rule, a fog customer does not really pick the closest fog node but rather voluntarily picks one of the fog nodes it can reach according to a few criteria such as dormancy, reputation, stack adjust, and so forth. For this situation, the fog node just needs to know the harsh area of the fog customer but can't do it unequivocally. Be that as it may, once the fog customer uses computing assets from various fog nodes in a territory, its area can come down to a little district, since its area must be in the intersection of the different fog nodes' inclusions. To save the area privacy in such a situation, one can use the strategy utilized in [51].

4.4.2 Access Control

Access control has been a solid tool to guarantee the security of the system and preserve the privacy of the client. Customary access control is generally tended to in the same manner as a trust domain. While due to the outsource idea of cloud computing, the access control in cloud computing is normally cryptographically executed for outsourced information. Symmetric key-based arrangement isn't versatile in key administration. A few public key-based arrangements are suggested for trying to accomplish fine-grained access control. Yu *et al.* have suggested a fine-grained information access control plot built on attribute-based encryption (ABE) [52]. Dsouza *et al.* proposed an arrangement-based asset access control in fog computing to help secure joint effort and interoperability between heterogeneous assets [53]. In fog computing, the challenge is how to configure access control spanning customer fog cloud while meeting the design objectives and asset constraints.

4.4.3 Intrusion Detection

This procedure is broadly conveyed in cloud system to alleviate attacks such as insider attack, flooding attack, port scanning, attacks on VM and hypervisor [54]; or in smart grid system to monitor control meter estimations and identify strange estimations that could have been engineered by attackers [55]. In fog computing, IDS can be conveyed on the fog node system side to identify intrusive conduct by monitoring and analyzing log record, access control arrangements and client login information. They can likewise be sent at the fog organize side to distinguish pernicious attacks, for example, denial-of-service (DoS), port scanning, and so on. Fog computing provides new chances to investigate how it can help with intrusion discovery on both the customer side and the brought together cloud side. Shi *et al.* have exhibited a cloudlet work-based security system which can identify intrusion to separate cloud, securing correspondence among cell phones, cloudlet and cloud [56]. There are likewise difficulties such as implementation of intrusion identification in geo-dispersed, huge scale, high-versatility fog computing environment to meet the low-dormancy necessity [57-60].

4.5 Conclusion

In this chapter, we examined the basics of fog computing, why we require fog computing and a few security and privacy issues in regard to fog computing. Fog computing is another computing architecture used worldwide to provide flexible assets at the system edge to nearby end clients which may require new thought to adjust to new difficulties and make changes (see Table 4.1 and Table 4.2).

Table 4.1 Summary of potential security issues found in fog applications.

Category of Attacks	Threats	Solutions	Impacts
Virtualization	• Hypervisor attacks • VM-based attacks • Weak or no Logical Segregation • Side channel attacks • Privilege Escalation • Service abuse • Privilege escalation attacks • Inefficient resource policies	• Multi-factor Authentication • Intrusion Detection System • User data isolation • Attribute/identity based encryption • Role-Based Access Control model • User-based permissions model • Process isolation	As all services & VMs are executing in a virtualized environment, its compromise will have adverse effect on all Fog services, data & users
Web security	• SQL injection • Cross-site scripting • Cross-site request forgery • Session/Account hijacking • Insecure direct object references • Malicious redirections • Drive-by attacks	• Secure code • Find & patch vulnerabilities • Regular software updates • Periodic auditing • Firewall • Anti-virus protection • Intrusion Prevention System	Exposure of sensitive information, attacker can become legitimate part of network, & enable malicious applications to install
Internal/ external communication	• Man-in-the-Middle attack • Inefficient rules/policies • Poor access control • Session/Account hijacking • Insecure APIs & services • Application vulnerabilities • Single-point of failure	• Encrypted communication • Mutual/Multi-factor authentication • Partial encryption • Isolating compromised nodes • Certificate pinning • Limiting number of connections • Transport layer security (TLS)	Attacker can acquire sensitive information by eavesdropping & get access to unauthorized Fog resources
Data security related	• Data replication & sharing • Data altering & erasing attacks • Illegal data access • Data ownership issues • Low attack tolerance • Malicious Insiders • Multi-tenancy issues • Denial of Service attacks	• Policy enforcement • Security inside design architecture • Encryption • Secure key management • Obfuscation • Data Masking • Data classification • Network monitoring	High probability of illegal file & database access, where attacker can compromise both user & Fog system's data
Wireless security	• Active impersonation • Message replay attacks • Message distortion issues • Data loss • Data breach • Sniffing attacks • Illegal resource consumption	• Authentication • Encrypted communication • Key management service • Secure routing • Private network • Wireless security protocols	Vulnerable wireless access points can compromise communication privacy, consistency, accuracy, availability & trustworthiness
Malware protection	• Virus • Trojans • Worms • Ransomware • Spyware • Rootkits • Performance reduction	• Anti-malware programs • Intrusion Detection System • Rigorous data backups • Patching vulnerabilities • System restore points	Malware infected nodes will lower the performance of the entire Fog platform, allow back-doors to the system & corrupt/damage data permanently

Table 4.2 Cloud computing vs. fog computing.

Category	Cloud Computing	Fog Computing
Target User	General Internet users.	Mobile users
Service Type	Global information collected from worldwide	Limited localized information services related to specific deployment locations
Hardware	Ample & scalable storage space and compute power	Limited storage, compute power and wireless interface
Distance to Users	Faraway from users and communicate through IP networks	In the physical proximity and communicate through single-hop wireless connection
Working Environment	Warehouse-size building with air conditioning systems	Outdoor (streets, parklands, etc.) or indoor (restaurants, shopping malls, etc.)
Deployment	Centralized and maintained by Amazon, Google, etc.	Centralized or distributed in reginal areas by local business (local telecommunication vendor, shopping mall retailer, etc.)

REFERENCES

1. Sagiroglu, S., & Sinanc, D. (2013, May). Big data: A review. In 2013 International Conference on Collaboration Technologies and Systems (CTS) (pp. 42-47). IEEE.

2. Alrawais, A., Alhothaily, A., Hu, C., & Cheng, X. (2017). Fog computing for the internet of things: Security and privacy issues. *IEEE Internet Computing*, 21(2), 34-42.

3. Tang, B., Chen, Z., Hefferman, G., Wei, T., He, H., & Yang, Q. (2015, October). A hierarchical distributed fog computing architecture for big data analysis in smart cities. In Proceedings of the ASE BigData & SocialInformatics 2015 (p. 28). ACM.

4. Marston, S., Li, Z., Bandyopadhyay, S., Zhang, J., & Ghalsasi, A. (2011). Cloud computingThe business perspective. *Decision support systems*, 51(1), 176-189.

5. Parkinson, S., Ward, P., Wilson, K., & Miller, J. (2017). Cyber threats facing autonomous and connected vehicles: Future challenges. *IEEE transactions on intelligent transportation systems*, 18(11), 2898-2915.

6. Stojmenovic, I., & Wen, S. (2014, September). The fog computing paradigm: Scenarios and security issues. In 2014 Federated Conference on Computer Science and Information Systems (pp. 1-8). IEEE.

7. Kim, J. Y., & Schulzrinne, H. (2013, December). Cloud support for latency-sensitive telephony applications. In 2013 IEEE 5th International Conference on Cloud Computing Technology and Science (Vol. 1, pp. 421-426). IEEE.

8. Bonomi, F., Milito, R., Zhu, J., & Addepalli, S. (2012, August). Fog computing and its role in the internet of things. In Proceedings of the first edition of the MCC workshop on Mobile cloud computing (pp. 13-16). ACM.

9. Buyya, R., & Srirama, S. N. (Eds.). (2019). *Fog and edge computing: principles and paradigms*. Wiley.

10. Vaquero, L. M., & Rodero-Merino, L. (2014). Finding your way in the fog: Towards a comprehensive definition of fog computing. *ACM SIGCOMM Computer Communication Review*, 44(5), 27-32.

11. Saharan, K. P., & Kumar, A. (2015). Fog in comparison to cloud: A survey. *International Journal of Computer Applications*, 122(3).

12. Dastjerdi, A. V., Gupta, H., Calheiros, R. N., Ghosh, S. K., & Buyya, R. (2016). Fog computing: Principles, architectures, and applications. In *Internet of things* (pp. 61-75). Morgan Kaufmann.

13. Schumacher, M., Fernandez-Buglioni, E., Hybertson, D., Buschmann, F., & Sommerlad, P. (2013). *Security Patterns: Integrating security and systems engineering*. John Wiley & Sons.

14. Satyanarayanan, M. (2015). A brief history of cloud offload: A personal journey from odyssey through cyber foraging to cloudlets. *GetMobile: Mobile Computing and Communications*, 18(4), 19-23.

15. Zissis, D., & Lekkas, D. (2012). Addressing cloud computing security issues. *Future Generation computer systems*, 28(3), 583-592.

16. Khan, S., Parkinson, S., & Qin, Y. (2017). Fog computing security: a review of current applications and security solutions. *Journal of Cloud Computing*, 6(1), 19.

17. Michael, A., Armando, F., Rean, G., Anthony, D. J., Randy, K. A. T. Z., Andy, K., ... & Matei, Z. A. H. A. R. I. A. (2010). A view of cloud computing. *Communications of the ACM*, 53(4), 50-58.

18. Bonomi, F. (2011, September). Connected vehicles, the internet of things, and fog computing. In The eighth ACM international workshop on vehicular inter-networking (VANET), Las Vegas, USA (pp. 13-15).

19. Wei, C., Fadlullah, Z. M., Kato, N., & Stojmenovic, I. (2014). On optimally reducing power loss in micro-grids with power storage devices. *IEEE Journal on Selected Areas in Communications*, 32(7), 1361-1370.

20. Atzori, L., Iera, A., & Morabito, G. (2010). The internet of things: A survey. *Computer networks*, 54(15), 2787-2805.

21. Kreutz, D., Ramos, F. M., Verissimo, P., Rothenberg, C. E., Azodolmolky, S., & Uhlig, S. (2015). Software-defined networking: A comprehensive survey. Proceedings of the IEEE, 103(1), 14-76.

22. Liu, K., Ng, J., Lee, V., Son, S., & Stojmenovic, I. (2014). Cooperative data dissemination in hybrid vehicular networks: Vanet as a software defined network. Submitted for publication.

23. Stojmenovic, I. (2014, November). Fog computing: A cloud to the ground support for smart things and machine-to-machine networks. In 2014 Australasian Telecommunication Networks and Applications Conference (ATNAC) (pp. 117-122). IEEE.

24. J_sang, A., Ismail, R., & Boyd, C. (2007). A survey of trust and reputation systems for online service provision. *Decision support systems*, 43(2), 618-644.

25. Damiani, E., di Vimercati, D. C., Paraboschi, S., Samarati, P., & Violante, F. (2002, November). A reputation-based approach for choosing reliable resources in peer-to-peer networks. In Proceedings of the 9th ACM conference on Computer and communications security (pp. 207-216). ACM.

26. Yi, S., Qin, Z., & Li, Q. (2015, August). Security and privacy issues of fog computing: A survey. In International conference on wireless algorithms, systems, and applications (pp. 685-695). Springer, Cham

27. Zhang, L., Jia, W., Wen, S., & Yao, D. (2010, April). A man-in-the-middle attack on 3g-wlan interworking. In 2010 International Conference on Communications and Mobile Computing (Vol. 1, pp. 121-125). IEEE.

28. Han, H., Sheng, B., Tan, C. C., Li, Q., & Lu, S. (2009, April). A measurement based rogue ap detection scheme. In IEEE INFOCOM 2009 (pp. 1593-1601). IEEE.

29. Balfanz, D., Smetters, D. K., Stewart, P., & Wong, H. C. (2002, February). Talking to Strangers: Authentication in Ad-Hoc Wireless Networks. In NDSS.

30. Bouzefrane, S., Mostefa, A. F. B., Houacine, F., & Cagnon, H. (2014, April). Cloudlets authentication in NFC-based mobile computing. In 2014 2nd IEEE International Conference on Mobile Cloud Computing, Services, and Engineering (pp. 267-272). IEEE.

31. Tsugawa, M., Matsunaga, A., & Fortes, J. A. (2014). Cloud computing security: What changes with software-defined networking? In Secure Cloud Computing (pp. 77-93). Springer, New York, NY.

32. Shin, S. W., & Gu, G. (2012, October). Cloudwatcher: Network security monitoring using openflow in dynamic cloud networks. In Network Protocols (ICNP) 2012 (pp. 1-6). IEEE.

33. McKeown, N., Anderson, T., Balakrishnan, H., Parulkar, G., Peterson, L., Rexford, J., ... & Turner, J. (2008). OpenFlow: enabling innovation in campus networks. ACM SIGCOMM Computer Communication Review, 38(2), 69-74.

34. Klaedtke, F., Karame, G. O., Bifulco, R., & Cui, H. (2014, August). Access control for SDN controllers. In Proceedings of the third workshop on Hot topics in software defined networking (pp. 219-220). ACM.

35. Yap, K. K., Yiakoumis, Y., Kobayashi, M., Katti, S., Parulkar, G., & McKeown, N. (2011). Separating authentication, access and accounting: A case study with OpenWiFi. Open Networking Foundation, Tech. Rep.

36. Wang, C., Wang, Q., Ren, K., & Lou, W. (2010, March). Privacy-preserving public auditing for data storage security in cloud computing. In 2010 proceedings ieee infocom (pp. 1-9). Ieee.

37. Cao, N., Yu, S., Yang, Z., Lou, W., & Hou, Y. T. (2012, March). LT codes-based secure and reliable cloud storage service. In 2012 Proceedings IEEE INFOCOM (pp. 693-701). IEEE.

38. Yang, K., & Jia, X. (2012). Data storage auditing service in cloud computing: challenges, methods and opportunities. World Wide Web, 15(4), 409-428.

39. Gennaro, R., Gentry, C., & Parno, B. (2010, August). Non-interactive verifiable computing: Outsourcing computation to untrusted workers. In Annual Cryptology Conference (pp. 465-482). Springer, Berlin, Heidelberg.

40. Parno, B., Howell, J., Gentry, C., & Raykova, M. (2013, May). Pinocchio: Nearly practical verifiable computation. In 2013 IEEE Symposium on Security and Privacy (pp. 238-252). IEEE.

41. Song, D. X., Wagner, D., & Perrig, A. (2000). Practical techniques for searches on encrypted data. In Proceeding 2000 IEEE Symposium on Security and Privacy. S&P 2000 (pp. 44-55). IEEE.

42. Wang, C., Cao, N., Ren, K., & Lou, W. (2012). Enabling secure and efficient ranked keyword search over outsourced cloud data. *IEEE Transactions on parallel and distributed systems*, 23(8), 1467-1479.

43. Cao, N., Wang, C., Li, M., Ren, K., & Lou, W. (2014). Privacy-preserving multi-keyword ranked search over encrypted cloud data. *IEEE Transactions on parallel and distributed systems*, 25(1), 222-233.

44. Rial, A., & Danezis, G. (2011, October). Privacy-preserving smart metering. In Proceedings of the 10th annual ACM workshop on Privacy in the electronic society (pp. 49-60). ACM.

45. Qin, Z., Yi, S., Li, Q., & Zamkov, D. (2014, April). Preserving secondary users' privacy in cognitive radio networks. In IEEE INFOCOM 2014-IEEE Conference on Computer Communications (pp. 772-780). IEEE.

46. Novak, E., & Li, Q. (2014, April). Near-pri: Private, proximity based location sharing. In IEEE INFOCOM 2014-IEEE Conference on Computer Communications (pp. 37-45). IEEE.

47. Lu, R., Liang, X., Li, X., Lin, X., & Shen, X. (2012). Eppa: An efficient and privacy-preserving aggregation scheme for secure smart grid communications. *IEEE Transactions on Parallel and Distributed Systems*, 23(9), 1621-1631.

48. Dwork, C. (2011). Differential privacy. *Encyclopedia of Cryptography and Security*, 338-340.

49. Wei, W., Xu, F., & Li, Q. (2012, March). Mobishare: Flexible privacy-preserving location sharing in mobile online social networks. In 2012 Proceedings IEEE INFOCOM (pp. 2616-2620). IEEE.

50. Le, D. N., Kumar, R., Mishra, B. K., Chatterjee, J. M., & Khari, M. (Eds.). (2019). *Cyber Security in Parallel and Distributed Computing: Concepts, Techniques*, Applications and Case Studies. John Wiley & Sons.

51. Gao, Z., Zhu, H., Liu, Y., Li, M., & Cao, Z. (2013, April). Location privacy in database-driven cognitive radio networks: Attacks and countermeasures. In 2013 Proceedings IEEE INFOCOM (pp. 2751-2759). IEEE.

52. Yu, S., Wang, C., Ren, K., & Lou, W. (2010, March). Achieving secure, scalable, and fine-grained data access control in cloud computing. In 2010 Proceedings IEEE INFOCOM (pp. 1-9). Ieee.

53. Dsouza, C., Ahn, G. J., & Taguinod, M. (2014, August). Policy-driven security management for fog computing: Preliminary framework and a case study. In Proceedings of the 2014 IEEE 15th International Conference on Information Reuse and Integration (IEEE IRI 2014) (pp. 16-23). IEEE.

54. Modi, C., Patel, D., Borisaniya, B., Patel, H., Patel, A., & Rajarajan, M. (2013). A survey of intrusion detection techniques in cloud. *Journal of network and computer applications*, 36(1), 42-57.

55. Valenzuela, J., Wang, J., & Bissinger, N. (2013). Real-time intrusion detection in power system operations. *IEEE Transactions on Power Systems*, 28(2), 1052-1062.

56. Shi, Y., Abhilash, S., & Hwang, K. (2015, March). Cloudlet mesh for securing mobile clouds from intrusions and network attacks. In 2015 3rd IEEE International Conference on Mobile Cloud Computing, Services, and Engineering (pp. 109-118). IEEE.

57. Le, D. N., Van, V. N., & Giang, T. T. T. (2016). A New Private Security Policy Approach for DDoS Attack Defense in NGNs. In Information Systems Design and Intelligent Applications (pp. 1-10). Springer, New Delhi.

58. Nguyen, L. D., Le, D. N., & Vinh, L. T. (2014, December). Detecting phishing web pages based on DOM-tree structure and graph matching algorithm. In Proceedings of the Fifth Symposium on Information and Communication Technology (pp. 280-285). ACM.

59. Urmila, T. S., & Balasubramanian, R. (2019). Dynamic Multi-layered Intrusion Identification and Recognition using Artificial Intelligence Framework. *International Journal of Computer Science and Information Security* (IJCSIS), 17(2).

60. Vasilomanolakis, E., & Mhlhuser, M. (2019). Detection and mitigation of monitor identification attacks in collaborative intrusion detection systems. *International Journal of Network Management*, 29(2), e2059.

CHAPTER 5

APPLICATION SAFETY AND SERVICE VULNERABILITY IN CLOUD NETWORK

Sudipta Sahana[1], Debabrata Sarddar[2]

[1] Department of CSE, JIS College of Engineering, Kalyani, Nadia, West Bengal, India
[2] Department of CSE, University of Kalyani, Nadia, West Bengal, India
 Email: ss.jisce@gmail.com

Abstract
 Cloud computing gives an in-manufactured stage to clients with simple and upon-request access to various framework level administrations for making virtual machines (VM) with productive use of equipment, computing and system assets. This enables clients to remotely execute a vast number of utilizations crosswise over different areas; for example, human services, utility administrations, e-administration, and so forth. Cloud computing is a standout amongst the present generally engaging innovation zones because of its cost-effectiveness and adaptability. Be that as it may, in spite of noteworthy interests, sending cloud computing in an undertaking framework presents critical security concerns. Effective usage of cloud computing in an endeavor requires legitimate arranging and comprehension of developing risks, threats, vulnerabilities, and conceivable countermeasures. This chapter examines security concerns of the three cloud computing models, specifically, software as a service (SaaS), platform as a service (PaaS) and infrastructure as a service (IaaS). It likewise examines cloud-based security tools, cloud data encryption, homomorphic encryption and access control (identity access for executives). Finally, the authors discuss the principal cloud computing security considerations and cloud computing security best practices. It also takes a look at the known vulnerability issues related to the applications and likewise the eventual fate of cloud applications.
 Keywords: Cloud computing, IaaS, SaaS, PaaS, cybersecurity, application vulnerability, cryptography, access control, data encryption, virtual machines

5.1   Introduction

Cloud computing is the delivery of various e facilities through the web. These assets integrate instruments and applications like storage, servers, databases, systems management, and programming. As opposed to keeping documents on a restrictive system storage or local storage equipment, cloud-based empowerment makes it feasible to keep them in a remote database. Before an electronic gadget approaches the web, it approaches the information and the product projects to run it. Cloud computing is a well-known substitute used by individuals and organizations for various reasons, including its cost-effectiveness, prolonged profitability, speed and proficiency, execution, and safety.

5.1.1   Introduction to Security Issues in Cloud Service Models

Cloud computing uses three conveyance models by which distinctive types of administrations are conveyed to the end node. The three conveyance models are SaaS, PaaS and IaaS, which give framework assets, application stage and programming as administrations to the purchaser. These models additionally place a diverse dimension of security prerequisite in the cloud condition.

IaaS is the establishment of all cloud administrations upon which PaaS is based; what's more, SaaS is also based upon it. Similarly, as capacities are acquired, so are the data security issues and dangers. There are significant trade-offs to each model in terms of coordinated highlights, unpredictability versus extensibility and security. On the off chance that the cloud administration supplier deals with just the security at some lower portion of the security design, the buyers progressively become in charge of executing and dealing with the security abilities. An ongoing study by the Cloud Security Alliance (CSA) and IEEE shows that undertakings across all divisions are eager to embrace cloud computing; however, security is required to both quicken cloud appropriation on a wide scale and react to administrative drivers. It likewise implies that cloud computing is forming its eventual fate; however, the nonappearance of a consistence domain is having a sensational sway over cloud computing's development. Associations utilizing cloud computing as an administration framework fundamentally prefer to look at the security and confidentiality issues for their businesses basic applications. Although ensuring the security of corporate information in the "cloud" is difficult, it is certainly feasible, as it provides distinctive administrations like SaaS, PaaS, and IaaS. However, each administration has its very own security issues [1, 2].

5.1.2   Security Issues in SaaS

Software as a service (SaaS) is a product arrangement display where applications are remotely facilitated by the application or specialist organization and made accessible over the internet to clients based on interest. SaaS offers clients significant benefits such as improved operational efficiency and diminished expenses. SaaS is quickly rising as the predominant conveyance for gathering the necessities of big business IT administrations. Nonetheless, most ventures are still ambivalent about the SaaS display because of the absence of understanding about the manner in which their information is stored and verified. The security [3] concerns are the most generally referred to motivation behind why undertakings are not inspired by SaaS. Therefore, tending to big business security concerns has risen as the greatest test for the reception of SaaS applications in the cloud. Therefore, in order to assuage client concerns about the security of information in these applications, merchants must address these issues head-on. There is solid trepidation about insider breaks along with other vulnerabilities [4] in the applications and frameworks' accessibility that could prompt loss of sensitive data and cash. Such difficulties can deter attempts to receive SaaS applications inside the cloud.

The following top security components ought to be deliberately measured as an indispensable part of the SaaS application advancement and sending process:

- Data Safety: In the case of SaaS, the undertaken resources are stored outside the scope of the venture. In the security system of the SaaS platform, sensitive resources are acquired from the enterprise produced by the SaaS application and kept at the SaaS merchant side.

- Data Region: In an SaaS environment, the consumer does not know about the storage location of the resources. In the scenario of the most basic components in any framework, resource trustworthiness and respectability stand out.

- Data Isolation: Multi-occupancy is one of the major characteristics of the cloud environment. Resources of different consumers are kept in an identical place but need to be isolated from client to client.

- Data Retrieval: Data retrieval is closely related to safety approaches facilitated by clients during information retrieval. Validation and approval of the product is facilitated outside of the corporate firewall.

- Web App Safety: Data breaches, vulnerability, accessibility, backup and identity of the executives and sign-on process of identity managemnt (IdM) or id of the executives are different concerns of SaaS.

5.1.3 Security Issues in PaaS

Platform as a service (PaaS) offers an incorporated arrangement of designer conditions in which an engineer, without having any hint about what is happening underneath the administration, can tap to assemble their applications. It offers engineers an administration that gives a total programming improvement of life cycle of executives, from planning to building applications to send to testing to maintain. Everything else occurs far from the perspective of the engineers. In the cloud side of PaaS these focal points can be useful to a programmer in order to use the PaaS cloud foundation for malware order and control and go behind IaaS applications [5].

In order for PaaS to fabricate applications over the stage, the vendor may recommend purposeful control to the consumer. However, any security lowers the application level, i.e, host and system theft avoidance will be handled by the vendor; furthermore, the supplier brings to the table solid affirmations that the information will remain difficult to reach between applications. Over this stage, PaaS is proposed to empower engineers to manufacture their own applications. Subsequently, it will generally be more extensible than SaaS, to the detriment of client prepared highlights. This trade-off stretches to security highlights and abilities, where the built-in capacities are less finished but there is greater adaptability to layer on extra security.

5.1.4 Security Issues in IaaS

Infrastructure as a service (IaaS) totally changes the manner in which engineers deploy their applications. Rather than going through widely with their very own data centers or managed hosting organizations or co-location facilities, and after that employing an activities staff to make it run, they can simply go to Amazon Web Services or one of different IaaS vendors, get a virtual server running in minutes, and pay for just the services they use. With cloud specialists like RightScale, enStratus, and others they could effectively become huge without stressing over things like scaling and extra security. To put it plainly, IaaS and other related services have empowered new companies and different organizations centered on their skills without stressing a lot over the provisioning and the executives of framework. IaaS totally masks the equipment behind it and enables clients to use a service without the fundamental complexities. The cloud has a convincing offer in terms of expense; however, out of the box IaaS just gives essential security (border firewall, load balancing and so on) and applications inside the cloud will require larger amounts of security given at the host [6].

IaaS is inclined to different degrees of safety issues depending on the cloud deployment model through which it is being conveyed. Public cloud represents a significant hazard whereas private cloud appears to have a lesser effect. Substantial security of infrastructure and disaster supervision is of most extreme significance if any harm is caused to the framework (either normally or purposefully). Infrastructure does not just relate to the equipment, where information is processed and stored, but also to the way in which data is being transmitted. In the era of typical cloud environment, data will be transmitted from sender to receiver through various numbers of third-party infrastructure gadgets.

5.2 Security Concerns of Cloud Computing

Cloud computing is being used by most of the organizations today. It makes work forms effective, versatile and conservative. It is net-driven, has an adaptable engineering and is effectively open. In any case, cloud can even now make organizations vulnerable. As per the survey, people mostly said that data security is the primary concern inhibiting cloud adoption [2, 7].

As organizations are moving their data to the cloud, they need to execute strategies and policies that will empower their workers to exploit cloud computing without affecting the security of corporate resources.

It is vital to distinguish the top security issues and find corrective measures.

5.2.1 Data Breaches

A data breach is an occurrence where data is stolen or taken from a framework without the knowledge or approval of the system proprietor. A small organization or a large-scale industry may endure a data breach. Hacked information may include sensitive, exclusive, or private data such as credit card info, client information, business data, or matters of national security.

The impacts of a data breach are quickly felt by an organization, causing harm to its reputation due the apparent "disloyalty of trust." Victims and their clients may also suffer financial losses should related records be a piece of the data stolen.

This can happen due to various reasons, some of which are explained below:

- Utilizing System Vulnerabilities: Obsolete software can create an opening that enables an intruder to inject malware into a PC and take information.

- Easy Passwords: It is so much easier to crack the simpler client passwords by the attacker, particularly if the words or expressions are contained in a secret key. That is the reason specialists advise against straightforward passwords.

- Drive-by Downloads: A threat or malware can be unexpectedly downloaded when surfing a compromised website. A drive-by download will commonly exploit a program, application, or working framework that is outdated or has security issues.

- Intended Malware Attack: Scammers use spam and phishing email in an attempt to trap the client to uncover client credentials by downloading infected files or guiding clients to compromised sites. Email is a typical path for malware to end up on your PC.

5.2.2   Hijacking of Accounts

Here the attacker utilizes a compromised email account to imitate the account holder. Commonly, account hijacking is brought about through phishing, sending spoofed messages to the client, credential guessing or various other attacking strategies. In most of the cases, an email account is connected to a client's different online activities, for example, social networks and bank account. The attacker can utilize the account to recover the individual's personal data, perform monitory transactions, make new accounts, and approach the account holder for cash or help with an illegal action.

Cloud account hijacking is a procedure in which an individual's or industry's cloud account is hacked or captured by an intruder. It is a typical strategy in identity theft in which the hacker utilizes the stolen account data to direct malevolent or unapproved action. At the point when cloud account hijacking happens, an attacker normally utilizes a compromised email account or other credentials to imitate the account holder.

While cloud computing conveys with it an abundance of advantages for organizations, including reduced capital costs and the resources required on an on-demand basis, it also gives digital culprits a domain ready for attack, since enormous amounts of information are housed in one location. Since the information is stored and fetched on gadgets and data is regularly shared crosswise over a wide range of clients, the risks represented by cloud account hijacking are ample.

5.2.3   Insider Threat

Insiders can be a significant threat to any industry. They can sidestep a major number of safety efforts utilizing their insight into and access to the restrictive frameworks. Computer emergency response team (CERT) experts work out techniques that enable stopping and recognizing insider threats that purposefully or inadvertently cause damage to the basic resources.

The nature of the threats plays a destructive role in spite of the computer environment the user is dealing with. For example, regardless of whether or not the information and applications are available on premises, public cloud, or cloud provider the risk of information exfiltration, information revealing, burglary, and similar events are ever present.

A major concern of insider threats is exactly how arbitrary they can be. It could be the accrual of a large amount of debt, a substance dependence, extortion, an individual's life suddenly becoming troubled, etc. It could likewise be angles nearer to work such as business reasons that include apparent poor pay, dread of being terminated, or feelings of being disregarded. All endeavors of all sizes must be concerned about insider threats.

Individuals who have been involved in cybersecurity for only a moment have heard the anecdotes about insider attacks carried out in ways such as planting rationale bombs and crushing loads of information. One such well-known episode is Omega Engineering, which involved an insider planting a logic bomb on a document server at one of Omega Engineering's assembling offices. The logic bomb effectively decimated software that ran the organization's manufacturing process. Another precedent is the city of San Francisco administrator who, as indicated by news reports, changed the credentials, preventing city employees from accessing the system for 12 days. There are also episodes involving the insiders behind the Department of Defense's Secret Internet Protocol Router Network (SIPRNet) and infamous NSA leaks.

5.2.4   Malware Injection

Malware refers to vindictive code that is dispatched to attack a single PC or an entire organization's system. It exploits target framework vulnerabilities such as a bug in authentic programming (e.g., a program or web application module) that can be infected.

A malware penetration can have devastating results such as stolen information, extortion or damaged system frameworks. Common malware types are ransomware, worms, Trojan, rootkits, backdoors, adware and spyware.

5.2.5   Abuse of Cloud Services

One of the specialties of cloud architecture is the capability to upscale and downscale resources per the requirements. This equivalent adaptability provides attackers with a dynamic domain in which to carry out their attacks. It is generally cheap to lease space from a cloud vendor and to utilize the CPU power and bandwidth capacity to initiate DDoS [5] attacks, run destructive sites, or control botnets. The answer to this issue isn't simple; an admirable approach can set down the rules, however, because of the mechanization that is engaged with provisioning new cloud cases, it is frequently too late before a cloud vendor distinguishes malicious cloud activity.

Another issue identified with the abuse of cloud administrations is cybercriminals exploiting the free trial period offered by some vendors. An example of this was the information shared by a vendor who had automated the provisioning of a free trial, which was thusly being white labeled and resold by a group of Chinese attackers!

The challenges in cloud service [7, 8] are the issues of service provider instead of customer; however, it can affect the client when the terrible cloud instances cause blockage on the cloud network in the case of a distributed denial-of-service (DDos) attack. This can lead to shared stage resource issues where the accessibility of a cloud instance is affected by the activity that is occurring somewhere else in the vendor platform.

5.2.6   Insecure APIs

Application programming interfaces (APIs) are utilized by cloud vendors and software developers to enable clients to communicate, oversee, and extricate data from cloud platform. APIs could be utilized, for instance, to assemble logs from an application, to furnish a combination of databases and storage segments [5], or to control explicit cloud data. APIs are also the direction in which a versatile application can associate with a site or backend benefits, and can give the capacity to validate clients as well as query data.

It is vital that the APIs are developed in view of security and contemplate sufficient confirmation and access control techniques [8] together with encryption technique to ensure that data isn't revealed. An example of a data breach that occurred because of an uncertain API happened at Moonpig, a web-based greeting card merchant. A versatile application utilizing static validation enabled the attackers to accumulate client data by just attempting all client IDs consecutively.

The main reason that APIs are a a security challenge in the cloud is that they are the open front door to the application and need to be available remotely. For organizations who follow a security by configuration method to deal with application advancement, they will ideally comprehend the security prerequisites around distributing APIs, and will find a way to guarantee that adequate validation, approval, and encryption are implicit, just as ensuring that the code itself doesn't contain any conspicuous vulnerabilities. Yet, tragically, a large number of companies have not yet grasped secure coding strategies, and release production code that isn't solidified enough.

5.2.7 Denial of Service Attacks

Denial-of-service (DoS) attack could be defined as a digital attack in which the attacker expects to render a gadget like a PC inaccessible to its proposed clients by intruding on the gadget's ordinary working. Commonly, DoS works by flooding an objective machine with solicitations until typical traffic is unfit to be prepared, and this results in denial of service to the expected clients [10, 11].

When thinking about cloud, a denial-of-service attack is an area that should be stressed upon data center administrators. New shortcomings have been triggered in the application foundation of big business as organizations have progressively been utilizing cloud services and virtualized data centers. At the same time, at the application foundation the DoS attacks are moving from brute-force floods of data to more harmful attacks.

For the organizations that are putting pivotal business information outside their offices, leaving their business dependent on proceeding with interchanges, this mix is progressively compromising. With the multi-occupant services winding up increasingly normal, the services of an inconsequential, yet co-founding, firm could be drastically influenced by attacks that have already taken place on an organization.

5.2.8 Insufficient Due Diligence

There is a knowledge gap that can help prevent sufficient exercise of due diligence when hiring a cloud service provider with cloud computing being a new implementation, especially in the hiring organizations. Customers can find a mismatch between what they expect and what a CSP can provide without knowing quite what they are contracting for. Therefore, asking the right questions is vital in order to understand the contractual obligations and liabilities of provider and customer. Service agreements may not be sufficient to discuss disclosure in the face of an incident. Whether the on-premise security controls will be effective in the cloud might not be confirmed by the enterprise architects. It's the prime task for the hiring organizations to make sure to choose a cloud provider that will not attempt to lock them in case the service should prove unsatisfactory, or if the organization wants to use services from another provider. Also, if the relationship needs to be terminated, the old cloud service provider must be willing and able to move on and delete the organization's data securely and efficiently.

In order to help make the organization understand the risks of adopting cloud computing technology, conducting due diligence is helpful. It can also provide a better understanding of their capacity and consumption needs, and thus prevents over-buying services.

5.2.9 Shared Vulnerabilities

In order to endorse multiple tenants which, share the underlying infrastructure, the cloud service providers use scalable infrastructure. There are hypervisors directly on the hardware layer, which help multiple virtual machines to run, while they themselves are running multiple applications. There are numerous attacks on the SaaS on the highest layer, where the access to the data of another application running in the same virtual machine is gained by the attacker. It is true for the lowest layers, where to gain access to all VMs on the same server the hypervisors can be exploited from virtual machines.

To a great extent, not all cloud hosting solutions and cloud computing services are secure. In this situation, threats can originate from other clients with the cloud computing service, and threats targeting one client could also have an impact on other clients. Hence, all layers of the shared technology can be attacked to gain unauthorized access to data such as CPU, RAM, hypervisors, applications, etc.

5.2.10 Data Loss

Data loss occurs at the hardware-based storage technology and the risk of data loss exists in cloud. In order to cope with this loss, proper security solutions are available like backups, security, redundancies and more.

Data could be lost in a variety of ways. For instance, sometimes the computers freeze and backup copies are lost, or sometimes technologies fail, or maybe servers crash and the information contained within is lost. Although most cloud storage providers go to great lengths to secure their networks and data, all attacks cannot be prevented. Software-as-a-service (SaaS) applications are a potential source of massive data loss. It is possible to have information mistakenly overwritten by users or by applications because these apps hold and continuously update large data sets. The old information could be overwritten by new information and data sets may be partially overwritten in the process. Also, there is a high chance of unintentional deletion of data. All of this may lead to a variety of problems like damage to the image, reputation and litigation from customers whose private information is exposed and/or lost.

Robust cloud storage options are provided by the technology service providers that provide ample storage, affordable pricing and, most importantly, robust security. Although data storage may never be perfect, there are solutions available to mitigate risks and provide security.

5.3 Security Tools in Cloud

Many IT organizations and business sectors have embraced the cloud computing technology in recent years. However, despite its growing popularity, there are a whole lot of security issues related to this infrastructure. Generally, these issues get ignored by cloud service providers who strive to meet customers' requirements at a profitable price. Hence, it is of utmost importance for the cloud service providers and cloud vendors to set security tools within the cloud infrastructure. These tools are required to perform penetration testing of the cloud infrastructure and ensure that the user data will be secured and protected at the optimum level.

Figure 5.1   Security tools in cloud.

5.3.1 Qualys

The security of devices and web apps can be achieved by Qualys,[1] which also assists users to remain in accordance with the principles of its cloud-only solution. The data about the hazards is constantly monitored and analyzed by the company and users are assured of the fact that there will hardly be any potential attack that can happen to the system. The software-as-a-service (SaaS) model played a pivotal role in Qualys being the first organization to provide vulnerability management systems as applications through the internet. It received an excellent rating from Gartner Group for these services. If malware exists in the system, it will provide the procedure to fix the bugs in the system. Once the bugs are removed, it will verify for the same. The cloud-based compliance and web application security offerings are two of the most significant features of Qualys. This company was involved in setting up the Cloud Security Alliance (CSA) and is a prominent member of the same.

5.3.2 CipherCloud

CipherCloud[2] helps business firms embrace cloud services while making sure that data security and regulatory compliance don't get compromised. It protects and secures the products that we use "as a service" such as Salesforce, Chatter, Box, Office 365, Gmail, Amazon Web Services, etc. Apart from all these services, it also offers some other services such as cloud control, threat protection, risk visibility, end-to-end encryption, data sovereignty, and global data protection compliance. CipherCloud is in two categories of security vendors classified by Gartner as cloud access security broker and cloud encryption gateway.

[1] https://www.qualys.com/
[2] https://www.ciphercloud.com/

5.3.3 Okta

Okta[3] is a software company which deals with identity and access management. It ensures that the access to all organizational data and services be given to appropriate and trustworthy persons. It keeps track of all the employees who are involved in retrieving information at the backend and frontend. Organizations are able to control and protect user authentication through cloud software provided by Okta, which also helps developers to create identity controls in applications, web services and devices. The IT organizations and business firms are highly benefited by Okta which enables applications such as Google Apps, Gmail, Workday, Salesforce, Slack, Box, SAP, Oracle, Office 365 to be managed with one login. Okta is also accessible from any kind of device. Privilege provisioning from one dashboard, implementing policies across devices, single sign-on options, etc., are some of the most prominent features of Okta. There is a provision for API authentication provided by Okta.

5.3.4 Skyline Networks

Skyline Networks[4] mainly focuses on offering internet access and other connectivity services through secure radio network. It offers a powerful and flexible network that can cover a wide range of areas and a high speed connectivity in multiplex and city centers. It offers a wide range of WLAN services and keeps the wireless network in good shape by continuously following up with customers throughout the WLAN deployment model starting with installation and continuing through validation, optimization and auditing. Skyline Networks can peer directly with other ISPs and allows management over traffic to whoever they choose. The network consists of various layers of redundancy. Skyline Networks offers additional services such as VoIP with PSTN termination, burstable offsite backup, remote access, LAN extension, IA redundancy services, etc., because the installation of links offers much higher bandwidths than the customers require.

5.3.5 Bitglass

Bitglass[5] offers clear security and protection of all the organizational data. The chances of data loss can be minimized and data visibility can be managed and controlled by Bitglass, which can be used in any device, be it computers or mobile devices. The IT organizations and firms have adopted the cloud thanks to Bitglass' Next-Gen Cloud Access Security Broker (CASB). Data security and regulatory compliance are two of the important features of CASB. The flow of sensitive data can be controlled with Bitglass cloud data loss prevention (DLP). It also monitors the application usage at the firewall and usage of unmanaged applications. The performance of the cloud can be improved by Bitglass, which also helps in encryption of uploaded data in the cloud. The business data present on the internet can be tracked by Bitglass and hence visibility can be well managed even when data gets uploaded into personal file-sharing services. The risk of mobile devices being lost can also be minimized using Bitglass.

---

[3]https://www.okta.com/
[4]www.skyline-networks.com/
[5]https://www.bitglass.com/

5.3.6 WhiteHat Security

The safety and protection of the software development life cycle can be ensured by the services offered by WhiteHat Application Security.[6] As a result, IT organizations and business firms have the luxury of having digital transformation without having to think about the security issues. Moreover, the organizations are able to provide secure applications without any delay as the breach between security and development has been reduced by WhiteHat Security. The organizational websites and the coding involved in maintaining the websites are all secured by WhiteHat Security. The data about the existing threat is given by a product included in WhiteHat Security so that the susceptibilities in the coding process can be prevented from scratch. The Sentinel product suite offered as a service enables the user to access the web apps. WhiteHat Security also aims to offer up date data about all the possible security attacks from the exterior of the network. Owing to its innovative platform, Gartner placed WhiteHat as a leader in application security testing multiple times.

5.3.7 Proofpoint

Proofpoint[7] offers software as a service and products that are primarily focused on security of email and is also concerned with the cloud-only services meant for organizations and business firms ranging from small- to medium-sized businesses. The other major responsibilities which are carried out by Proofpoint are the prevention of loss of outgoing data, social media, mobile devices, digital risk, encryption of email, etc., which are all achieved through "software as a service" offered by Proofpoint. Besides safeguarding the data, it also ensures that it will not be able to decrypt any of the data. Proofpoint has become quite popular in the market and its importance has been realized by a large number of users who have started to use the same for security of email and to avoid the loss of data.

5.3.8 docTrackr

docTrackr[8] is a very important security layer that keeps track of all the proceedings related to file-sharing services such as Box and Microsoft Sharepoint. The primary objective of docTrackr is to prevent any document sent by the user from being accessed, changed or tampered with. docTrackr can set user privileges on their document and can share the document with their choice of persons. Moreover, it gives users the provision to track their document and lets them know the identity of the person who is trying to access their data illegally and without permission. Moreover, the document can also be fetched to the user's side and can be unshared if they don't want their document to be accessible or modified by others.

5.3.9 Centrify

A wide range of products and services are dependent on Centrify, whose primary objective is identity and access management, just like Okta. An organization is all about having several types of users from employers to employees to users. The main objective of Centrify

---

[6]https://www.whitehatsec.com/
[7]https://www.proofpoint.com/
[8]https://www.crunchbase.com/organization/doctrackr

is to treat the users and employees in the same way and make them gather in one central area; and then the concerned organization uses its enforced rules, regulations and policies to supervise and manage them. Anyone attempting to sign in via on-premise software or cloud through any part of the Centrify network will be tracked and protected by Centrify. Samsung Knox is one of the key products associated with Centrify.[9] Single sign-on options for gadgets running Knox are offered by Samsung Knox and Centrify plays an active role in enabling IT sectors to control these gadgets.

5.3.10 Vaultive

Vaultive[10] is a software company that is primarily focused on offering a cloud data encryption platform to assist the cloud-based services and applications. Founded in 2009 by Ben Matzkel and Maayan Tal, it is a network-layer proxy, which indicates there is no requirement of any premise device for Vaultive to be placed in the middle of their network and the internet. Vaultive gives users the provision to use the cloud-based services of an organization and encrypt their data if the organizations are not trustworthy. Vaultive aims at assisting users in safeguarding more applications apart from Office 365 and Exchange. Vaultive is continuously striving to stretch their responsibilities for effective management of software dealing with customer relationships, communication services, file-sharing applications, etc.

5.3.11 Zscaler

Zscaler[11] is a network security company that offers a whole lot of services such as web security, antivirus, vulnerability management, sandboxing and firewalls. It also works in mobile and IOT environments. This company also deals with forensics of automated threats and prevention of malware against all possible cyberattacks. Founded in 2008 and headquartered in the United States, it offers a cloud-based approach to security as a service.

Zscaler ensures the simplicity of setting up these products and is quite economical as compared to traditional securities. The other services offered by this organization are prevention of advanced persistent threats and spear phishing. The organization's products supervise all the traffic that flows within and out of the network. It is not necessary to filter the total traffic from one central point. Depending on the user's requirement, they can analyze and supervise specific networks in the cloud. The safety of the Android devices can be ensured within the organization, which is supervised by making use of a special mobile online dashboard.

5.3.12 SilverSky

SilverSky[12] is a software company which is mainly concerned with solutions of cloud-based security. It was founded in 1997 and its headquarters are located in Northeastern United States. Although it is really difficult for organizations to cope with the demands of escalating security requirements in the regular operations of their official activities and businesses, the cloud-based security solutions of SilverSky help in cost reduction, com-

---

[9]https://www.centrify.com/
[10]https://vaultive.com/
[11]https://www.zscaler.com/
[12]https://www.crunchbase.com/organization/silversky

plexity management, and check whether all the requirements comply with the policies of the organization. Clients who are not at all concerned with security but are aiming for high goals from a business point of view greatly benefit from SilverSky. It ensures that the cloud security solutions are quite simple, manageable and economical.

SilverSky also offers a wide range of cloud-controlled security and application services apart from providing security for advanced cloud-based email and a software for threat management. Apart from IT organizations, SilverSky also serves the purpose of some other sectors such as finance, healthcare, retail, etc.

Last but not the least, SilverSky also helps to meet the compliance aspects related to the management of healthcare data by organizations and the safety and security of online payment systems for the organizations accepting online payments. SilverSky also helps in upgrading and updating clients' systems against all the latest threats that can have a severe impact on business aspects and disrupt regular activities.

5.4   Cloud Service Vulnerabilities

Cloud security vulnerabilities can be embodied in different ways, and if not rapidly removed can lead directly to data breaks and infringement of privacy. To stop the security attacks in the cloud requires a great amount of attention, consistent research, and routine checking of the system to identify, address, and resolve problems [12, 13].

Cloud safety is a common duty between the cloud vendors and the endeavor. The measure of engagement per entity is based upon cloud offerings the enterprise uses and whether it is a public, private, or hybrid cloud. Service level understandings should detail what a venture is and isn't in charge of with regards to security.

In spite of which entity is in charge of verifying the cloud network, it's indispensable for the two parties to perceive and enforce it to shield the cloud from security vulnerabilities. The most transcendent cloud security vulnerabilities are given below.

5.4.1   Visibility and Control Reduction at the Consumer End

While changing over resources/tasks to the cloud, companies lose some perceivability and authority over those resources/tasks. When utilizing external cloud benefits, the accountability regarding some policies and architecture moves to the cloud vendor.

Based on the cloud service model utilization that a real move towards accountability relies upon, a change in perspective is prompted for offices in connection to security event monitoring and logging. Companies need to carry out checking and examining of data about applications, administrations, information, and clients, where system-based security event monitoring and logging are not utilized, which is accessible for on-premises IT.

5.4.2   On-Demand Self-Service Simplifies Unauthorized Use

Cloud service providers make it awfully simple to arrange new start-ups. The self-administration provisioning highlights of the cloud empower a company's workforce to arrange extra features from the cloud vendor on an on-demand basis without IT assent. The act of utilizing software in a company that isn't maintained by the company's IT sector is ordinarily alluded to as shadow IT.

Because of the lower expenses and simplicity of actualizing PaaS and SaaS items, there is a likelihood of unapproved utilization of cloud administrations increments. Be that as it may, administrations provisioned or utilized without IT's knowledge present dangers to a company. The illegitimate use of cloud services could result in an expansion in malware attacks or information exfiltration since the company is unfit to secure assets it doesn't know about. The illegitimate use of unapproved cloud benefits likewise diminishes a company's visibility and control of its system and information.

5.4.3   Web-Based Organization APIs Can Be Compromised

Cloud vendors uncover a lot of application programming interfaces (APIs) that clients use to oversee and associate with cloud administrations. Companies utilize these APIs to arrange, oversee, organize, and screen their resources and these client APIs are utilized by the company. Indistinguishable programming vulnerabilities from an API for a working framework, library, and so forth are carried by these APIs.

Threat actors search for vulnerabilities in the executives APIs. Whenever found, these vulnerabilities can be transformed into effective attacks, and organization cloud resources can be undermined. From that point, aggressors can utilize company resources to execute further attacks against other clients.

5.4.4   Separation among Multi-Tenant Fails

Abuse of framework and system vulnerabilities inside a service provider foundation, platforms, or applications that help multi-tenancy can prompt an inability to keep up partition among occupants. This breakdown can be utilized by an assailant to obtain access with one company's asset to another company's or client's assets or information. Multi-tenancy expands the attack surface, leading to an expanded possibility of information leaking if the segregation controls come up short.

This attack can be cultivated by abusing vulnerabilities in the vendor's applications, hypervisor, or equipment, subverting coherent disengagement controls or attacks on the CSP's administration API. Till date there has not been a reported security disappointment of a vendor's SaaS stage that has brought about an outside aggressor accessing occupants' information.

5.4.5   Incomplete Data Deletion

Threats related to information removal exist in light of the fact that the client has decreased visibility into where their information is physically stored in the cloud and a diminished capacity to check whether their information is securely removed. This hazard is concerning in light of the fact that the information is spread over various distinctive capacity gadgets inside the service provider's framework in a multi-tenancy condition. Likewise, removal strategies may vary from vendor to vendor. Companies will most likely be unable to confirm that their information was safely erased and that remainders of the information are not accessible to attackers. These risk increases as an agency utilizes more cloud service.

5.4.6   Stolen Credentials

In case a user's cloud credentials are accessed by an attacker, the vendor's services could be admitted by the attacker to provision additional data, as well as target the company's resources. The cloud computing resources could be influenced by the attacker to target the company's admin users, other organizations using the same cloud service provider, or the provider's administrators. The agency's structure and information could be admitted by an intruder who gains access to a vendor administrator's cloud identity.

A cloud service provider and an organization have different managerial roles. On one hand the vendor's administrator has access to the cloud service provider (CSP) network, systems, and applications of the cloud's infrastructure; on the other hand, the consumer's administrators have access only to the organization's cloud implementations. In addition to this, the administrator has supervision rights over more than one consumer and supports several services.

5.4.7 Increased Complexity Strains IT Staff

Intricacy could be brought into IT tasks after moving to the cloud. The organization's current IT staff are required to gain proficiency with another model that will take care of overseeing, incorporating, and working in the cloud. The limit and ability level to oversee, incorporate, and maintain the relocation of benefits and information in the cloud must be controlled by the IT staff, notwithstanding their present obligations regarding on-premises IT.

Key management and encryption systems become progressively mind-boggling in the cloud. To include the intricacy, the administrations, systems, and apparatuses accessible to log and screen cloud benefits commonly shift crosswise over CSPs. Because of innovation, strategies, and usage techniques, there may likewise be emanant dangers/hazards in half-breed cloud executions which include intricacy. This additional unpredictability results in an expanded potential for security holes in an organization's cloud and on-premises usage.

5.4.8 Vendor Lock-In Complicates Moving to Other CSPs

Vendor lock-in becomes an issue when an organization considers moving its assets/operations from one CSP to another. The organization discovers that the cost/effort/schedule time necessary for the move is much higher than initially considered due to factors such as non-standard data formats, non-standard APIs, and reliance on one CSP's proprietary tools and unique APIs.

This issue increases in service models where the CSP takes more responsibility. As an agency uses more features, services, or APIs, the exposure to a CSP's unique implementations increases. These unique implementations require changes when a capability is moved to a different CSP. If a selected CSP goes out of business, it becomes a major problem since data can be lost or cannot be transferred to another CSP in a timely manner.

5.4.9 Insiders Abuse Authorized Access

Malicious insiders are those people in the organization who misuse their authorized access, which adversely impacts the organization. All the vital data of the organization can be infiltrated when insiders such as employees, staff and trusted business partners abuse their authorized access to critical assets. It is lot more difficult to detect malicious insiders than harmful outsiders as those insiders have valid access to the company's information and are involved in regular official activities of the organization. There are some other adverse effects of these malicious insiders such as intentional disruption of information technology, stealing of information and insider fraud. This type of threat can be mitigated through proper training of employees, background verification of all staff and applying the rule of least privilege.

5.4.10 Stored Data is Lost

All the vital information and data of cloud customers can be lost due to a number of factors. One of those factors can be unintentional removal of information by the cloud service providers. Apart from some natural disaster, there can be loss of cloud information due to negligence in storage, which might happen due to failing to understand the storage model of cloud service provider (CSP). This threat can also arise due to the encryption key being lost by the cloud customers. Apart from the issue of malicious insiders, hardware or software failure, power failure, presence of bugs in software, administrator faults, malicious activities, such as injecting virus and SQL injection, are some of the prominent reasons as to why the stored data of customers in the cloud can be lost. The lost data can be restored through proper backup procedures and a disaster recovery device.

5.4.11 CSP Supply Chain Can Be Compromised

An organization is adversely affected when vulnerable elements in the supply network get targeted. It is a form of cyberattack which can happen in any organization. Talking from the cloud point of view, the third parties strongly disagree with the necessities that the CSP is entrusted with offering the organization and this problem arises when the infrastructural or operational parts get outsourced by CSP. There has to be a proper assessment of all the compliances set up by the CSP and the organization should play an active part in that. There may be an escalation of the threat to an agency if there is a lack of imposition of the necessities on the supply chain. The probability of the occurrence of this kind of threat is enhanced as an increased number of services offered by CSP is used by IT organizations and business firms.

5.4.12 Inadequate Due Diligence Amplifies Cyber Threat

The issue of insufficient due diligence often plays a role in affecting the organizations and firms in an adverse manner. The transition of the organizational data and business data to the cloud infrastructure is often done without having the full knowledge of all the security aspects related to this infrastructure. They blindly decide that they are going to move their sensitive and confidential data to the cloud infrastructure without considering the safety measures which should be taken by the cloud service provider to safeguard the organizational data. There should be an effective cybersecurity policy that should be put into place. When the organizations conduct due diligence, they should check for some of the factors that need to be adopted such as cybersecurity insurance, security program assessment (SPA), etc.

5.5 Cloud Computing Security Best Practices

Since the inception of the cloud computing era, security has been the biggest worry among organizations. Based on security concerns, some safety measures can be taken to overcome this problem [14, 15]. Some of cloud's computing security best practices are given below.

5.5.1 Cloud Data Encryption

Cloud data encryption ensures that data available in the cloud is encrypted both in transmission media and cloud storage. Organizations and companies need to adopt an info-driven strategy to ensure their sensitive data so as to make preparations for safe guarding of complex and developing situations of virtualization, cloud management, and portability. Organizations should execute information security arrangements that give continuous protection in sensitive resources, including cloud data security enhancement through encryption and cryptographic key management. A complete stage for cloud security and encryption also ought to convey powerful access controls and key administration capacities that empower associations to cost-effectively and extensively influence encryption to address security goals.

5.5.2 Identity and Access Management

Identity and access management is a procedure that is amalgamated with company's IT framework. An identity management and access privilege system has been included in the system. These frameworks get to control programming, a client database, and the management tools for controlling the access privilege, evaluating and authorization. At the point when a client is added to the framework, system admin utilizes an automated provisioning framework to set up consents dependent on access control systems, work duties and workflows; authorize least benefit to confine special access and to solidify cloud assets; and provide role-based access privilege and monitor the same through session checking.

5.5.3 Network Segmentation

Network segmentation is a very successful system to confine the effect of network attack. Security specialists have known for quite a while that network segmentation is a helpful advance in ensuring their networks and, luckily, this should be possible as adequately as possible inside virtual and private cloud frameworks. Although some planning and technical configuration might be required, network segmentation best practices are as of now a key control to stop the intruders, avert data breaches and meet consistence necessities.

5.5.4 Disaster Recovery

Disaster recovery in cloud computing is reinforcement and restore methodology that includes reserving and maintaining duplicates of electronic records in a cloud environment as a safety effort. The objective of cloud disaster recovery allows a company to regain the resources if any breakdown occurs due to natural calamity or human intervention. Cloud data centers provide full disaster recovery benefits by replicating the servers [6] between the data center along with system configuration for quick recovery.

5.5.5 Vulnerability Management

Vulnerability management is a way of distinguishing, characterizing, remediating, and moderating vulnerabilities, particularly in software and firmware. Vulnerabilities are found in each IT resource that is created and must be recognized at the beginning periods of advancement and remediated. Vulnerability management is indispensable to PC security and system security. Monitoring vulnerabilities, reviewing security and fixing known vulnerabilities should be done on a regular basis.

5.5.6 Monitoring, Altering and Reporting

For safety reasons, there is continuous monitoring of client activity in every platform and instance. An effort is made to incorporate all data from the cloud service provider (if accessible) with data from in-house and other service providers to get an encompassing picture of what's going on with the user's personal data. Alerting notifies the user of any changes done in cloud data, which is reported to the concerned authority.

5.6 Conclusion

Cloud computing has a significant number of advantages, yet it faces difficulties and analysis because of its compromising security implementation. There ought to be complex security strategies set up when managing the cloud applications. Likewise, applications ought to implement more layers of security; for example, multiple factor verification must be introduced to guarantee that information is appropriately verified. Information in transmission media must be encoded and marked to guarantee secrecy and honesty. Likewise, most business associations should utilize a hybrid cloud platform since this guarantees the individual data is supervised inside private clouds and not stored on public clouds. This mitigates the threat of personal data being compromised.

REFERENCES

1. Kandukuri, B. R., & Rakshit, A. (2009, September). Cloud security issues. In 2009 IEEE International Conference on Services Computing (pp. 517-520). IEEE.

2. Le, D. N., Kumar, R., Mishra, B. K., Chatterjee, J. M., & Khari, M. (Eds.). (2019). *Cyber Security in Parallel and Distributed Computing: Concepts, Techniques, Applications and Case Studies*. John Wiley & Sons.

3. Bose, R., Sahana, S., & Sarddar, D. (2017). An Adaptive Cloud Communication Network Using VSAT with Enhanced Security Implementation. In Proceedings of the First International Conference on Intelligent Computing and Communication (pp. 117-125). Springer, Singapore. DOI 10.1007/978-981-10-2035-3_13

4. Chou, T. S. (2013). Security threats on cloud computing vulnerabilities. *International Journal of Computer Science & Information Technology*, 5(3), 79.

5. Sahana, R. B. S., & Sarddar, D. (2015). An enhanced storage management scheme with search optimization for cloud data center. *Int J Appl Eng Res*, 10(12), 32141-32150.

6. Sahana, S., Bose, R., & Sarddar, D. (2016). Harnessing RAID mechanism for enhancement of data storage and security on cloud. *Brazilian Journal of Science and Technology*, 3(1), 12. DOI 10.1186/s40552-016-0024-5.

7. Murray, A., Begna, G., Nwafor, E., Blackstone, J., & Patterson, W. (2015, April). Cloud service security & application vulnerability. In SoutheastCon 2015 (pp. 1-8). IEEE.

8. Xiong, D., Zou, P., Cai, J., & He, J. (2015, August). A Dynamic Multi-domain Access Control Model in Cloud Computing. In International Symposium on Security in Computing and Communication (pp. 3-12). Springer, Cham.

9. Le, D. N., Kumar, R., Nguyen, G. N., & Chatterjee, J. M. (2018). *Cloud Computing and Virtualization*. John Wiley & Sons.

10. Somani, G., Johri, A., Taneja, M., Pyne, U., Gaur, M. S., & Sanghi, D. (2015, December). DARAC: DDoS mitigation using DDoS aware resource allocation in cloud. In International Conference on Information Systems Security (pp. 263-282). Springer, Cham.

11. Le, D. N., Van, V. N., & Giang, T. T. T. (2016). A New Private Security Policy Approach for DDoS Attack Defense in NGNs. In Information Systems Design and Intelligent Applications (pp. 1-10). Springer, New Delhi.

12. Le Dang, N., Le, D. N., & Le, V. T. (2016). A new multiple-pattern matching algorithm for the network intrusion detection system. *IACSIT International Journal of Engineering and Technology*, 8(2).

13. Morrow, T., Pender, K., Lee, C., & Faatz, D. (2019). Overview of Risks, Threats, and Vulnerabilities Faced in Moving to the Cloud. CMU/SEI-2019-TR-004. Software Engineering Institute, Carnegie Mellon University.

14. Ryan, M., & Lucifredi, F. (2018). *AWS System Administration: Best Practices for Sysadmins in the Amazon Cloud.* " O'Reilly Media, Inc.".

15. Morrow, T., LaPiana, V., Faatz, D., & Hueca, A. (2019). *Cloud Security Best Practices Derived from Mission Thread Analysis.*

PART II

SECURITY DESIGNS FOR THE INTERNET OF THINGS AND SOCIAL NETWORKS

CHAPTER 6

IOT SECURITY AND PRIVACY PRESERVATION

BRIGHT KESWAN[1], TARINI CH. MISHRA[2], AMBARISH G. MOHAPATRA[3], POONAM KESWANI[4]

[1] Department of Computer Applications, Suresh Gyan Vihar University, Jaipur, India
[2] Department of Information Technology, Silicon Institute of Technology, Odisha, India
[3] Silicon Institute of Technology, Odisha, India
[4] Akashdeep PG College, Jaipur, Rajasthan, India
Email: kbright@rediffmail.com, tarini@silicon.ac.in, ambarish.mohapatra@gmail.com, poonamkeswani777@gmail.com

Abstract

The Internet of Things (IoT) envisages a scenario where billions of devices (smart things, servers, communication equipment) are connected to each other and offers services to various entities irrespective of distance over a network. IoT is one of the major revolutions that has happened in the recent past. This new area provides unprecedented benefits and level of comfort and has the capability to drive the world when its full potential is unleashed. However, all of this may come at the cost of compromised privacy in this complex paradigm. The overall goal of an IoT system is about connection services, data collection mechanism and data sharing and analysis. As IoT systems interact with humans, it is prone to cause a threat to individual privacy as well. Here, the need for privacy and security cannot be gauged in a narrow sense of confidentiality. Success of an application is proportional to the IoT framework, emphasizing the employed security mechanism. The market pertaining to IoT application is growing exponentially. To preserve privacy and data security a competent IoT framework has to be envisaged. The framework selected must have the capability to identify applications (preferably cloud-based IoT application) by centralizing the data source, which can overcome the privacy challenge of the user (user-centric privacy) or the network (network-centric privacy).

Keywords: IoT, big data, privacy and security, smart devices and equipment

6.1   Introduction

The past decade has witnessed a drift towards the way people maintain their attributes, which is mainly due to cost-effective technologies that have enabled these devices to be an integral part of a so-called human-oriented network and as a result creates the Internet of Things (IoT) [1]. Primarily, if we want to define IoT it would be something like: "It is a collection of sensor nodes which provide the capability of sensing, processing and sending the data required over the internet and at the receiving end the data are analyzed."

In some contexts IoT can be defined as follows: "Internet of Things allows people and things to be connected at anytime and anyplace with anything and anyone, ideally using any path/network and any service" [2].

The Internet of Things can also be defined as "a world where physical objects are seamlessly integrated into the information network, and where the physical objects can become active participants in business processes. Services are available to interact with these 'smart objects' over the Internet, query their state and any information associated with them, taking into account security and privacy issues" [3].

It is predicted that by the year 2020 more than 50 billion devices will be connected to various IoT platforms in a way to help society find new and innovative solutions for social, automation, energy conservation, security, wearable computing, industrial, manufacturing and many more applications. These devices will primarily act as a bridge between the physical world and the computing paradigm.

However, establishing, maintaining and realizing the visualization of these devices has really been the challenge nowadays. That means establishing these connections has some peer technical issues. Firstly, the cost of these devices has to be considered. The initial design of the sensor networks has to be cost-effective. Secondly, the degree of convenience of establishing the actual connection among the devices where most of the nodes are supposed to be untethered. Thirdly, all these devices run on batteries, so the power consumption and form factor of these devices are to be considered so as to provide a longer operational lifetime of these devices [4].

In addition to the above, the IoT comes with several constraint factors. Primarily, the user of the IoT network has a high dependency factor on the type of application. However, as the IoT devices are very small in size, it is very difficult to perform any kind of audit and quality/traffic control of these devices because it is very difficult to identify and tag each of them. The data are vulnerable in IoT application and can be manipulated and used by any unauthorized entities [1].

Technically, the IoT architecture is based on communication tools for the purpose of providing infrastructure and aiding data transfer among things reliably and securely. An industrial aspect to IoT will require a higher degree of reliability so that a system will be resilient enough to withstand node failures, authentication on data and information, implementation of access control mechanism by the information provider over the data provided and, finally, the privacy measures of a user [5].

According to Weber [5], various challenges will persist as a result of the large number of devices connected and data exchanged among devices in a network, and any security or privacy breach will have a huge impact on the involved stakeholders. New measures have been suggested to ensure the system's flexibility to attacks, client data privacy, access control and data encryption.

Finally, we can infer that the primary issues, apart from the technical issues in IoT, are primarily related to the privacy of a user and data security, which can be referred to as the social and ethical challenges of IoT. These challenges can be monitored through some stringent policies, which can be referred to as the legal challenges of IoT. So, in this chapter the challenges related to IoT are broadly divided into three categories, namely, Ethical issues, Legal issues and Social issues. However, this chapter focuses mainly on energy conservation using IoT.

6.2 Review of Existing Technology

Al-Fuqaha *et al.* have surveyed the IoT in a generalized way [6]. They have mentioned various IoT architectures, opportunities in the market with IoT elements, communication parameters, protocol standards, challenges and research opportunities in IoT.

In another survey, Derhamy *et al.* have surveyed the commercialized aspect of various IoT frameworks. Moreover, they have compared various approaches, protocols, industrial usage and hardware and application development [7]. In [8] there is a brief overview of the current IETF standards of IoT.

The research community has primarily focused on the security and privacy aspect of IoT and has addressed the same at various forums. There are four vital perceptions of security and privacy concerns of IoT [9]. Firstly, there is a limitation on applying IoT security, such as computational power and battery life, and a solution to this problem has to be worked out. Secondly, various IoT attacks, such as remote and local, are classified. Thirdly, the focus should be on authorization and authentication of IoT devices and the architecture and mechanism of the devices are to be done accordingly.

Finally, the security concerns of all the IoT layers need to be analyzed properly. Privacy and security in all the IoT layers are analyzed in [10, 11] and most of the security flaws exist in the IoT layers [12]. These flaws have emerged from different communication protocols used across sensor networks. To check access and availability of the network to an eligible user, Sicari *et al.* proposes an authorization access model and security framework [13]. Security challenges in middleware and an approach to overcome it have been described in [14]. In IoT middleware, a huge number of devices are able to incur various secured properties. Hence, approaches to available middleware are to be analyzed properly considering the familiar security and privacy issues. Moreover, each security approach is to be evaluated properly.

6.3 Research Design

Knowing the impact of IoT on society is useful to understand the capacity of the IoT applications, namely, materialization, a process where information is gathered using sensor nodes, automation, where a system is assigned a responsibility to fulfill an activity, and transformation, a procedure where the process is redefined.

Primarily, IoT products are designed and deployed to empower themselves so as to control and secure their personal data and information [15]. So, the user must be sensitized as to how to interact with the IoT framework as far as the data transaction is concerned [16]. This research design basically states the most feasible way in which a user can interact with the IoT maintaining a user's ethical gratitude, legality and social dignity.

The choices a user opts for certainly vary from the point of view of privacy, legality and society. But other choices that a user makes can arise from other issues due to the degree of interconnection established among these devices. Therefore, the resemblance of other ethical products can motivate socially accountable users. Similarly, ethics can provide a sustainable business model in IoT technology and can ensure a high level of social autonomy with a justifiable legal aspect and can promote a market place.

This model focuses on authorizing and allowing the user to make a choice irrespective of the issues. Ethics are neither properly defined nor levied; rather it is up to the user's choice. The values are designed as a matter of right of the user in line with the IoT architecture. Development and improvement of the user's ability to choose independently will definitely result in substantial challenges in IoT technology. Some of the characteristics of such options are human behavior, consciousness and autonomy outcome of the predefined implementation of IoT objects. Here, a user acts as an autonomous subject rather than being an automated mechanism in the IoT platform [17]. The user's actions, such as cognizance, autonomy and thought process, indicate the user's limitations.

The user's attributes will be in danger of being desensitized if the user is not made aware of the ethical, legal and social impact of IoT [18]. The IoT objects are supposed to develop the attributes in a user which can regulate the ethical activity in the society without questioning its legitimacy [19]. It is probable that any user who can be trained to establish and control IoT objects can make its environment smarter [20]. However, these applications are a result of joint growth which includes a bit of conviction on the part of all users, which in turn increases with societal needs. The conviction can be made clear with the help of proper legislation and accountability that can ensure a proper ownership of a service [21].

Table 6.1   Challenges in IoT.

Sl. No.	Challenges	Explanation
1	Fiscal agenda of protection of data where it is not directed to the user	The Fiscal agenda of data protection limited to the IoT environment, its application and services provided
2	Imperfect evidence on the significance of data expose	The user however has imperfect information as far as the consequence on the disclosed data is concerned and its vulnerability, which in turn affects the decision making. In IoT this problem is more prevalent and pertains towards data transparency with respect to IoT applications [25].
3	Big enough space pertaining towards outcome of data exposure	The intelligence required towards making an appropriate option large enough so as to use the IoT services ineffectively.
4	Emotional favoritisms	The pursuit of instantaneous profits, such as easy access to IoT infrastructure, is likely to promote undesirable outcomes.
5	Compromises among needs towards data collection and processing data and privileges considered towards privacy	There is an undesirable bizarre between the needs for data collection and innovation for the realization of IoT environment and user. Here the challenge is to properly legitimate the dynamic environment [26].
6	Implementation cost privacy enhancement and data protection	It signifies the implementation cost of various methods towards data protection, privacy and societal benefits. The question arises here about the ownership of this cost. Whether agency or the user will bear the cost is the real challenge in this case.
7	Accountability	The challenge here is again about the ownership of the legal accountability of the user data. From economic point of view a data exposure is enough to shut down a business.
8	Identity of an entity	As it is discussed that there is a blurred separation between on-line and off-line data and therefore it is susceptible towards a breach in privacy [27].
9	Digital divide	Every user is different in their trends in accessing IoT objects and related applications. The risks related to the discussed issues primarily depend on the level of proficiency of the user in using the IoT infrastructure.
10	Correspondence to controlling outlines	Two aspects can be taken into account; firstly the degree of progress of IoT technology vis-à-vis the pace at which the effective legislation are formulated, secondly the amount of modification required on the existing IoT infrastructure and the cost of this modification [28].
11	Sustenance in dynamic situation	The usability of IoT services and applications with the processing capabilities and storage of data are liable to change dynamically.

The proposed design must be a component in developing futuristic technology that can lead to a better ethical result and make the technology socially responsible [22]. The expectation is that ethical values support the social paradigm and so the design of the system is properly legitimated. The type of the technology can vary depending on the protocols used to satisfy the internet architecture but the objective in the design is pragmatic. Hence, the requirement of the ethics in IoT is to lessen the risk of social vulnerabilities [23].

The privacy in a design process can be considered as practice to inculcate awareness regarding the methods by which ethics and legislations are impounded on the technical design of an IoT system where the privacy focuses on the norms that can encourage lucidity and can preserve the social dignity of a person [24]. In the design approach itself the user is provided with predefined security.

Finally, the proposed design will have, firstly, a capacity to provide the user with control over the data collected and in addition the user can also freely decide the distribution of the data and services related to the user, which can promote the ethical attributes of a human being, an agency, cognizance and autonomy. Secondly, it will be capable of a proper legislation with respect to time. Thirdly, it will have the capability to support change, which means the design must be dynamic. And lastly, it will have the capability to observe and ascertain personal relations to promote social values.

6.4 Methodology

6.4.1 AWS IoT

Figure 6.1 shows an AWS IoT architecture that consists primarily of a device gateway, a device shadow, a rule engine and a registry [25].

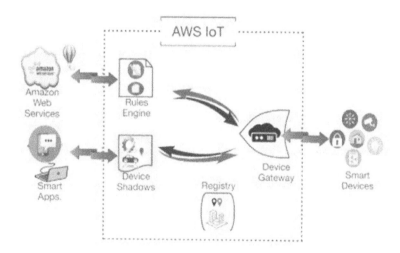

Figure 6.1 AWS IoT architecture.

A device gateway is placed between connected devices and cloud. It allows devices to communicate using message queue telemetry transport (MQTT) protocol. MQTT being an old protocol, it is used in AWS because it is fault tolerant, has high intermittent connectivity, efficiently uses network bandwidth, has a small footprint in device memory and provides a publish/subscribe model for one to many connections across devices [26]. Security among IoT devices and related applications exist because of transport layer security (TLS) over MQTT [27]. TLS is a successor to secure socket layer (SSL). Device gateway also supports WebSocket and HTTP 1.1 protocols [28], AWS Lambda[1] [29], AWS Management Console2 services [30].

Moreover, Amazon provides multilayer security in AWS IoT, applying security at each level of its tech stack. Figure 6.2 shows the design of the security architecture that is based on the Message Broker service with identity service.

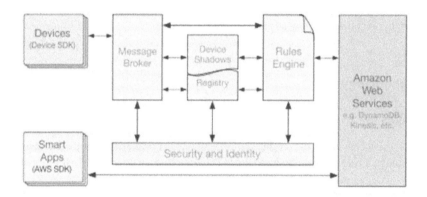

Figure 6.2   AWS IoT security mechanism.

6.4.2 ARM Mbed IoT

IoT applications can also be designed based on ARM microcontrollers using ARM Mbed [31]. Mbed has its own ecosystem to provide all requirements to build both standalone and networked IoT applications [32]. Using Mbed an IoT product will be scalable and secured. Other Mbed tools such as ARM microcontrollers, Mbed OS, Mbed cloud and Mbed device connector can also be integrated into an IoT device.

Mbed OS,[2] Mbed cloud, the device connector and the Mbed library along with various ARM hardware are the basic building blocks of the IoT platforms designed on ARM products. Mbed OS, which is the backbone of all the services [32], is an open-source stack operating system designed especially for embedded application development. ARM Cortex-M, a modular microcontroller, is suitable for many smart applications such as smart home. Mbed OS represents the device-side component and stands on the top of a device security module, called Mbed uVisor.

Figure 6.3 shows the architecture of the Mbed OS. The architecture shows the event-driven capabilities. Apparently, Mbed doesn't support a multithreading environment. Mbed provides a core operating system and drivers that simplify hardware layer connectivity. A suite of protocols in Mbed along with various APIs provide better security and management of devices.

---

[1] https://aws.amazon.com/lambda/
[2] https://www.mbed.com/

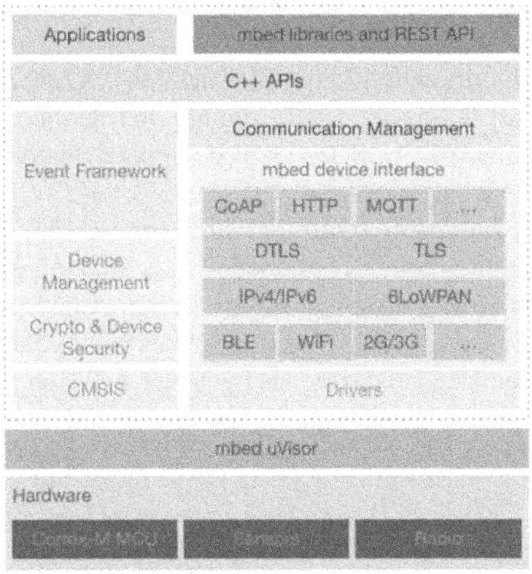

Figure 6.3   Mbed OS architecture.

Similarly, Figure 6.4 provides a broader view of the Mbed architecture. The hardware layer is for the IoT-enabled devices, and Mbed OS takes place all the components. The client library is used to interact with higher layers. The libraries encapsulate the functionality of the Mbed OS for connecting physical devices with the connector service and support OMA lightweight machine-to-machine (LWM2M)[3] compliance [33].

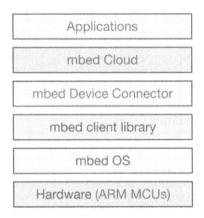

Figure 6.4   ARM Mbed IoT architecture.

The Mbed device connector connects IoT devices to cloud with a bare minimum requirement of connection infrastructure [34]. There is compatibility with Mbed OS which is accessed using corresponding libraries. Moreover, it is compatible with the REST API. This is useful for making market-ready applications. End-to-end trust is implemented using TLS with protocols such as CoAP, TCP, UDP and LWM2M.

[3]https://www.mbed.com/en/platform/mbed-os/

6.4.3 Azure IoT Suite

Microsoft has its own IoT suite called Azure IoT suite [35]. Azure IoT suite provides all the typical application support that is expected from any IoT service. Moreover, it addresses scaling, telemetry patterns and big data. Azure supports many platforms, devices and programming languages.

Figure 6.5 shows the Microsoft Azure IoT architecture [36]. There is a gateway to connect IoT devices to Azure cloud. The inbound data are stored in the cloud for further processing. Azure Machine Learning and Azure Stream Analytics provide a mechanism for real-time data analytics over cloud. Azure provides bi-directional communication between devices and the cloud backend services by Azure IoT Hub [37].

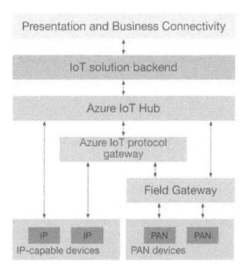

Figure 6.5   Azure IoT architecture.

6.5   Implication and Findings

6.5.1   Ethical

There are four factors that can affect the privacy information of an individual. Firstly, the unauthorized method of surveillance and the data collection mechanism; secondly, the data generation mechanism and the pattern of usage of data; thirdly, the authentication process and how the ownership in this case is handled; finally, the security aspect of the information and the mechanism to increase the security of the data collected.

A huge collection of data related to an individual and promotion of sophisticated surveillance techniques are some of the greatest concerns in user privacy, which in turn makes privacy more susceptible to being breached. However, it has been found that in some cases individuals have no objections to sharing personal data when a service provider is trusted and when the service is beneficial [38].

Also, it has been found that when the control of IoT objects exceeds the data congregation, controlling the exposure of the collected information is required; therefore, there must be a controlled diffusion process. But, in a web of application a controlled diffusion is apparently not possible [39] because the data control mechanism is closely associated with other techniques such as limited use of sensor, legislation and authorization [40]. Hence, a user is liable for a transparent and guaranteed service, thereby providing the data to the actual owner because the data control involves the data owner, sensor manufacturer and legislation authorities [41].

Authentication of services can be done centrally, but it gives rise to a new challenge in terms of access control. Similarly, handshakes between sensors and services have the same risk factor involved with respect to identity [41]. The extent of security provided by IoT application and services is another key aspect of privacy. IoT objects collect a large amount of data and process data through sensors and are always on the verge of being attacked by hackers. Hence, a proper encryption approach must be present so that a sensor cannot share adequate information so as to limit the breach of private data.

6.5.2 Legal

To build the user's trust in the IoT infrastructure the legislation over the data protection must be properly framed keeping the new and fast changing technology in mind. Several principles can be adopted that can frame the rules which can be deployed in IoT applications [42, 43].

Announcement and agreement are good principles to adopt, though it is complicated. In the framing of this principle a list of options is presented to the users and they can decide how to handle the data. But, in IoT there is no such communication component between a user and sensors. However, the traditional methods of adopting this principle cannot hold well because of the large-scale implementation of IoT devices in the ecosystem. In addition to this, the number of users of the IoT ecosystem keeps on increasing every day. Hence, it is compulsory for the IoT devices to provide data on how information is gathered and used [44, 45].

Moreover, the user of the IoT system has some responsibilities. A must for the producers of IoT devices are extensive agreements which include sensible security in the manufactured devices. Additionally, multiple checks on the authentication of data is the foundation stone of any IoT application. The user, who is the owner of the data, must monitor the usage of their data by any third party which promotes the transparency in data usage.

One question arising here is whether or not the IoT ecosystem needs governance similar to that of the internet. This IoT governance can frame rules, norms, usage decision making and much more. Moreover, this governance system can regulate the legislation of security, protocols, interoperability and standards.

6.5.3 Social

The IoT and its infrastructure are increasing day by day and research is ongoing in this field. But, the policies related to IoT must have social significance, thereby making the new technology more adoptable and accessible. This is the time to frame the rules for IoT infrastructure because alteration of the infrastructure in the future according to social demand would be practically impossible [46-49].

In the future, there is a possibility that every household will follow rules to implement energy conservation and will be bound to use IoT devices at home. However, although this will definitely make life easier it should not be required of users. IoT is supposed to be beneficial but must not take away the autonomy of a person. An IoT product must disclose its drawbacks and advantages to a user. In any IoT device safety must be a primary concern.

So, the IoT device must be surrendered when it comes to making a choice between human life and the IoT ecosystem, because there is no way that an IoT device can replace a human being.

No one can encourage or force others to share their private information. Any pressure to do this must be prosecuted immediately and would be marked as illegal. Complete protocols must be available to all users and agencies who are supposed to be the actors of the IoT ecosystem and they must be properly followed. It is necessary to address having complete and competent regulations and legislation on issues related to IoT.

6.6 Future Scope

Solid growth in the field of IoT has been noticed. In a very short span of time it has become an emerging field in product marketability and research. So, there is a shift to providing a singular IoT element to application frameworks that can support standardized IoT suite with regulations and protocols. However, because of the various implications of security and privacy many solutions have been proposed to overcome these constraints. Moreover, there are requirements of designing new philosophies in terms of identifying security and privacy concerns in distributed data sources and other upcoming cloud-based applications. A comparative analysis of the various frameworks is a necessity based on various hardware-software requirements and security. Because immunity against attacks is one of the most important contemporary issues facing the Internet of Things, measures for verifying the security of each framework with various security features will continue to be highlighted in the future [50].

6.7 Conclusion

The evolution of the IoT infrastructure is exponential and can cause intense changes in various areas. The smart grid is a major area of concern which can promote smart energy conservation techniques and paradigm. In this chapter, we explored different issues involved in energy conservation in IoT with reference to ethical, legal and social aspects. We did an intense survey of the literature related to privacy concerns, data collection, and legislation over information sharing and societal impact of IoT. We demonstrated different challenges that can take place in these areas of concern.

We conclude that if the IoT is not properly managed there will be constant concern over the ethical aspect of it. Without proper legislation the societal dignity of a person is definitely going to be affected, even if it is also the responsibility of the user to sensitize themselves against the potential risks of the IoT.

From a societal aspect, we also conclude that there aren't any foolproof methods or representatives that can monitor all the activities of the IoT infrastructure, thus making the ecosystem absolutely secure. Legislation to preserve the user's dignity is obligatory and can promote an IoT infrastructure that is trustworthy and useful.

However, this chapter is limited in scope and more in-depth work is required for more sensitization of a person towards legislation and its association with ethics.

REFERENCES

1. AboBakr, A., & Azer, M. A. (2017, December). IoT ethics challenges and legal issues. In 2017 12th International Conference on Computer Engineering and Systems (ICCES) (pp. 233-237). IEEE.

2. Azure M. Azure iot hub. https://azure.microsoft.com/en-us/services/iot-hub/.Online; accessed: April 2017.

3. Baldini, G., Botterman, M., Neisse, R., & Tallacchini, M. (2018). Ethical design in the internet of things. *Science and engineering ethics*, 24(3), 905-925.

4. Jayakumar, H., Raha, A., Kim, Y., Sutar, S., Lee, W. S., & Raghunathan, V. (2016, January). Energy-efficient system design for IoT devices. In 2016 21st Asia and South Pacific Design Automation Conference (ASP-DAC) (pp. 298-301). IEEE. DOI:10.1109/aspdac.2016.7428027

5. Weber, R. H. (2010). Internet of Things-New security and privacy challenges. *Computer law & security review*, 26(1), 23-30.

6. Al-Fuqaha, A., Guizani, M., Mohammadi, M., Aledhari, M., & Ayyash, M. (2015). Internet of things: A survey on enabling technologies, protocols, and applications. *IEEE communications surveys & tutorials*, 17(4), 2347-2376.

7. Derhamy, H., Eliasson, J., Delsing, J., & Priller, P. (2015, September). A survey of commercial frameworks for the internet of things. In 2015 IEEE 20th Conference on Emerging Technologies & Factory Automation (ETFA) (pp. 1-8). IEEE.

8. Sheng, Z., Yang, S., Yu, Y., Vasilakos, A. V., McCann, J. A., & Leung, K. K. (2013). A survey on the ietf protocol suite for the internet of things: Standards, challenges, and opportunities. *IEEE Wireless Communications*, 20(6), 91-98.

9. Yang, Y., Wu, L., Yin, G., Li, L., & Zhao, H. (2017). A survey on security and privacy issues in Internet-of-Things. *IEEE Internet of Things Journal*, 4(5), 1250-1258.

10. Kumar, J. S., & Patel, D. R. (2014). A survey on internet of things: Security and privacy issues. *International Journal of Computer Applications*, 90(11).

11. Vikas, B. O. (2015). Internet of things (iot): A survey on privacy issues and security. International Journal of Scientific Research in Science, *Engineering and Technology*, 1(3), 168-173.

12. Borgohain, T., Kumar, U., & Sanyal, S. (2015). Survey of security and privacy issues of internet of things. arXiv preprint arXiv:1501.02211.

13. Sicari, S., Rizzardi, A., Grieco, L. A., & Coen-Porisini, A. (2015). Security, privacy and trust in Internet of Things: The road ahead. *Computer networks*, 76, 146-164.

14. Fremantle, P., & Scott, P. (2017). A survey of secure middleware for the Internet of Things. *PeerJ Computer Science*, 3, e114.

15. Mohapatra, A. G., Keswani, B., Lenka, S. K. (2017). Optimizing Farm Irrigation mechanism using feedforward neural network and structural similarity index. *Int J Comput Appl*, 4(7), 135-141.

16. Mohapatra, A. G., Keswani, B., & Lenka, S. K. (2017). Soil npk prediction using location and crop specific random forest classification technique in precision agriculture. *International Journal of Advanced Research in Computer Science*, 8(7).

17. Kyriazis, D., & Varvarigou, T. (2013). Smart, autonomous and reliable Internet of Things. Procedia Computer Science, 21, 442-448.

18. Mohapatra, A. G., Lenka, S. K., & Keswani, B. (2018). Neural network and fuzzy logic based smart DSS model for irrigation notification and control in precision agriculture. Proceedings of the National Academy of Sciences, India Section A: Physical Sciences, 1-10. DOI: 10.1007/s40010-017-0401-6

19. Lenka, S. K., & Mohapatra, A. G. (2016). Hybrid Decision Model for Weather Dependent Farm Irrigation Using Resilient Backpropagation Based Neural Network Pattern Classification and Fuzzy Logic. In Proceedings of First International Conference on Information and Communication Technology for Intelligent Systems: Volume 1 (pp. 291-302). Springer, Cham.

20. Arendt, H. (2013). *The human condition*. University of Chicago Press.

21. Trappeniers, L., Roelands, M., Godon, M., Criel, J., & Dobbelaere, P. (2009, October). Towards abundant DiY service creativity. In 2009 13th International Conference on Intelligence in Next Generation Networks (pp. 1-6). IEEE.

22. Kounelis, I., Baldini, G., Neisse, R., Steri, G., Tallacchini, M., & Pereira, A. G. (2014). Building trust in the human? internet of things relationship. *IEEE Technology and Society Magazine*, 33(4), 73-80.

23. Brey, P. A. (2012). Anticipating ethical issues in emerging IT. *Ethics and Information Technology*, 14(4), 305-317.

24. Cavelty, M. D. (2014). Breaking the cyber-security dilemma: Aligning security needs and removing vulnerabilities. *Science and engineering ethics*, 20(3), 701-715.

25. Amazon. Components of awsiot framework. https://aws.amazon.com/iot/how-it-works/. Online; accessed: April 2017

26. Hunkeler, U., Truong, H. L., & Stanford-Clark, A. (2008, January). MQTT-SA publish/subscribe protocol for Wireless Sensor Networks. In 2008 3rd International Conference on Communication Systems Software and Middleware and Workshops (COMSWARE'08) (pp. 791-798). IEEE.

27. Dierks, T., & Rescorla, E. (2008). The transport layer security (TLS) protocol version 1.2 (No. RFC 5246).

28. Amazon. Amazon iot protocols. http://docs.aws.amazon.com/iot/latest/ developerguide/protocols.html. Online; accessed: April 2017.

29. Amazon. Amazon lambda. https://aws.amazon.com/lambda. Online; accessed: April 2017.

30. Amazon. Amazon management console https://aws.amazon.com/console. Online; accessed: April 2017.

31. ARM: Arm mbed IoT device platform: http://www.arm.com/products/ iot-solutions/mbed-iot-device-platform

32. ARM. mbed device connector. https://www.mbed.com/en/platform/cloud/mbed-device-connector-service/. Online; accessed: April 2017.

33. ARM. mbedos. https://www.mbed.com/en/platform/mbed-os/. Online; accessed: April 2017.

34. mbed A. mbed client. https://www.mbed.com/en/platform/mbed-client/. Online; accessed: April 2017.

35. Microsoft. Tap into the internet of your things with azure iot suite. https://www.microsoft.com/en-us/cloud-platform/internet-of-things-azure-iot-suite. Online; accessed: April 2017.

36. Azure M. Microsoft azure iot reference architecture. https://azure.microsoft.com/en-us/updates/microsoft-azure-iot-reference-architecture-available/.Online; accessed: April 2017.

37. Amazon. Awsiot framework. https://aws.amazon.com/iot. Online; accessed: April 2017.

38. Dratwa, J. (2014). Ethics of security and surveillance technologies. Brussels: Brussels.

39. Culnan, M. J., & Armstrong, P. K. (1999). Information privacy concerns, procedural fairness, and impersonal trust: An empirical investigation. Organization science, 10(1), 104-115.

40. Atziori, L., Iera, A., & Morabito, G. (2010). The Internet of Things: A Survey. *Computer Networks*.

41. Baldauf, M., Dustdar, S., & Rosenberg, F. (2007). A survey on context-aware systems. *International Journal of Ad Hoc and Ubiquitous Computing*, 2(4), 263-277.

42. Azure M. Communication protocols. https://azure.microsoft.com/en-us/documentation/articles/iot-hub-devguide-messaging/#communication-protocols. Online; accessed: April 2017.

43. Amazon. Amazon s3. https://aws.amazon.com/s3. Online; accessed: April 2017.

44. Amazon. Amazon dynamodb. https://aws.amazon.com/dynamodb. Online; accessed: April 2017.

45. Amazon. Amazon machine learning. https://aws.amazon.com/machine-learning. Online; accessed: April 2017

46. Azure M. Azure iot protocol gateway. https://azure.microsoft.com/en-us/documentation/articles/iot-hub-protocol-gateway/. Online; accessed: April 2017.

47. Puar, V. H., Bhatt, C. M., Hoang, D. M., & Le, D. N. (2018). Communication in Internet of Things. In Information Systems Design and Intelligent Applications (pp. 272-281). Springer, Singapore.

48. Zhou, J., Cao, Z., Dong, X., & Vasilakos, A. V. (2017). Security and privacy for cloud-based IoT: Challenges. *IEEE Communications Magazine*, 55(1), 26-33.

49. Yang, W., Wang, S., Zheng, G., Yang, J., & Valli, C. (2019). A Privacy-Preserving Lightweight Biometric System for Internet of Things Security. *IEEE Communications Magazine*, 57(3), 84-89.

50. Dehghantanha, A. (2019). *Handbook of Big Data and IoT Security*. Springer.

CHAPTER 7

AUTOMATION MOVIE RECOMMENDER SYSTEM BASED ON INTERNET OF THINGS AND CLUSTERING

Lalit Mohan Goyal[1], Mamta Mittal[2], Asheesh Sharma[3]

[1]1Department of Computer Engineering, J. C. Bose University of Science and Technology, YMCA, Faridabad, India

[2] Department of Computer Science and Engineering, G. B. Pant Engineering College, New Delhi, India

[3] Edfora Infotech Private Limited, New Delhi, India

Email: mittalmamta79@gmail.com

Abstract

This chapter discusses an intricate movie genre recommender engine based on K-means clustering combined with a powerful Pearson correlation similarity measure. This system takes basic information from users, asks them to enter a rating for movies and uses machine learning algorithms to provide a recommended genre. It also makes it possible to quickly predict movie ratings based on the user's choices. It gives the user a real-time review of the movie from those who have just watched it by calculating the polarity using sentiment analysis either via their voice or by text or by review in simple numerical form from the device keypad. It also includes a device consisting of NFC and Arduino combined with a powerful beacon to provide a perfect IoT device to automatically authenticate the reviews with real-time updating.

Keywords: IoT, NFC, Arduino, beacons, machine learning

7.1 Introduction

The internet is a tool that has revolutionized the computer and communication world. Taking into account the impact made by the internet on education, communication, business, science and government, the web is one of the most effective manifestations in all of mankind's history. The web's advancement is a continuous process. The Internet of Things (IoT) [1] can be considered to be the next web development. Its interfaces consist of distinctive components to the web as opposed to various individuals. IoT is comprised of free accumulation of different, reason manufactured systems. It considers numerous individual systems like transport [2, 3], vitality, training and so forth combined with security, investigation and administration capacities. Therefore, IoT winds up being more effective [4]. The IoT has taken an enormous leap in its capacity to assemble, break down and convey information that we can transform into information, knowledge and ultimately wisdom. IoT is needed for the following reasons:

- Many networks, like transport, education, business, home, etc., are connected. IoT enables the quick and accurate retrieval of data located in different domains.

- It allows communication to take place independent of location.

- It presents a huge window of opportunity for creation of applications in the areas of automation, sensing and machine-to-machine communication.

- It improves resource utilization ratio.

- It improves the relationship between nature and human beings by framing a scholarly element by incorporating human culture and physical framework.

- It reduces operational cost. In the case where there are aged patients in the home, the personal body network helps them communicate with the doctor, thereby reducing operational cost.

- Thus, IoT can be considered to be a revolutionary application that has the ability to dramatically improve the way people work, learn, live, and entertain.

The development of IoT [5-7] has enabled an automated movie environment powered by a proximity sensing device, namely, beacon and NFC (near-field communication) technology, and backed with powerful review analysis. The real-time problems that we face every day include not knowing what we would really enjoy watching, wasting time standing in long queues to see it, and not being able to see how a movie is really performing all around the world [8]. To solve the above problems, this chapter presents a product that combines powerful automation tools like Arduino, Beacon technology and NFC to automate the current system and give customers what they really want [9]. It is a product that will not only ensure true reviews given by those who have just watched the movie but also update other users. The powerful learning algorithm helps users understand the genre and gives them a worldwide view of users' feelings about the performance of the movie they want to see.

This chapter uses a combination of K-means and Pearson similarity measure to power up the movie genre recommender engine. The reasons for such a combination originated for the following purposes: To analyze and give an overall review based on user comments with the application of text mining, IoT and NFC; To use social media like Twitter and Facebook to fetch reviews of people, performing sentiment analysis and come up with the polarity of reviews; To make the system that is server based and non-local for future analysis [10]; To ensure easy maintenance, maintain data consistency and provide better performance; To increase the efficiency through automation; To give user quick tips through powerful analysis of social media through a powerful algorithm and presenting it in a unique visual form [11-15].

All these challenges have motivated us to revolutionize the current system and come up with a product that can help users visualize and understand what they really want. We have also tried to develop a product to ensure that users have a hassle-free experience when ordering food, rating visualizations and rating submissions. Thus, researchers came up with the idea of combining the powerful machine learning algorithms with IoT devices like Arduino, NFC and Beacon technology to solve the challenges efficiently [14, 16].

We aim to automate the current system at the movie theater venue, from booking of tickets to ordering of food, in such a way that vendors can know about the quality of various services. A system is proposed to capture reviews in real-time from text, voice and numeric keypad in order to give real-time analysis of any ongoing movie [11]. This chapter is organized as follows: Section 7.2 describes the IoT and its related technologies, Section 7.3 describes related researches, Section 7.4 presents the proposed work, Section 7.5 shows performance analyses. Finally, the conclusions that can be drawn from the information presented are given in Section 7.6.

7.2 Background

7.2.1 Characteristics of IoT

- Ambient Intelligence: The system will act in full interoperable manner and it will be able to auto-organize itself depending on the context, circumstance and environment.

- Event Driven: The system will act depending upon the notification received by the other entities in the system.

- Flexible: More numbers of nodes or devices can be connected.

- Semantics Sharing: This property enables the device to send and share resources.

- Complex Access Technology: There are several networks used in IoT, thus in order to access them a different complex technology is needed.

7.2.2 Evolution of IoT

The term "Internet of Things" was coined by Kevin Aston in 1999. Kevin Aston is a British innovation pioneer who helped to establish the Auto-ID focus at the Massachusetts Institute of Technology (MIT).[1] The work at MIT was focused on Auto-ID in the field of arranged radio recurrence recognizable proof (RFID) and detecting advancements [3]. The lab consisted of seven research colleges situated in four distinct locations. Subsequently, a wide range of gadgets were associated and IoT was instituted. *The Internet of Things* was seventh in the series of ITU web reports initially published in 1997 under the title "Challenges to the Network." In 2005, 6.3 billion individuals living on earth and 500 million

---

[1]www.mit.edu/

gadgets were associated with the web, i.e., less than 0.08% for every person. Thus, IoT didn't yet exist. Due to the explosive growth of smartphones and tablet PCs, the number of devices connected to the internet increased. Thus, Cisco Internet Business Solutions Group (CIBSG)[2] has estimated that 25 billion devices by 2015 and 50 billion devices by 2020 would be connected to the internet.

7.2.3   Trends in IoT

- In 2000, there was a need for on-demand logistics. Thus, RFID tags are used to facilitate routing, inventory and loss prevention. This is helped in supply chain management.

- In 2010, there was a need for cost reduction. Thus, IoT will be used in security, healthcare, transport, and food safety. This will help in vertical market application.

- The challenging task in deploying IoT is the ability of all devices to receive global signals. This can be done by locating different objects and people in the network, which helps in ubiquitous positioning.

- Over the next few years, tele-operations and telepresence will be invented which can monitor and control distant objects.

7.2.4   Requirements of IoT

The IoT needs the following in order to establish a better communication [17]:

- A shared comprehension of the circumstance of its clients and their gadgets.

- A shareware framework unavoidable correspondence system to handle and pass on data to where it is applicable.

- An analytic tool which aims for autonomous and smart behavior.

7.2.5   IoT Elements

- Appliances: These are made up of sensors, actuators and embedded communication appliances. Sensors to sense the correct signals at the right time by the desired routers or switches and actuators connected to electrical signals for desired actions.

- Middleware: This is data storage to store the voluminous data that needs to be transferred from one application domain to another computing tool for data analysis.

- Presentation: A simple graphical user interface, which will be easy to understand, visualize and interpret.

Besides this, basic network elements like routers, desired protocols and switches may be required. After learning the various elements required by IoT, we can now define it as follows: "The multiplication of gadgets in a correspondence organizes to make IoT, wherein sensors and actuators mix consistently with the world around us, and the data is shared crosswise over stages so as to build up a typical working picture."

---

[2]https://www.cisco.com/

7.2.6 Architecture of IoT

A system is a likely example of event-driven architecture [18]. The devices react to the event produced by other devices. Keeping in mind the end goal to acknowledge maximum capacity of distributed computing and also detecting, a consolidated structure with cloud at the middle is by all accounts generally reasonable. This provides adaptability for separating related costs as well as versatility. Detecting specialist organizations can join the system and offer their information utilizing capacity in the cloud; investigative instrument engineers can provide their product devices; man-made brainpower specialists can provide their information mining and machine learning apparatuses helpful in changing over data to learning; lastly, PC illustration fashioners can offer an assortment of representation devices.

- *Aneka Cloud Computing Platform*: Aneka is a .net-based application advancement platform as a service (PaaS) which can use stockpiling and process assets of both open and private mists. It offers a runtime domain and an arrangement of APIs that empower engineers to assemble application utilizing various programming models like task programming, string programming and so forth.

- *Addressing of Things*: The ability to uniquely identify things is critical. The original idea of the Auto-ID Center is based on RFID tags and unique identification through the electronic product code; however, it has evolved into objects having an IP address or URL. The addressing should be unique, reliable, persistent and scalable. But this is a critical task to achieve. The IPv4 supports this to some extent. The device or object should be able to hold its address when the network crashes. Scalability of address should be sustainable. Addition of network and device must not hamper the performance of the device. Uniform resource name (URN) is the standard used for addressing things.

7.2.7 Application Domain of IoT

Healthcare Sector: The IoT has numerous uses in the medical field. It may incorporate a wearable staff emotional support network to find both specialists and patients in the health network any time of day. It might likewise incorporate IoT-based information frameworks to distinguish an adverse drug reaction in patients. The blend of sensors, Wi-Fi, and so on is helpful in the observing of imperative elements of the body, such as temperature, pulse, heart rate and cholesterol levels, and to invigorate the heart muscle in the event of heart attack and so on. Implantable remote identifiers can be embraced to store well-being records of individuals with chronic illness. IoT applications enormously affect unassisted living and support for the maturing populace by identifying day by day living and bolster utilizing wearable and surrounding sensors and checking perpetual infection. IoT devices can convey normal alarms, e.g., the remote observing of patients with medical issues such as coronary illness, sugar levels, and circulatory strain.

Retail, Supply Network and Logistics: Actualizing the IoT in retail, coordination and inventory network administration has its own particular points of interest. Smart shelves can progressively track the items present. Stocks can be observed through radio frequency identification (RFID) labels to alert the shop proprietor as to when to make new requests. Quick installment arrangements can be influenced through label perusing registration focuses. For pharmaceutical items, security and well-being is of most extreme significance. Following them through the store network and checking their status with sensors guarantees a quality item for the end client. Medications require certain storage conditions, thus observing their condition en route and on the racks is indispensable. IoT offers the chance to follow maintenance and repair over the production network, with the goal that reviews can be issued when quality issues emerge.

Transportation: The IoT offers various arrangements in the transportation field. Toll frameworks, screening of travelers and products on planes to meet security requirements, checking out where to turn in the parking lot, and robotized following of travelers and baggage are some of the applications for IoT in transport. Applications in the automotive industry incorporate the utilization of "smart things" to screen and report everything from weight in tires to the closeness of different vehicles. RFID advances give constant information in the assembly of autos. Flexible autonomous vehicles will eventually be able to induce other drivers on the road. For protected and content drivers, there are applications which detect the driver's actions and contrast them with the detected practices of other drivers on the roads. The flying industry is undermined by the issue of wrong parts, which is a maintenance problem that can be addressed using the IoT.

Home Automation: Because remote applications are abundant, their scope of use is generally extensive, such as the use of smart metering which has ended up being notable for estimating energy usage and transmitting the information to the electricity supplier. Sensors for temperature and moistness provide information that naturally alters the comfort level in a room.

Environment Monitoring: Day by day, the use of remote devices is growing as part of the promising business of eco-friendly applications for safeguarding the environment. Remote observation of woodland fires, conceivable outcomes of seismic tremors, potential surges and contamination reduce the impact of natural disasters. The remote business offers the chance to screen the oil and gas workforce under normal conditions, following the location of gas and oil spills as a way to lessen the danger of mishaps.

Agriculture: During the occurrence of a disease outbreak or natural disaster, such as a flood, etc., the progressive research into the identification of people/animals with the use of RFID labels is quite beneficial. In order to upgrade the efficiency of agricultural land there is a need for automation in farming. To fulfill such a purpose, smart planning and research is going on in China to design horticultural equipment which can work with ICT technologies, like websites, mobile phones, satellite route frameworks, and distributed computing, to be used as a guide to help in the organization of a rural motorized age and which is slated for use in equipment countrywide. The orders regarding the dispatch of the developed machines and their advancement, etc., are all done properly, and they are dependent on several factors like climate, their development time and how to transport them from one place to another and so on. This can be done by a proper survey which includes the demand for farm machinery, data gathering, measuring farmland range and estimation of item yields. RFID sensors are very helpful in environmental monitoring, which directly affects agriculture and also helps during the food supply chain process.

Education: IoT can empower collaboration with physical spaces for learning purposes or correspondence. Scientists from the Department of Computer Science at the University of Waseda in Japan are dealing with an enlarged calligraphy framework that supports calligraphy students self-education by giving critiques. The framework screens the learners with a web camera and tells them if their arm movements will result in a terrible shape.

Telecommunications: The IoT increases the likelihood of combining diverse advancements, such as the Global System for Mobile Communications (GSM), near-field communications (NFC), Bluetooth, global positioning systems (GPS), sensor systems, etc., to make new administrations. Remote communication between the IoT and broadcast network takes place over a significant distance.

Insurance: In vehicle protection, electronic recorders are set in autos to record speed and impart the data to the backup system to evaluate the hazard. GPS beacons are utilized to combat auto theft. Dynamic misfortune counteractive action in transportation can be prevented with markers and sensors. Early discovery of risks through sensors averts water and fire damage. Auto-ID Labs in Zrich are currently working on the IoT applications identified with protection. The IoT Swarm networking application enables clients to contact their safety net provider with their advanced mobile phone. E-bicycles rely on nonstop operation of GPS-based beacons. This decreases bike theft and enhances the well-being of cyclists. Water claims caused by obsolete or rusted pipes are an issue. Since early detection is key to averting water damage and related cases, different sensors can be used to recognize small water spills in rooms. An SMS message is sent to alert inhabitants and the programmed valves close the central water pipe.

7.2.8 IoT Technology

Various advancements in IoT technology can be found throughout the extensive variety of literature [5, 7], some of which are recorded below:

- *RFID*: Radio-recurrence recognizable proof (RFID) utilizes radio waves to distinguish things. As opposed to standardized tags, RFID labels can be perused far from the viewable pathway. They track things progressively to yield essential data about their area and status. Early uses of RFID include programming thruway toll gathering, tracking stock, inventory network administration for huge retailers, preventing counterfeit pharmaceuticals, and checking on patients with e-wellbeing. Embedding RFID labels under the skin for restorative purposes, e-government applications (e.g., in driver's licenses and international IDs) and RFID-empowered telephones are some of the applications.

- *Sensor Networks*: Recognizing changes in the physical status of things is also fundamental for recording changes in the earth. In such manner, sensors assume a vital part in conquering any hindrances between physical and virtual universes, and empower things to react to changes in their physical condition, creating data and bringing issues to light about the specific circumstance. Sensor systems are not required to be associated with the internet and frequently dwell in remote locales, vehicles and structures having no internet access.

- *Microcontrollers*: Microcontrollers are PC chips that are intended to be implanted into objects. Implanted knowledge in things appropriates the power generated in the system, and engages things and gadgets in the system to make free choices.

- *Protocols*: Machine-to-machine interfaces and conventions of electronic correspondence set the tenets of engagement for at least two hubs of a system. Web Protocol (IP) has turned into the standard for all information correspondence and it is simple to move things over the internet in this way. Cases of conventions that can be utilized as a part of low-control radio for correspondence are: Link Layer, ISA 100A, Wireless HART, ZigBee and IPv6. The internet convention for lower power radio IPv6 assumes a major role in the IoT. The upside of IPv6 is that it addresses the difficulties of various existing frameworks working together. Since this interoperability is conceivable, the arrangement of items associated by means of the internet can be built up similar to the way the internet was created. The adaptation of IP being used right now, IPV4, underpins just 4.3 billion one of a kind addresses; a small amount of what is required to dole out a name and area to everybody and everything.

- *Biometrics*: Biometrics empowers innovation to perceive individuals and other living things, instead of lifeless articles. Associated ordinary articles could perceive approved clients by biometric identification using unique marks, voice prints, iris/eye scan or other biometric innovations.

- *Machine Vision*: Machine vision can be a channel for conveying a similar sort of data that RFIDs empower. It is an approach that can screen objects having no on-board sensors, controllers or remote interfaces. For instance, cameras on commonplace PDAs can capture pictures of articles; utilizing picture preparing calculations, far off servers can distinguish such questions and report data about them. Brilliant segments can execute diverse arrangements of activities, as indicated by their environment and the undertakings they are intended for. For example, gadgets can coordinate their vehicle, adjust to their particular surroundings, self-arrange, self-keep up, and self-repair and in the end even assume a dynamic part in their transfer.

- *Actuators*: Actuators identify an approaching sign and react by changing something in nature. Actuators, for example, engines, pneumatics and power through pressure, can move protests and pump liquids. A transfer, for instance, is an actuator that flips a mechanical switch, and would thus be able to make a decent number of reactions happen, for example, empowering brightening, warming framework, perceptible caution, etc.

- *Location Technologies*: Location-aware technology is able to discover the current location of people and track them. Sensors assume a part; however, that approach does not fulfill reasonable requirements for geo areas, bringing about the ascent of remote methodologies such as GPS and cell towers. Radar, LIDAR and sonar can identify the relative area of things, contingent upon their electromagnetic, optical and acoustic properties. A few things transmit their own radio, light or potentially solid, keeping in mind the end goal to uncover their whereabouts to individuals and machines. The end goal of programmed recognizable proof of labeled items is to rapidly look into data or start a particular activity; utilizing standardized identifications for connecting real protests virtual data has various downsides when contrasted with a RFID-empowered component with relating versatile RFID perusers such as near-field communication (NFC)-empowered cell phones. Near-field communication is a short-run remote availability standard that empowers correspondence between gadgets when they are brought inside a couple of centimeters of each other through attractive enlistment.

- *Ambient Technologies*: Ambient advances allude to electronic situations that are sensitive and receptive to the nearness of individuals. In a world surrounded by knowledge, gadgets work to assist individuals in completing their regular day-to-day tasks in simple, characteristic ways utilizing data and insight that is hidden in the system associating these gadgets. The encompassing insight worldview expands upon inescapable processing, universal registering, profiling practices and human-driven PC collaboration planning.

- *Bar Codes*: A standardized tag is an optical portrayal of machine-coherent information and can be seen on most items in retail businesses to accelerate the checkout procedure. These straight symbologies or one-dimensional (1D) standardized tags convey information in vertical parallel lines with shifting space and line width. The lesser-known two-dimensional (2D) standardized tag or grid code is likewise an optical portrayal that looks like squares or rectangles that contain many small, individual dots, which have much more machine-coherent information and can ordinarily be seen on bigger bundling holders to help with stockroom coordination and quality control. Examples of 2D network codes are QR, DataMatrix and Semacode. The "QR" in QR Code is derived from "Quick Response," as the creator intended the code to allow its contents to be decoded at high speed. A DataMatrix code consists of high-contrast black and white modules arranged in either a square or rectangular pattern. The data to be encoded can be content or crude information. The code can be perused rapidly by a scanner, which enables the media (e.g., a package) to be followed. Semacode is machine-comprehensible ISO/IEC 16022[3] information framework images which encode URLs. Semacodes are primarily aimed at being used with PDAs which have built-in cameras. A URL can be converted into a sort of scanner tag resembling a crossword puzzle, which is known as a "tag." Labels can be immediately captured with a cell phone camera and decoded with a perused application to acquire a site address. It will then be possible to reach this address by means of the phone's program.

7.2.9   The Present and Future of IoT

Today, IoT is still an evolving technology [6]. By using IoT certain work can be done at the right time without human intervention, making life easier. Smartphones have been developed which have diverse applications which help in instant messaging and sharing of files with people across the world within seconds. Thus, smartphones can be considered as the first invention of IoT. A few years later, there would be many applications of IoT which would make the lives of human beings more efficient and comfortable. Smart houses keep track of household activities even in the absence of the occupants. In the area of medicine and the healthcare sector, patients can be connected to their doctors via the internet. Thus, patients are able to see their doctors without going to their office or hospital. Because of the advent of IoT, our future lives will be safer, more secure and more comfortable.

7.2.10   IoT Challenges

There are certain barriers which affect the development of IoT technology [9]. They are detailed below:

- *Addressing of Things*: Since various things are connected to the network, it would be difficult for the developers as well as the users to identify these things. A unique addressing scheme should be adopted in order to eliminate this problem and also make the elements scalable. Deployment of IPv6 eliminates this problem.

- *Sensor Energy and Power Management*: Many things in the IoT and its sensors will be battery powered. The sensors within things should be designed in such a way to be self-sustaining, thereby reaching their full potential.

---

[3]https://www.iso.org/standard/44230.html

- *Security*: With the amount of information being sent inside the IoT, security is an absolute necessity. Utilizing a security convention is basic to secure the IoT, which ensures equipment security and secures existing availability.

- *Storage*: The IoT has brought about an era of colossal amounts of information which must be stored, handled and exhibited in a consistent, effective and effortlessly interpretable shape. Thus, a good database should be designed in order to store the data. The design of a proper retrieval strategy and algorithm helps in retrieving the correct results based on the situation and the data in the sensor.

- *Managing Complexity*: Since many networks are designed and many objects are added to the network, managing the complex network is a big issue. This requires designing a proper network architecture and protocol.

- *Rapid Evolution*: The IoT is constantly evolving. More devices are being added every day. Thus, managing these trends is a complex issue. The network should be made scalable.

- *Standard*: A unique standard must be defined for IoT, especially in the areas of security, privacy, architecture and communication.

7.2.11 Scope of IoT

Sooner rather than later, the internet and remote advancements will interface diverse sources of data, such as sensors [13], cell phones and automobiles, in an increasingly tighter way. The quantity of gadgets which interface with the internet seems to be expanding exponentially. These billions of parts deliver, expend and prepare data under various conditions, such as strategic applications, processing plants and airplane terminals, and also in the work and regular day-to-day existence of individuals. The general public needs new, versatile, good and secure answers for both the administration of the perpetually connected, intricately organized, vast Internet of Things (IoT), and also for the support of different plans of action. The extent of research in the IoT could be both to make a system to contemplate areas inside the given field and furthermore to unmistakably characterize the different research goals. Among the numerous business areas inside the IoT condition, the focus can be on the smart home, well-being and security, and automotive IoT business spaces as a beginning stage of general IoT activity to investigate. Other imperative IoT business areas, for example, vitality, coordination, retail, office, industry, and so forth, ought to dependably be remembered, as they could bit by bit show up under the scope for exploration as the IoT continues to extend its reach.

7.3 Related Works

Estimote Beacons and Stickers [,1 2] are small wireless sensors that can be attached to any location or object. They broadcast tiny radio signals which a smartphone can receive and interpret, unlocking micro-location and contextual awareness. Android is a mobile operating system (OS) [3, 19] developed by Google, based on the Linux kernel and designed primarily for touchscreen mobile devices such as smartphones and tablets. Android's user interface is based on direct manipulation, using touch gestures that loosely correspond to real-world actions, such as swiping, tapping and pinching, to manipulate on-screen objects, along with a virtual keyboard for text input. In addition to touchscreen devices,

Google has further developed Android TV [17, 18] for televisions, Android Auto for cars, and Android Wear for wrist watches, each with a specialized user interface. Arduino [20] is a software company, project, and user community that designs and manufactures computer open-source hardware and microcontroller-based kits for building digital devices and interactive objects that can sense and control physical devices. These systems provide sets of digital and analog I/O pins that can interface with various expansion boards (termed shields) and other circuits.

Near-field communication (NFC) [5, 7] is a set of communication protocols that enable two electronic devices, one of which is usually a portable device such as a smartphone, to establish communication by bringing them within 4 cm of each other. NFC-enabled portable devices can be provided with apps, for example, to read electronic tags or make payments when connected to an NFC-compliant apparatus. Earlier close-range communication used technology that was proprietary to the manufacturer for applications such as stock ticket, access control and payment readers [13]. Other works can be seen in [15, 16].

7.4 Proposed System

In the proposed system, the user demands that automation be established in the current system so that it would be fruitful for both the user and the managers [6]. This would help users avoid daily issues and allow managers to analyze user data more carefully, calculating new trends and making a decision that would help them increase profits to new limits. Products would not only provide a hassle-free experience to the consumer but will help them enjoy an automated environment with a variety of features that understand their true desires [9]. Since the system is verified with valid as well as invalid data and is run with an insight into the necessary modifications that may be required in the future, it can be maintained successfully without much hassle. This system depends on two main popular users: admin and customer. The implementation is done by making a prototype of the proposed product due to limitation of resources and time.

The proposed prototype is shown in Figure 7.1.

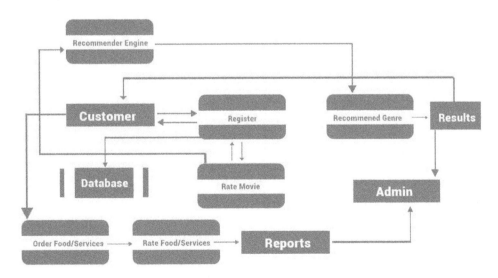

Figure 7.1   Workflow of the proposed system.

The prototype has been built using a combination of technologies. A description of the proposed model is given below:

- Step 1: Creation of recommendation engine using K-means clustering combined with the Pearson correlation similarity measure.

- Step 2: Selection of dataset and building the utility matrix.

- Step 3: Building of web application using Flask framework.

- Step 4: Incorporating the recommender logic in the Flask backend.

- Step 5: Making the user interface for the front end of the web app.

- Step 6: Implementation of the android app with a rich user interface.

- Step 7: Programming the NFC tag and android app to communicate with each other easily.

- Step 8: Making the app communicate with the beacon.

- Step 9: Programming the Arduino to work according to purpose.

- Step 10: Building the complete hardware for the product by combining all three at once.

- Step 11: Making the Arduino communicate with Python.

- Step 12: Making a system capable of recording reviews and generating and updating a real-time graph based on sentiments calculated from the voice or taken from the Arduino device.

The above model is implemented with the help of different technologies like R language, Python and machine learning packages for analyzing the database.

7.5 Implementation

The implementation is done to make a prototype of the proposed product using a combination of technologies, namely, Python,[4] Flask Framework,[5] Arduino Language,[6] Android, Java, R Programming, NFC and Beacon Programming. MovieLens data sets [6, 9] were collected. It consists of 100,000 ratings (1-5) from 943 users on 1682 movies; each user has rated at least 20 movies; simple demographic info for the users (age, gender, occupation, zip) is requested. The data were cleaned up; users who had less than 20 ratings or did not have complete demographic information were removed from this data set. Some interfaces of the proposed system that have been implemented and tested successfully are shown below (Figures 7.2-7.8).

---

[4]https://www.python.org/
[5]flask.pocoo.org/
[6]https://www.arduino.cc/

Figure 7.2 A screen user after rating

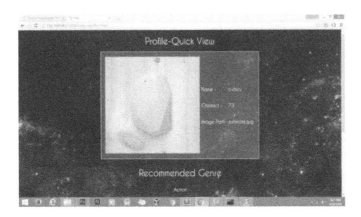

Figure 7.3 Recommendation.

Figure 7.4 A device to capture user reviews and combine technologies like NFC and beacon into a single device.

Figure 7.5 Right side view of the device showing how beacon is incorporated on it.

Figure 7.6 The app home screen. The second image happens when NFC is connected.

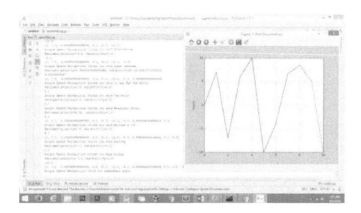

Figure 7.7 Screen showing real-time data updates that reflect reviews recorded by voice or Arduino-based keyboard.

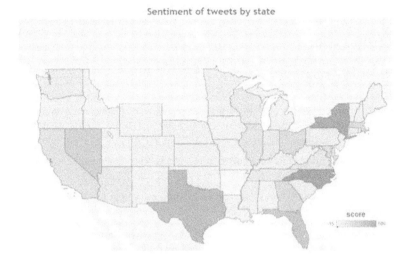

Sentiment of tweets by state

Figure 7.8   Heat map showing the popularity of a movie.

7.6   Conclusion

This chapter proposed a new intricate movie genre recommender engine based on K-means clustering combined with the Pearson correlation similarity measure. The implementation of text mining to generate average rating to check the polarity of the text would help in checking the overview of the rating and interfacing with the emerging IoT device to automate the current system. The system has endless opportunities and can be used in day-to-day life. The perfect real-time performance of reviews would help readers understand movie content in a better manner. As the technology is improving every day, it is highly possible that soon all phones will be NFC enabled, which would make the product very usable and cheap and would help in automating every area of our day-to-day lives. Therefore, future investigations are going to make this application generic for the complete automation of the current system and even suitable for blind people so that they can also enjoy it without difficulty.

REFERENCES

1. Santos, L., Schleicher, S., & Caldas, L. (2017), Automation of CAD models to BEM models for performance based goal-oriented design methods. *Building and Environment*, 112, 144-158.

2. Choi, J. H. (2017). Investigation of the correlation of building energy use intensity estimated by six building performance simulation tools. *Energy and Buildings*, 147, 14-26.

3. Mahata, A., Saini, N., Saharawat, S., & Tiwari, R. (2016, December), Intelligent Movie Recommender System Using Machine Learning, In International Conference on Intelligent Human Computer Interaction Springer, Cham, pp. 94-110.

4. Katarya, R., & Verma, O. P. (2016). An effective collaborative movie recommender system with cuckoo search. *Egyptian Informatics Journal*.

5. Alenljung, B., Lindblom, J., Andreasson, R., & Ziemke, T. (2017), User Experience in Social Human-Robot Interaction. *International Journal of Ambient Computing and Intelligence* (IJACI), 8(2), 12-31.

6. Guesgen, H. W., & Marsland, S. (2016), Using Contextual Information for Recognising Human, Behaviour. *International Journal of Ambient Computing and Intelligence* (IJACI), 7(1), 27-44.

7. Mishra, D., Gunasekaran, A., Childe, S. J., Papadopoulos, T., Dubey, R., & Wamba, S. (2016). Vision, applications and future challenges of Internet of Things: A bibliometric study of the recent literature. Industrial Management & Data Systems, 116(7), 1331-1355.

8. Isinkaye, F. O., Folajimi, Y. O., & Ojokoh, B. A. (2015). Recommendation systems: Principles, methods and evaluation. *Egyptian Informatics Journal*, 16(3), 261-273.

9. Meddeb, A. (2016). Internet of things standards: who stands out from the crowd, *IEEE Communications Magazine*, 54(7), 40-47.

10. Botta, A., De Donato, W., Persico, V., & Pescap, A. (2016). Integration of cloud computing and internet of things: a survey. *Future Generation Computer Systems*, 56, 684-700.

11. Chen, R., Bao, F., & Guo, J. (2016), Trust-based service management for social internet of things systems, *IEEE Transactions on Dependable and Secure Computing,* 13(6), 684-696.

12. Dong, X., Dong, X., Chang, Y., Chang, Y., Wang, Y., Wang, Y., & Yan, J. (2017), Understanding usage of Internet of Things (IoT) systems in China: Cognitive experience and affect experience as moderator, *Information Technology & People*, 30(1), 117-138.

13. Kolias, C., Stavrou, A., Voas, J., Bojanova, I., & Kuhn, R. (2016), Learning Internet-of-Things Security" Hands-On", *IEEE Security & Privacy*, 14(1), 37-46.

14. Roca, D., Nemirovsky, D., Nemirovsky, M., Milito, R., & Valero, M. (2016), Emergent Behaviors in the Internet of Things: The Ultimate Ultra-Large-Scale System. *IEEE Micro*, 36(6), 36-44.

15. Sattar, A., Ghazanfar, M. A., & Iqbal, M. (2017). Building Accurate and Practical Recommender System Algorithms Using Machine Learning Classifier and Collaborative Filtering. *Arabian Journal for Science and Engineering*, 1-19.

16. Bourkoukou, O., El Bachari, E., & El Adnani, M. (2017). A Recommender Model in E-learning Environment. *Arabian Journal for Science and Engineering*, 42(2), 607-617.

17. Shah, M., Parikh, D., & Deshpande, B. (2016, March), Movie Recommendation System Employing Latent Graph Features in Extremely Randomized Trees, In Proceedings of the Second International Conference on Information and Communication Technology for Competitive Strategies, 42-56.

18. Petersen, D., Steele, J., & Wilkerson, J. (2009, April), WattBot: a residential electricity monitoring and feedback system. In CHI'09 Extended Abstracts on Human Factors in Computing Systems, 2847-2852.

19. Doshi, S., Bakre, P., Agrawal, R., & Kosamkar, P. (2016), Movie Recommender System: Movies4u. *International Journal of Engineering Science*, 38-74.

20. Wang, W., Zhang, G., & Lu, J. (2016), Member contribution-based group recommender system, *Decision Support Systems*, 87, 80-93.

CHAPTER 8

SOCIETAL IMPLICATIONS OF EMERGING TECHNOLOGIES (SMAC) AND RELATED PRIVACY CHALLENGES

Manikant Roy, Amar Singh, Sukanta Ghosh, Nisha Sethi

Lovely Professional University, Punjab, India
Email: manikantroy@gmail.com, amar.rana80@gmail.com, sukantaghoshmca@hotmail.com, nisethi85@gmail.com

Abstract

Will machines be surpassed by human intelligence? Will automation take away jobs from humans? Or even more terrible, will machines be able to take over humans? These are some of the many questions that come to mind when talking about today's emerging network technologies: social, mobile, analytics and cloud (SMAC). Technology is changing more rapidly than ever and so is life! The daily life of humans has become more sophisticated because of technological advancements, but these advancements also pose challenges which have implications for society such as algorithmic bias, privacy breach, data breach, etc. This chapter will present the various effects of SMAC on society and possible solutions to any privacy-related problems.

Keywords: Social media, analytics, cloud, privacy

Security Designs for the Cloud, IoT, and Social Networking.
Edited by Dac-Nhuong Le *et al.* Copyright © 2019 Scrivener Publishing

8.1 Introduction to Data Analytics

Data is the next most expensive commodity after oil. Data is not much different from the crude oil we get from oil depots. Organizations from almost every sector are generating a large volume of data on a regular basis. Merely collecting large amounts of data will not serve any purpose and cannot be used directly for the profit of the company. Organizations can extract very useful information from this data which can further support complex decision making; hence, there is a need for data analytics [1].

The art and science of refining data to fetch useful insight which further helps in decision making is known as "Analytics." In terms of marketing jargon there are different categorizations of analytics [2], namely:

Figure 8.1   Data analytics categorizations.

- Descriptive Analytics

- Diagnostic Analytics

- Prescriptive Analytics

- Exploratory Analytics

- Predictive Analytics

- Mechanistic Analytics

- Casual Analytics

- Inferential Analytics

Let's explore them one by one.

8.1.1 Descriptive Analytics

Descriptive analytics is a primary phase of information handling that makes an outline of historical information to yield valuable data and conceivably sets up the information for further analysis. The principal focal point of descriptive analytics is to abridge what has occurred in an organization. Data aggregation and data mining techniques sort out the data and make it conceivable to recognize examples and connections in it that would not generally be unmistakable. Descriptive analytics examines the raw data or content to answer questions such as: *What happened and what is happening in an organization?*

Descriptive analytics is portrayed by traditional business intelligence and visualizations such as bar charts, pie charts, line graphs, or the created stories. Descriptive analytics are helpful in light of the fact that they enable us to learn from past practices, and see how they may impact future results. Any good data scientist may attempt to utilize the aftereffects of descriptive analytics and further change the data or patterns or example analysis to estimate future patterns in business [3, 4].

Some examples of descriptive analytics are summarizing past events such as regional sales, customer attrition, or success of marketing strategies or findings of general trends in popular travel destination or trending techniques, etc.

8.1.2 Diagnostic Analytics

Recognizing what has happened is important, however, it isn't sufficient to make a confident decision. Hence, diagnostic analytics is used to answer the question "Why has this happened?" Various techniques such as drill-down, data discovery, data mining and correlations can be used to figure out the answer to the question. Diagnostic analytics investigates data to endeavour to comprehend the reasons for occasions and practices. Intuitive data representation tools enable managers to effectively pursue, channel and look at individuals by bringing the data together [5].

The main function of diagnostic analytics is to identify anomalies, drill into the analytics and determine the casual relationships. On the basis of the results of descriptive analysis, analysts must recognize areas that require further examination since they bring up issues that can't be addressed only by taking a look at the information. Analysts then must identify the data sources that will help them explain these anomalies. Finally, the hidden relationships are revealed by considering events that might have caused the recognized anomalies.

Examples of diagnostic analytics can be some form of social media marketing campaign where the user is interested in retrieving the number of likes or reviews. Diagnostic analytics can help to filter out thousands of likes and reviews into a single view to see the progress of the campaign.

8.1.3 Prescriptive Analytics

Prescriptive analytics is the third and last category of business analytics, which likewise incorporates descriptive and predictive analytics. Prescriptive analytics contributes by answering exact inquiries with a "laserlike" focus [2].

There are lots of examples associated with predictive analytics. The healthcare industry uses prescriptive analytics to achieve a patient population by computing the number of patients who are clinically overweight.

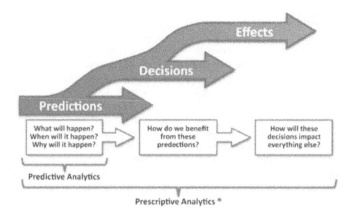

Figure 8.2   Prescriptive analytics.

8.1.4   Exploratory Analytics

Exploratory data analysis alludes to the basic procedure of performing introductory examinations on information to find designs, to spot abnormalities, to test theories and to check presumptions with the assistance of outline insights and graphical portrayals [6]. Exploratory analytics is an investigative methodology that principally centers around distinguishing general examples in the crude information to recognize anomalies and highlights that probably won't have been foreseen utilizing other expository methods.[1]

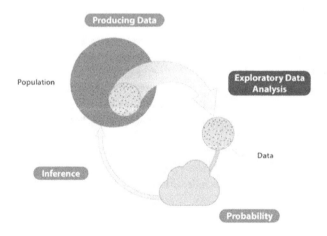

Figure 8.3   Exploratory data analysis.

For example, if you want to go to a theater to watch a movie, the analysis and searching you do to select a movie to watch is nothing but your exploratory analytics.

[1] https://bolt.mph.ufl.edu/6050-6052/unit-1/

8.1.5   Predictive Analytics

Prescriptive analytics answers the question "What is probably going to happen?" It is when past data is combined with guidelines, algorithms, and external data to control the probable future consequence of an event. The objective of predictive analytics is to enable you to go over exactly what has occurred and give the most ideal appraisal of what is probably going to occur in the future [7].

In business, predictive models exploit designs found in recorded and value-based information to recognize risks and opportunities. Models catch connections among numerous variables to permit evaluation of risk or potential related with a specific set of conditions, controlling basic leadership for decision making.

Predictive analytics can be utilized in keeping banking frameworks to distinguish fraud detection cases, measure the dimensions of credit chances, and expand the strategically pitch and up-move openings in an association.

8.1.6   Mechanistic, Causal and Inferential Analytics

Mechanistic analytics allow data scientists to recognize clear modifications in procedures or even variables which can result in altering of variables. The outcomes of mechanistic analytics are resolved by calculations in engineering and physical sciences [8, 9].

Causal analytics allow data scientists to symbolize what is probably going to happen if one module of the variable is altered. In this approach, you should trust a number of arbitrary variables to regulate what's likely to occur next, even though you can use non-arbitrary studies to infer the answer from connections.

Inferential analytics methodology takes different world philosophies into account to regulate certain features of the huge population. In inferential analytics, it is essential to take a smaller section of data from the population and use that as a basis to conclude parameters about the larger population.

8.2   Privacy Concerns Related to Use of Data Analytics

The intensity of data analytics is great, notwithstanding that for all conceivable positive business outcomes, there is a similar number of new security concerns created. As personal data is increasingly being gathered up by giant organizations, massive amounts of information have turned out to be accessible for real uses as well as for disreputable purposes. In this context we will discuss some key areas and significant risks associated with data analytics [10-13].

8.2.1   Immoral Actions Based on Analyses

Data analytics can be utilized by giant organizations to provide a greater assortment of business choices that don't consider the human lives that are included. The possibility of uncovering personal data should be considered, which, although not unlawful, can harm the life of an individual. Data stores, for example, NoSQL, have numerous security vulnerabilities, which are a danger to privacy. A noticeable security blemish is that it can't scramble information amid the labeling or logging of information or while conveying it into various gatherings, when it is collected.

8.2.2   Discrimination

With data analytics, attempting to select job candidates, provide promotions, etc., may go wrong if the analytics are not accurately objective. This is known as "automated discrimination." For instance, a financial organization may not be able to ascertain an applicant's race with a credit application, but could deduce race based upon a wide range of data, collected online, using data analytics to then turn down a loan to an individual.

8.2.3   Privacy Breaches

The activities taken by organizations as a consequence of data analytics may breach the privacy of those involved, and lead to embarrassment and even lost jobs and lives. For example, if a woman goes shopping during her pregnancy, due to data analytics the data may be transferred to family members or others from who the woman may be hiding her condition. This might put the woman in an embarrassing situation; hence, it is the ultimate case of privacy breach.

8.2.4   Inaccuracy of Data Analytics

The predictions and conclusions of data analytics are not always accurate. The data files used for data analysis can frequently contain imprecise data, or use data models that are inappropriate to particular individuals, or simply be faulty algorithms. This can simply result in off the mark decision making by the organization.

8.2.5   E-Discovery Angst

The e-discovery process generally involves organizations to recognize and yield documents applicable to legal action. When dealing with the millions of documents that organizations have in their repositories, this becomes expensive and time-consuming. A data analytics using an approach called "predictive coding" is used on the large repositories to more quickly narrow down the documents necessary for legal action. There is distress involved in using such analytics to yield documents, as an organization may suspect that all the necessary documents are not being counted.

To conclude, data analytics holds great potential for important innovations, improving upon all segments of organizations and bringing benefits to individuals. Nevertheless, organizations that choose to use big data analytics must govern the connected privacy and information security effects before they actually put analytics into use.

8.2.6   Understanding Cloud Basics

Cloud Computing: The term "cloud" comes from the network design that was used by network engineers to represent the location of various network devices and their interconnection. The shape of this network design was like a cloud so the name cloud was given to it. Cloud is publicly available to users but it is privately owned and provides access to IT hardware and software resources. Computing means designing and building hardware and software systems for a wide range of purposes. Thus, cloud computing refers to an environment that provides computing powers (CPU, memory, network speed, etc.) to customers. The main advantage of cloud computing that makes it different from the traditional on-premises services is its pay-as-you-go service model. This model saves cost, time and resources of the customers. This involves the user activity for timely provisioning and deprovisioning of resources. Multi-tenancy and flexibility are two other key components of the cloud model. Multi-tenancy empowers the sharing of same service instances among various tenants whereas flexibility is the capability of cloud for mounting up and down resources as current service demands.

Advantages of Cloud: There are many advantages of cloud computing. It helps in reducing cost by replacing physical datacenters with virtual datacenters. With virtualization, the users are not bothered about the physical location of datacenters and other resources as they are available to the users on demand. Users have to take care of selecting the datacenter which is in close proximity to them. Other advantages include broad network access, resource management, rapid elasticity and resilient computing [14].

Cloud Service Models:

- SaaS: Software as a service is the service that cloud provides to the user for providing various software services to them. This means that the user can access the applications running on the provider's site by using any thin client interface or program interface that can be used to access that application. This means the user need not install, buy or run that software, instead renting the same from any cloud provider.

- IaaS: Infrastructure as a service is another service model for realizing the whole infrastructure on a desktop. This provides the capability to provision processing, virtual machines, servers, storage, load balancers, networks, etc.

- PaaS: Platform as a service develops various other applications such as database web servers and development tools.

There are also other service models like data as a service, science as a service, etc.

Figure 8.4   Cloud service models.

Deployment Models of Cloud:

- *Private Cloud*: This cloud service is provided solely for an organization and is operated by an organization or third party, i.e., the cloud is accessible to the specific organization.

- *Public Cloud*: This cloud infrastructure is made available to the public and the cloud is owned by the organization selling cloud services.

- *Community Cloud*: This cloud infrastructure is shared by various organizations and supports a specific goal. These services may be managed by an organization or any third party.

- *Hybrid Cloud*: This cloud infrastructure is a composition of two or more clouds. Information on the private, public, community and hybrid deployment models is compiled in Table 8.1 below, which summarizes information about their management, infrastructure and accessibility.

Table 8.1   Summary of the management, infrastructure and accessibility of deployment models.

Deployment Model	Managed By	Infrastructure Owned By	Infrastructure Located At	Accessible and Consumed By
Public	Third party provider	Third party provider	Off-premise	Untrusted
Private	Organization	Organization	On-premise Off-premise	Trusted
	Third party provider	On-premise Off-premise	On-premise Off-premise	
Community	Organization /Third party provider	Organization/Third party provider	On-premise /Off-premise	Trusted
Hybrid	Both organization and third party provider	Both organization and third party provider	Both on-premise and off-premise	Trusted or Untrust

Nowadays, many government and private organizations have been shifting to cloud-based services in order to reduce their investments in IT infrastructure and resources. Although this shift has brought many advantages over the traditional computing approaches, there are also concerns over the potential risks of implementing cloud-based technologies as it encompasses many technologies, including networks, load balancing, transaction management, databases, operating systems, virtualization and resource scheduling. Therefore, the security issues related to these technologies are applicable to cloud computing also.

These risks mostly cover six specific areas of the cloud computing environment where equipment and software require substantial security attention [1]. These six areas are:

1. Security of data at rest.

2. Security of data in transit.

3. Authentication of users/applications/processes.

4. Robust separation between data belonging to different customers.

5. Cloud legal and regulatory issues.

6. Incident response.

Encryption is the best option to secure data at rest as well as in transition. In addition to encryption, integrity protection mechanisms and authentication also ensure the security of data in transit. So, strong encryption and authentication mechanisms ensure the security of data at rest and in transition.

Another concern is the separation between the users' data from one another. To mitigate this challenge many cloud providers use various virtual machines to store the data of the customers separately. Cloud providers must have strong policies and practices that address legal and regulatory matters.

8.3 Issues

There are many cloud security threats that include threat to confidentiality, integrity and availability, and encryption is best for securing the data at rest as well as in transit. In addition, authentication and integrity protection mechanisms ensure that data only goes where the customer wants it to go and is not modified in transit [15-19].

8.3.1 Challenges

Challenges include regulatory, security and privacy issues [20-22].
   The advantages in cloud computing are:

- *A Virtualized Datacenter*: Allows you to access computer services without regard to where, exactly, the datacenter is located and the hardware that the services are running on. However, you do want to select a datacenter that is in close proximity to users.

- *Reduced Operational Costs*: Similar to using virtual machines, cloud computing uses resources more efficiently. In addition, inconsistent availability and high operational costs are reduced by providing pooled resources, elasticity, and virtualization technology.

- *Datacenter/Server Consolidation*: A virtual infrastructure helps consolidate servers by hosting multiple virtual machines on a virtualization host. Although the cloud uses a virtual infrastructure, the cloud goes one step further by helping consolidate datacenters by moving servers from your current datacenter to the cloud. In fact, the cloud can also be used to expand current datacenters. You can consolidate servers by hosting multiple virtual machines on a virtualization host.

- *Improved Resilience and Agility*: With the correct applications, the cloud-computing model improves resiliency and agility.

8.3.2 Services of Cloud

- *Productivity Services*: Allow users to work and collaborate. An example of productivity services is Office 365,[2] which allows users to create and share documents.

- *Storage Services*: Provide a storage platform for data. By storing data on the cloud, the data can be accessed by any user or device. An example of storage services is Azure storage.

- *Communications Services*: Provide communications between users. Examples of communication services include Exchange Online and Skype for Business Online. Exchange Online[3] provides email, calendar, and contact sharing and Skype[4] for Business Online provides instant messaging, computer-to-computer audio and video calls, and screen sharing.

---

[2] https://office365.com/
[3] https://products.office.com/en/exchange/exchange-online
[4] https://www.skype.com/

- *Search Services*: Provide search functionality in custom applications. In addition, they can provide a search engine and storage of data that can be accessed on an application programming interface (API). An example of search services is Azure Search cloud computing, which is intended to save costs because of the pay-as-you-go model and because of the economies of scale (because cloud computing offers scalability as long as you are willing to pay for the growing resources).

In a traditional, on-premises datacenter, you will need to pay for the following:

- *Server Costs*: All hardware components and the cost of hardware support. Of course, when purchasing servers, don't forget to design fault tolerance and redundancy, such as clustering of servers, redundant power supplies, and uninterruptable power supplies.

- *Storage Costs*: All hardware components and the cost of hardware support. Based on the application and level of fault tolerance, centralized storage can be very expensive. For larger organizations, you can create tiers of storage where more expensive fault-tolerant storage is used for critical applications and lower priorities use a cheaper form of storage.

- *Network Costs*: All hardware components, including cabling, switches, access points, and routers. It also includes WAN connections and internet connections.

- *Backup and Archive Costs*: The cost to back up, copy, or archive data to the cloud or datacenter. Options might include backing up to the cloud or backing up from the cloud.

- *Business Continuity and Disaster Recovery Costs*: Along with server fault tolerance and redundancy, you have to think about how to recover from disaster and continue operating should the worst scenario occur. This should consist of creating a data recovery (DR) site. It could also include backup generators.

- *Datacenter Infrastructure Costs*: Costs for electricity, floor space, cooling, and building maintenance.

- *Technical Personnel*: Based on the technology used, you will need technical expertise and manpower to install, deploy, and manage the systems at the datacenter.

8.4 Social Media

8.4.1 Introduction

Social media is an integral part of life in today's era! Usage of social media is increasing exponentially [23, 24]. It connects known people as well as those we don't know, which leads to the creation of a social system in virtual world. Due to the exponential growth and usage of social network, data is generated in large amounts, which presents opportunities as well as challenges. Online social network (OSN) analysis is the computational method to analyze, visualize and understand the various insights. The online social network can be classified into the two broad categories shown in Figure 8.5 below.

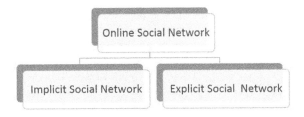

Figure 8.5 Social network.

Explicit social networks (e.g., Facebook,[5] LinkedIn,[6] Twitter[7] and Myspace[8]) are where the users define the network by explicitly connecting with other users, possibly, but not necessarily, based on shared interests. An implicit social network could be ephemeral and lasts only as long as is necessary, unlike a majority of explicitly created networks. Furthermore the online social network can be classified based on interactions on chatting platforms like WhatsApp,[9] Facebook Messenger,[10] etc., where both users need to be simultaneously online for real-time communication, whereas in social platforms like blogs, e-mail or Quora users need not be online simultaneously.

8.4.2 Societal Implication of Social Network

The social network is a boon as well as a curse. Due to the popularity of social network sites like Facebook, Twitter, etc., the world has been transformed into a global village. Social media has had a large impact on society in many ways. It has also had very serious repercussion on society [25].

Some of the serious challenges of the social network are:

- Fake news and content

- Seeing is no longer believing

- Individual privacy concerns

- Data theft and misuse

- Changing work culture

- Algorithmic bias on online platform

8.5 Conclusion

Currently our life has been taken over by the SMAC (Social Mobile Analytics and Cloud), and we are dependent on technology more than ever. Hardly any aspect of life is untouched

---

[5]https://www.facebook.com/
[6]https://www.linkedin.com/j
[7]https://twitter.com/
[8]https://myspace.com/
[9]https://www.whatsapp.com/
[10]https://www.facebook.com/messenger/

by technology. Knowingly or unknowingly, human lives are now technology driven. Technology makes our life better but at the same time also has a few threats. One of the challenging aspects of technology usage is to maintain the privacy of the user. Social, mobile, analytics and cloud are technologies which access vital information about the user's activity and identity, hence it has become very important to have proper privacy measures in place to protect the users.

REFERENCES

1. Delen, D., & Demirkan, H. (2013). *Data, information and analytics as services.*

2. Song, S. K., Kim, D. J., Hwang, M., Kim, J., Jeong, D. H., Lee, S., ... & Sung, W. (2013, December). Prescriptive analytics system for improving research power. In 2013 IEEE 16th International Conference on Computational Science and Engineering (pp. 1144-1145). IEEE.

3. Grover, P., & Kar, A. K. (2017). Big data analytics: a review on theoretical contributions and tools used in literature. *Global Journal of Flexible Systems Management*, 18(3), 203-229.

4. Sharda, R., Asamoah, D. A., & Ponna, N. (2013, June). Business analytics: Research and teaching perspectives. In Proceedings of the ITI 2013 35th International Conference on Information Technology Interfaces (pp. 19-27). IEEE.

5. Jiggins, J. (2012). Diagnostic research in support of innovation. *NJAS-Wageningen journal of life sciences*, 60, 115-121.

6. Gibson, D., & de Freitas, S. (2016). Exploratory analysis in learning analytics. Technology, *Knowledge and Learning*, 21(1), 5-19.

7. Shmueli, G., & Koppius, O. R. (2011). Predictive analytics in information systems research. MIS quarterly, 553-572.

8. Holsapple, C., Lee-Post, A., & Pakath, R. (2014). A unified foundation for business analytics. *Decision Support Systems*, 64, 130-141.

9. Daniel, B. (2015). Big Data and analytics in higher education: Opportunities and challenges. *British journal of educational technology*, 46(5), 904-920.

10. Wang, G., Gunasekaran, A., Ngai, E. W., & Papadopoulos, T. (2016). Big data analytics in logistics and supply chain management: Certain investigations for research and applications. *International Journal of Production Economics*, 176, 98-110.

11. Jayakrishnan, M., Mohamad, A. K., & Yusof, M. M. (2018). Assimilation of Business Intelligence (BI) and Big Data Analytics (BDA) Towards Establishing Organizational Strategic Performance Management Diagnostics Framework: A Case Study. *Journal of Digital Information Management*, 16(1).

12. Bose, R. (2009). Advanced analytics: opportunities and challenges. *Industrial Management & Data Systems*, 109(2), 155-172.

13. Phillips-Wren, G. E., Iyer, L. S., Kulkarni, U. R., & Ariyachandra, T. (2015). Business Analytics in the Context of Big Data: A Roadmap for Research. CAIS, 37, 23.

14. Le, D. N., Kumar, R., Nguyen, G. N., & Chatterjee, J. M. (2018). *Cloud Computing and Virtualization*. John Wiley & Sons.

15. Legg, P. A. (2016, June). Enhancing cyber situation awareness for non-expert users using visual analytics. In 2016 International Conference On Cyber Situational Awareness, Data Analytics And Assessment (CyberSA) (pp. 1-8). IEEE.

16. Singh, H., Manhas, P., Maan, D., & Sethi, N. (2016). Cloud Computing Security and Privacy Issues-A Systematic Review. *IJCTA*, 9(11), 4979-4992.

17. Le, D. N., Kumar, R., Mishra, B. K., Chatterjee, J. M., & Khari, M. (Eds.). (2019). *Cyber Security in Parallel and Distributed Computing: Concepts, Techniques, Applications and Case Studies*. John Wiley & Sons.

18. http://www.sifytechnologies.com/blog/5-focus-areas-for-data-center-security/

19. https://www.ibm.com/blogs/cloud-computing/2013/04/04/how-cloud-computing-is-impacting-everyday-life/

20. Mller, O., Junglas, I., Brocke, J. V., & Debortoli, S. (2016). Utilizing big data analytics for information systems research: challenges, promises and guidelines. *European Journal of Information Systems*, 25(4), 289-302.

21. Puar, V. H., Bhatt, C. M., Hoang, D. M., & Le, D. N. (2018). Communication in Internet of Things. In Information Systems Design and Intelligent Applications (pp. 272-281). Springer, Singapore.

22. Arpaci, I. (2017). Antecedents and consequences of cloud computing adoption in education to achieve knowledge management. *Computers in Human Behavior*, 70, 382-390. DOI: 10.1016/j.chb.2017.01.02

23. Hussain, A., & Vatrapu, R. (2014, May). Social data analytics tool (sodato). In International Conference on Design Science Research in Information Systems (pp. 368-372). Springer, Cham.

24. Kurka, D. B., Godoy, A., & Von Zuben, F. J. (2015). Online social network analysis: A survey of research applications in computer science. arXiv preprint arXiv:1504.05655.

25. Shaharudin, M. S., Fernando, Y., Jabbour, C. J. C., Sroufe, R., & Jasmi, M. F. A. (2019). Past, present, and future low carbon supply chain management: A content review using social network analysis. *Journal of cleaner production*, 218, 629-643.

CHAPTER 9

IMPLEMENTATION OF REST ARCHITECURE-BASED ENERGY-EFFICIENT HOME AUTOMATION SYSTEM

Shankey Garg[1], Jyotir Moy Chatterjee[2], Dac-Nhuong Le[3]

[1]NIT Raipur, Chhattisgarh, India
[2] LBEF (APUTI), Kathmandu, Nepal
[3] Haiphong Unviersity, Haiphong, Vietnam
 Email: shankeygarg1793@gmail.com, jyotirm4@gmail.com, nhuongld@dhhp.edu.vn

Abstract

The Internet of Things (IoT) envisions a reality where each gadget, anywhere, could be associated. This would create a reality where lights automatically turn on, entryways open upon the arrival of relatives and remain closed to unfamiliar persons, coffee makers turn on when the morning alarm goes off, and many more applications. The IoT isn't the internet, yet it could be called a system of gadgets which are associated with the internet. Much research related to the utilization of IoT is currently being conducted. In this chapter we try to explain how we can mechanize the home with automation using Arduino and REST engineering. The outcome likewise indicates how the utilization of Arduino and REST engineering is beneficial when contrasted with other accessible resources in the field of IoT. The proposed framework can possibly give adaptable answers to address current issues such as energy conservation, energy awareness, cost cutting and so on.

Keywords: IoT, REST, Arduino Uno

9.1   Introduction

Sir Kevin Ashton coined the term "Internet of Things" in 1999; and the hard-working research group at the Auto-ID Center worked on radio frequency identification (RFID) technology and many more emerging technologies. At that time the general definition of IoT including objects and connectivity was not proposed. Also, a precise and accurate explanation has still not been found [1]. The IoT has turned into a famous innovation for the future, in which an expansive number of everyday life smart items, such as sensors, actuators and so on, are associated with the internet [2]. The sensors and actuators are commonly outfitted with various types of microcontrollers, transceivers and protocols for various purposes as required. Numerous works are being done in the field of automation. Here the main focus is correspondence management to detect and control information [3]. These tools, i.e., sensors or actuators, are associated with one another to exchange their detected information to concentrated servers, where data, on the whole, is saved and is accessible to specific clients having appropriate privileges [4]. The exchange of information to and from one sensor/actuator node to another sensor/actuator center or an IoT server is accomplished over another correspondence perspective known as machine-type communication (MTC) or machine-to-machine (M2M) communication [5]. A brief description of REST architecture which is used in the proposed system is given here. Why REST is most suitable for implementing IoT is also explained.

This chapter describes how these devices could be combined with the use of technology to develop a smart system which could be controlled by any android tablet or device through URL. With the help of the above-mentioned tools, techniques and architecture we tried to develop a cost-effective, simple, and user-friendly system capable of automating home appliances. We used a voice recognition application on the smart device to operate the appliances through voice. This application best serves handicapped people as they are not capable of going from switch to switch to turn devices on or off.

Smart systems are being proposed and developed which are user friendly, cost-effective and easy to install and use in real time. Nowadays, most of the scientists and experts are finding ways to develop systems that are energy efficient for use in smart homes [6-11].

9.2   Related Work

A system based on IoT is being developed which will enhance performance, thereby reducing the overall energy utilization of any household or organization, and will also contribute towards the fulfillment of the dream of a smart house/building [12]. As we know, IoT gives us the power to interact with smart devices and we can easily integrate this real-world data and knowledge into the digital world [13]. With this goal in mind, we need to focus on the different aspects which should be remembered when designing such systems. Reference [8] provides step-by-step instructions for executing the idea of IoT for verifying whether an LPG stove is on or off, aided by an Android application.

9.3   RESTful Web Server

The RESTful web server is a `REST` established web framework where everything is a resource. A RESTful server, which is highly maintainable, scalable and lightweight, is mostly used to create API for web-based applications [14]. `REST` is the acronym for

Representational State Transfer. It utilizes HTTP protocol for data communication and all the components that are involved in the communication are accessed by the standard HTTP version. REST is web-based architecture and it treats every component as a resource which is easily accessible by HTTP standards [15]. The REST server gives ingress to the resources and the REST client accesses and presents the resources. All the resources involved will be recognized by their respective URIs or their global IDs. Representations used by the REST are Text, JSON and XML. Out of these, JSON is the most commonly used representation.

As discussed earlier, each component involved is treated as a resource. The resource here may be in the form of text file, html page, image type, video or any other type of data. The REST server gives access to these resources and the clients, and handles and modifies these resources according to the requirements. A resource in the REST can be treated in the form of an object of the object-oriented programming language or as an entity of the database. Once we recognize these resources, then its characterization can be easily decided utilizing the standard format. There's no confinement on the configuration of a resource that is represented [16]. One can get any representation format for the same resource like the server. These representations may be in the form of JSON representation or it can be an XML representation. The REST server is dependable for sending the resource to the customer in the organization so that the user gets it [15]. A RESTful web server makes the utilization of the HTTP protocol a mode of information exchange between the client and the server. The client sends a message in the format of http request and the server responds to it in the form of http response; this this request and response method is called messaging. The content of the message can be the message data and metadata.

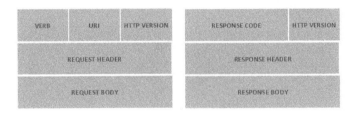

Figure 9.1   HTTP request and response.

9.4   Why and How REST is More Suitable for IoT

RESTful web service does not have any official standard, unlike the SOAP-based web services. Whenever the client refers to the web resources through the URL, representation of the resource is returned, which in turn places the client application in the state. While using the same with IoT framework, sensors get the data with the help of RFIDs, which is then sent with a MIME type format [15]. Here, a sensor or the data of the sensor could be seen as a resource on the web; one can also find a way to connect to the resources, if required. RESTful web service is a suitable method to merge HTTP and web service, in addition to which it also builds a URL to every resource, which makes it easy for the client to use these URL sets to get what is required [16].

In this work, we named a resource feed that consists of data like URL, region, state, etc. Generally, one feed characterizes one node that senses and one can have complete data of the resource with a particular URL, like http://iotarch.com/index/. In this work, for sending the data to switch an appliance on or off we used URL. REST uses HTTP methods (GET, POST, PUT and DELETE) to manipulate the resources.

9.5 Architecture of Arduino-Based Home Automation System

The architectonics of the Arduino-based home automation system are shown in Figure 9.2.

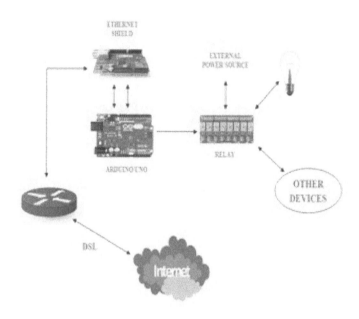

Figure 9.2   Architecture of Arduino-based home automation system.

9.6 Implementation Details

In this system we have utilized an Arduino UNO board along with Ethernet Shield to support local network connectivity (here, the android tablet is connected to the same network wirelessly) [17]. We designed an android application which is capable of recognizing the voice and work according to the command that is given by voice in English. We programmed Arduino UNO in the way that the client sends directions from the Android tablet to the Arduino board. The Arduino thusly transmits the guidelines to the gadgets associated by means of hand-off. We actualized our code utilizing work in Arduino capacities and libraries to help the ideal interface. We also adapted some codes from a variety of sources.

9.7 Why Arduino?

In the proposed system we used Arduino UNO board rather than the other options available [7]. Because if we compare Arduino with other options like Raspberry Pi, we will find that Arduino is better for the following reasons [18]:

- Although Raspberry Pi is available with more options, Arduino is more suitable to satisfy the needs of the system at a cheaper price.

- In relation to the software part, Arduino's simplicity makes it much easier to code in the IDE.

- Arduino is more real-time and analog than Raspberry Pi.

- It is easier to code in Arduino IDE than in the Linux used in Raspberry Pi.

- Arduino is much better than Raspberry Pi for the hardware-based projects.

9.8 Result Analysis

Presently, the assembled device could be used to automate a maximum of eight appliances. In the initial stage, we connected a bulb and a fan. These devices work efficiently with the smartphone as well as the system through URL. Since we have taken power directly from the system which at most could provide a 5 volt supply, if we want to add more appliances then we could do so using a 5 volt external supply through an adapter. Furthermore, we could use sensors with the system in order to detect motion or to detect the presence of live objects in the locality. The beauty of home automation is that it can help the user turn appliances off or on as required from any location through the smart devices. Also, it can be used to turn on devices like air conditioners, lights, etc., before entering the house, so that the user can have cool air upon arrival. A detailed analysis of the consumption of electric power without and with the use of the IoT is given in Table 9.1 below. The energy consumption is monitored by means of the number of units consumed per day. These values are recorded for both cases. After recording the number of units consumed in 15 days for both cases, we calculated the electricity bills in both scenarios. At the initial stage a total of three appliances were used for the analysis of the electricity consumption. The appliances included one light bulb and two fans.

Table 9.1 Power ratings of the appliances.

Sl. No.	Appliance	Power Ratings (Watt)
1	CFL Bulb	20
2	Ceiling Fan	50
3	Wall Fan	30

The data from Table 9.1 is used to calculate the power consumption of the room for one month. We will perform the same task two times, firstly without the use of IoT and secondly with the use of IoT. In both cases we will be calculating the overall power consumption in 30 days and accordingly we will calculate the electricity bill in both scenarios.

Assumption: We have supposed the total consumption for 30 days as 1000 Watts. 1 Unit = 1 kWh, so

$$total\ consumption = 1000\ watts \times 24\ hrs \times 30\ days = 72000\ Watts/hour \quad (9.1)$$

We are interested in changing it into Units; thus, $1\ unit = 1\ kWh$.
So, total Consumed units:

- 720000/1000 ($k = kilo = 1000$).

- Total Units = 720. Cost/unit is 9.

- So, Electricity bill = 720 x 9 = 6480.

9.8.1 Power Consumption without Automation

Here, we will calculate the power consumption of the appliances mentioned in Table 9.1. Now we will calculate the total power consumption as well as the estimated cost of electricity for 30 days by using the above-mentioned calculations.

Table 9.2   Calculation of power consumption (without IoT).

Sl. No.	Appliance	Power Ratings (Watt)	Hours Per Day	Total Consumption Per Day	Overall Consumption
1	CFL Bulb	20	13	260	
2	Ceiling Fan	50	9	450	27,600 Watts/Hour
3	Wall Fan	30	7	210	

From Table 9.2, we have arrived at the value of total consumption for 30 days as 27,600 Watts/Hour. Now, we will convert it into units:

$$27,600/1000 = 27.6$$

Total units consumed in 30 days are 27.6 Units.
We have assumed the cost of 1 Unit as 9 (Could be in $, £, €, INR, DHR, Riyal, etc.). So,

$$27.6 \times 9 = 248.4$$

9.8.2 Power Consumption with IoT

Here, we will calculate the power consumption of the appliances mentioned in Table 9.1. The only difference is that now we have automated the appliances using IoT. We are calculating the total power consumption as well as the estimated cost of electricity for 30 days by using the above-mentioned calculations.

From Table 9.3, we have arrived at the value of total consumption for 30 days as 18,900 Watts/Hour. Now, we will convert it into units:

$$18,900/1000 = 18.9$$

Total units consumed in 30 days are 18.9 Units.
We have assumed the cost of 1 Unit as 9 (Could be in $, £, €, INR, DHR, Riyal, etc.). So,

$$18.9 \times 9 = 170.1$$

Table 9.3 Calculation of power consumption (with IoT).

Sl. No.	Appliance	Power Ratings (Watt)	Hours Per Day	Total Consumption Per Day	Overall Consumption
1	CFL Bulb	20	10	200	
2	Ceiling Fan	50	5	250	18,900 Watts/Hour
3	Wall Fan	30	6	180	

9.8.3 Total Power Consumption Analysis

From the calculations performed in the previous subsection we have arrived at the following result:

Table 9.4 Calculation of power consumption (with and without IoT).

Sl. No.	Appliance	Power Ratings (Watt)	Total Consumption Per Day (Without Automation)	Total Consumption Per Day (Without Automation)
1	CFL Bulb	20	260	200
2	Ceiling Fan	50	450	250
3	Wall Fan	30	210	180

Now, we will calculate the overall consumption for 30 days for both cases. Using the values taken from Table 9.4 we get the results shown in Table 9.5. below.

Table 9.5 Cost calculation (with and without IoT).

Sl. No.	Appliance	Total Consumption for 30 Days in Watt/hour (Without Automation)	Electricity Bill @9 per unit (Without Automation)	Total Consumption for 30 Days in Watt/hour (Without Automation)	Electricity Bill @9 per unit (Without Automation)
1	CFL Bulb	7,800	70.2	6,000	54
2	Ceiling Fan	13,500	121.5	7,500	67.5
3	Wall Fan	6,300	56.7	5,400	48.6

We have seen from Table 9.5 that the value of total consumption and total cost varies in both scenarios. The total electricity consumption without the utilization of automated system is more as compared to the total consumption through the utilization of automated system. Similarly, the total cost without the use of automated system is more as compared to the price with the utilization of automated system.

A comparison of power consumption and cost in both scenarios are shown in Figure 9.3 and Figure 9.4.

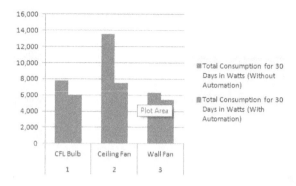

Figure 9.3   Comparison of power consumption.

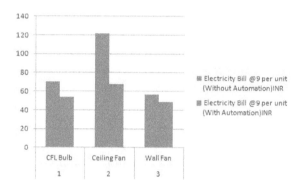

Figure 9.4   Comparison of cost (in INR).

9.9   Conclusion and Future Scope

In this chapter, a design for IoT has been proposed, which guarantees an energy productive use of the resources. We have suggested the details of how we can automate home appliances utilizing Arduino and `REST` framework. The outcome also demonstrates how the utilization of Arduino and `REST` platform is helpful when contrasted with other accessible resources in the field of IoT. The proposed system has the potential to provide flexible solutions to challenges such as energy conservation, energy awareness, cost cutting, etc. The key task of implementing the system is to automate the appliances [19].

This work could be further enhanced and used for many applications. Some of them are:

- Existing work could be effectively extended and used for automation of high-power consuming gadgets like air conditioners, room heaters and so on.

- The work could likewise be elaborated by the utilization of sensors, actuators and IP cameras to detect movement and take video so as to direct the room temperature as required.

- In the next stage of the proposed system we will be using PIR (passive infrared) sensors to detect the presence of a human body in a locality through infrared radiations.

- Several different sensors, such as IR sensors, ultrasonic sensors, motion sensors, etc., could also be assembled with the device and implemented according to the requirement [7].

- With this smart gadget, we can monitor energy, as it enables us to monitor the pointless use of energy [20].

REFERENCES

1. Miorandi, D., Sicari, S., De Pellegrini, F., & Chlamtac, I. (2012). Internet of things: Vision, applications and research challenges. *Ad hoc networks*, 10(7), 1497-1516.

2. Said, O., & Masud, M. (2013). Towards internet of things: Survey and future vision. *International Journal of Computer Networks*, 5(1), 1-17.

3. Said, O., & Masud, M. (2013). Towards internet of things: Survey and future vision. *International Journal of Computer Networks*, 5(1), 1-17.

4. Bello, O., & Zeadally, S. (2016). Intelligent device-to-device communication in the internet of things. *IEEE Systems Journal*, 10(3), 1172-1182.

5. Balamuralidhara, P., Misra, P., & Pal, A. (2013). Software platforms for internet of things and M2M. *Journal of the Indian Institute of Science*, 93(3), 487-498.

6. Moser, K., Harder, J., & Koo, S. G. (2014, October). Internet of things in home automation and energy efficient smart home technologies. In 2014 IEEE International Conference on Systems, Man, and Cybernetics (SMC) (pp. 1260-1265). IEEE.

7. Da Xu, L., He, W., & Li, S. (2014). Internet of things in industries: A survey. *IEEE Transactions on industrial informatics*, 10(4), 2233-2243.

8. Garg, S., MoyChatterjee, J., & KumarAgrawal, R. (2018, August). Design of a Simple Gas Knob: An Application of IoT. In 2018 International Conference on Research in Intelligent and Computing in Engineering (RICE) (pp. 1-3). IEEE.

9. Puar, V. H., Bhatt, C. M., Hoang, D. M., & Le, D. N. (2018). Communication in Internet of Things. In Information Systems Design and Intelligent Applications (pp. 272-281). Springer, Singapore.

10. Chatterjee, J. M., Kumar, R., Khari, M., Hung, D. T., & Le, D. N. (2018). Internet of Things based system for Smart Kitchen. *International Journal of Engineering and Manufacturing*, 8(4), 29.

11. Le, D. N., Kumar, R., Nguyen, G. N., & Chatterjee, J. M. (2018). *Cloud Computing and Virtualization*. John Wiley & Sons.

12. Serra, J., Pubill, D., Antonopoulos, A., & Verikoukis, C. (2014). Smart HVAC control in IoT: Energy consumption minimization with user comfort constraints. *The Scientific World Journal*, 2014.

13. Khan, R., Khan, S. U., Zaheer, R., & Khan, S. (2012, December). Future internet: the internet of things architecture, possible applications and key challenges. In 2012 10th international conference on frontiers of information technology (pp. 257-260). IEEE.

14. Ferreira, H. G. C., Canedo, E. D., & de Sousa, R. T. (2013, October). IoT architecture to enable intercommunication through REST API and UPnP using IP, ZigBee and arduino. In 2013 IEEE 9th international conference on wireless and mobile computing, networking and communications (WiMob) (pp. 53-60). IEEE.

15. Zhang, X., Wen, Z., Wu, Y., & Zou, J. (2011, May). The implementation and application of the internet of things platform based on the REST architecture. In 2011 International Conference on Business Management and Electronic Information (Vol. 2, pp. 43-45). IEEE.

16. Balamuralidhara, P., Misra, P., & Pal, A. (2013). Software platforms for internet of things and M2M. *Journal of the Indian Institute of Science*, 93(3), 487-498.

17. Kodali, R. K., Jain, V., Bose, S., & Boppana, L. (2016, April). IoT based smart security and home automation system. In 2016 international conference on computing, communication and automation (ICCCA) (pp. 1286-1289). IEEE.

18. Soumya, S., Chavali, M., Gupta, S., & Rao, N. (2016, May). Internet of Things based home automation system. In 2016 IEEE International Conference on Recent Trends in Electronics, Information & Communication Technology (RTEICT) (pp. 848-850). IEEE.

19. Baraka, K., Ghobril, M., Malek, S., Kanj, R., & Kayssi, A. (2013, June). Low cost arduino/android-based energy-efficient home automation system with smart task scheduling. In 2013 Fifth international conference on computational intelligence, communication systems and networks (pp. 296-301). IEEE.

20. Weiss, M., & Guinard, D. (2010, December). Increasing energy awareness through web-enabled power outlets. In Proceedings of the 9th International Conference on Mobile and Ubiquitous Multimedia (p. 20). ACM.

CHAPTER 10

THE VITAL ROLE OF FOG COMPUTING IN INTERNET OF THINGS

VIKRAM PURI[1], JOLANDA G TROMP[1], CHUNG VAN LE[1], NHU GIA NGUYEN[1], DAC-NHUONG LE[2]

[1]Duy Tan University, Danang, Vietnam
[2] Haiphong University, Haiphong, Vietnam
Email: purivikram@duytan.edu.vn, jolanda.tromp@duytan.edu.vn, levanchung@duytan.edu.vn, nguyengianhu@duytan.edu.vn, nhuongld@dhhp.edu.vn

Abstract

Research regarding the Internet of Things (IoT) has spread all over the world where everything is connected to the internet to exchange, process, and collect data from day-to-day activities and environmental surroundings. Nowadays, IoT efficiently supports and enables any normal device to become "smarter," but in the majority of cases it is not capable of hosting application services. Fog computing (FC) is introduced as a technology to overcome this limitation and also acts as a bridge to complete the gap between the IoT and remote data services bureau. Fog-enabled IoT is a new archetype that enhances the platform capability of cloud computing by allocating different services, such as enhanced security and reduced latency, and reduces bandwidth on the edge of the network. This chapter overviews the engagement of FC to unlock the potential of IoT services and also discusses the security and privacy issues of IoT. The principles of FC are discussed, highlighting different IoT domains that are related to fog computing. The community adopted research direction is also highlighted in this chapter.

Keywords: IoT, fog computing

10.1   Introduction

The Internet of Things (IoT) continues to play a vital role in the development of technology. With the aid of the internet, it involves everything from "smart" devices (smartphones, tablets, health monitoring devices) to non-data exchanging "dumb" things such as traditional lights and old devices [1]. Internet-connected devices not only exchange data but are also involved in the storage and processing of data. In addition, people are also becoming a part of IoT technology, exchanging data with servers through their smartphones and tablets. According to the Gartner report [2], 20 billion devices will be connected by 2020 and the McKinsey Institute predicted that the economic potential of IoT applications would be increasing to $11 trillion per year by 2025 [3]. Cisco [4] also estimated that in the same period of time, 26.3 billion devices will be connected through machine-to-machine devices, smartphones, wearable devices, televisions, LEDs or some other connected devices. IoT technology is mandatory for the implementation of an unknown number of innovative services but the direct use of these services is not enough in most cases. IoT devices collect a large amount of data [5] from the sensors, and store and process data to make it visual (see Figure 10.1). However, less processing speed, less storage, and limited power source make IoT devices incapable of performing all the tasks. To overcome these limitations, the most popular platform utilized is called the cloud computing platform. The cloud platform is categorized into three types: private cloud, public cloud, and hybrid cloud. The services can be accessed through the deployment policies and various models include infrastructure as a service, platform as a service and software as a service. Public cloud is where services are available across the internet. The distinctive features of the cloud services is that they are highly flexible to unknown user demands, and deployment and maintenance investment is equal to negligible. Public clouds are dedicated to a specific organization. Data packets are totally isolated and delivered via an encrypted secured network. The main features of the private cloud services are their uncompromising security and privacy, high flexibility, and highly efficient service level. Hybrid cloud is a fruitful synergy of public and private cloud services. The services are decided [6] based on the requirements such as security technical policies, scalability, cost and efficiency. They are highly flexible from a security, performance and cost point of view. Reliability in the multiple data centers is also high (see Figure 10.2).

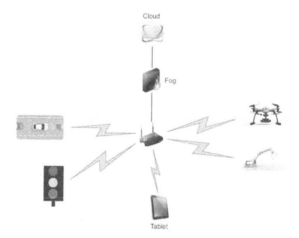

Figure 10.1   Integration of fog computing and IoT devices.

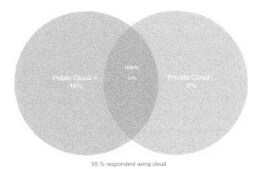

95 % respondent using cloud

Figure 10.2   Cloud computing categorization.

Quintessential IoT applications work on the principle of real-time requirement, which is difficult to fulfill by traditional cloud computing. Fog computing [7] is the ideal solution to overcome these challenges and also provides extended services with high flexibility and low cost. Fog computing is used to extend and unlock the key potential of cloud computing towards elasticity, transparency, virtualization [8], and networking. In addition, fog computing extends the cloud so that it is nearer to the things that can be easily accessible on IoT data.

OpenFog Consortium (OFC) [9] predicted from the survey of 451 research proposals that globally the potential worth of the fog computing market would be $4 billion by 2019 and will increase to up to $18 billion by 2020.

The main aim of this chapter is to discuss the role of fog computing in the IoT. The synergy of IoT and fog computing is more beneficial in various contexts such as network security, gaming, and exchange of delivery packets. This chapter provides an overview of the fog computing principle and paradigm and also highlights the IoT domains that are integrated with fog computing. We also highlight the security and privacy challenges regarding the integration of fog computing with the IoT.

The remainder of the chapter is as follows: Section 10.2 discusses the related studies regarding the integration of IoT and fog computing; Section 10.3 highlights the fog computing principle and IoT application domains; Section 10.4 highlights the privacy and security challenges regarding fog computing with IoT; Section 10.5 covers issues in fog computing regarding security and privacy; and Section 10.6 gives some final thoughts on the topic.

10.2 Related Studies

Bonomi *et al.* [1] discussed essential qualities of fog computing in IoT services and applications such as internet-connected vehicles, smart grid, smart cities as well as wireless sensor and actuator network. The author also illustrated the cooperative role of fog and cloud computing. Vaquero and Rodero-Merino [2] explored fog computing, as well as comprehending technologies that include virtualization in networking, sensor networks, and cloud network; they also highlighted the issues and challenges in the implementation of fog computing. Aazam and Huh [3] proposed architecture on the smart gateway integrated with fog computing to overcome the challenge of data trimming. The proposed architecture is also tested through some parameters, including basic upload delay, Jitter, upload delay regarding the bulk data and synchronization. Yi *et al.* [4] discussed fog computing and concepts related to fog computing, application scenarios. The authors also highlighted challenges and issues with respect to design and implementing fog computing system and illustrated new opportunities related to quality of service, security, privacy as well as data resource management. Yannuzzi *et al.* [7] explored the challenges of mobility, reliability and scalability in the scenario of IoT for a large geographical area and also discussed cooperation of fog computing with IoT. Fog computing and related technologies' work are discussed by Stojmenovic and Wen [5]. The researchers considered a case study to explore the security in the fog computing system and also investigated hidden features for examining CPU and memory consumption on devices. Iorga *et al.* [9] presented documentation on fog and mist computing and their relation to cloud-based models. The authors also characterized important features in fog computing, including baseline strategies and models in deployment services.

Mahmud *et al.* [8] analyzed the challenges concerning fog computing acting as an intermediate layer between the backend processing and sensors and also discussed the current scenario in fog computing. The researchers also presented taxonomy with respect to the research gap in the field of fog computing.

The studies discussed in this section illustrate that synergy of IoT and fog is thought of as key to unlocking the potential of IoT. We will examine different IoT domains related to fog computing as well as security and privacy issues in subsequent sections.

10.3 IoT Principles and Applications

To overcome the integral limitation of cloud computing data centers and IoT, fog computing was introduced by Cisco in 2012 [10]. This section covers the fog computing paradigms and different IoT domains in fog computing. According to IEEE 1934, fog computing is a horizontal, system-level architecture that distributes the resources and services such as network storage to end users throughout the length of cloud to devices continuum.

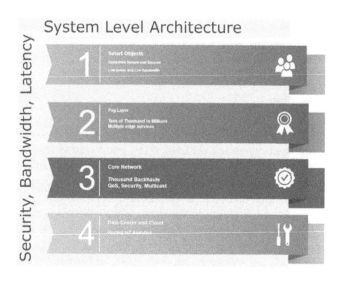

Figure 10.3   System-level architecture.

In the system-level paradigm (see Figure 10.3), everything that lies between the things and cloud is not limited to only sensor devices, edge layer, cloud layer, radio waves as well as particular protocol [11].

Cloud computing-based architecture has faced the following challenges: 1) latency, 2) devices/sensors/processing units, 3) nodes location, 4) separation gap between the clients and server, 5) end-user privacy, 6) malware attacks, 7) deployment.

Fog computing acts as a bridge between two different sides, one is IoT devices and the second is cloud computing and its services. Fog computing is able to overcome these challenges and provides high-level computation, and processing interaction between the end devices and cloud. For wide deployment, fog computing supports some services to make real-time interactions device to device and device to cloud for increasing time sensitivity. According to the previous studies [12], fog computing overcomes the following challenges of IoT.

1. *Security*: Usually those devices that have less storage and run on battery power sources have limited security. Fog computing acts as a substitute to update the old firmware and security credential.

2. *Network Disturbance*: If there is any disruption, such as lack of internet connectivity and reduced computing time due to overuse of data occurring at cloud services, fog computing works independently to overcome these issues.

3. *Save Bandwidth*: Fog computing enables hierarchical data processing along with data from cloud to things. With the aid of data processing, less bandwidth is used because it works on application demands.

4. *Latency Constraint*: Fog computing helps to manage, process, and analyze data from the end user to backend unit, such as servers, which helps to maintain time sensitivity in most of the applications.

10.4   Different IoT Domains

The unification of IoT and fog computing opens many pathways to various IoT applications (see Figure 10.4). This section presents an overview of various IoT applications [13-20].

10.4.1   Autonomous Cars

Autonomous cars are the future of the automobile industry according to the Cisco white paper [21]. Integration of fog computing and IoT enables automatic driving with hands-free devices, which means there is no involvement of a third party such as a human being. Expected in the next few years, autonomous cars will take over the automobile market and every new car will communicate through the internet to nearby cars. Fog computing is the backbone for autonomous vehicles to provide security, privacy, and real-time interaction. To reduce collisions and accidents, fog computing is the best way to make connections because, like the cloud approach, it does not connect through a centralized server.

10.4.2   Healthcare

The healthcare field is the toughest and most sensitive as it is directly involved with people's lives. The Internet of Medical Things [16, 22] enables several services for patient

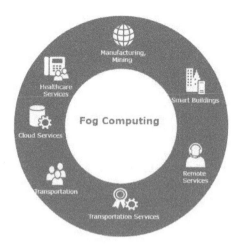

Figure 10.4   Applications of IoT with fog computing.

care, but due to its instability and centralized server it's not suitable for emergency situations. Some solutions provided by fog computing are as follows:

1. It reduces the response time, which usually makes the difference between life and death.

2. It is accessible in remote environments where there is little or no connectivity.

3. Fog computing security makes health-related sensitive data secure.

10.4.3   Smart Home

Fog computing is entering the field of smart home design to make devices smarter and secure. Smart homes will benefit from the introduction of fog computing in IoT devices. The presence of fog computing means if there is no internet connectivity it would recover quickly from this situation. It also improves the data latency, consumes less bandwidth, secures the data and maintains privacy. Last but not least, it provides a UI interface to integrate every device with the aid of the internet.

10.4.4   Industry 4.0

Nowadays, everything is moving towards a new revolution as industries move forward to become Industry 4.0. The main purpose of Industry 4.0 is to integrate the IoT, automation, augmented reality, cloud computing, big data, and connectivity. In addition, fog computing plays a vital role in Industry 4.0 to fulfill the latency requirement and also is a key player between devices and cloud services to enable real-time management.

10.5   Issues in Fog Computing Regarding Security and Privacy

Work is categorized into four types: 1) Authentication, 2) Trust, 3) Attacks, 4) End-user privacy, and 5) Secure communication between fog nodes.

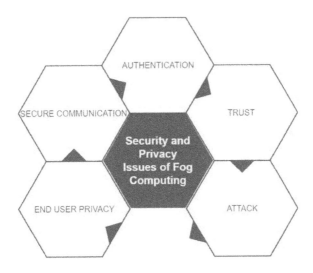

Figure 10.5   Components of security and privacy of fog computing.

10.5.1 Authentication

Authentication of networked devices is the most significant and difficult issue for the security of fog computing. Authentication is an essential requirement to secure authorized entry of any node, because to access the fog services, a device's first step is to connect to the fog network after authentication. Different types of authentication are applied to secure the fog computing network; however, some of them are still not suitable and do not work properly, such as certificates and PKI (public key infrastructure), due to unavailable resources. In addition, the biometric technique, such as using face or fingerprint authentication, is also an efficient technique to secure the network from malicious attacks and is also an efficient way to access the network. A certificate authority (CA) provides authentication to devices that need to connect to the fog network; in this case, authentication is offered as a service. This model helps to secure the fog network from the unauthorized node or malicious nodes from service requests.

Especially in the case of mobile nodes, the nodes enter or exit the fog layer very frequently. It's mandatory to provide uninterrupted services to join new fog nodes for registering in the fog layer.

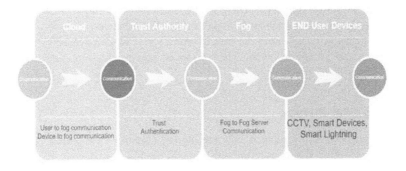

Figure 10.6   Trust authentication at cloud and fog layer.

10.5.2 Trust

Trust plays a most vital role in making a reliable and secure relation between the fog node and edge devices. Mostly, a fog node is considered a major component to ensure the privacy and security of the end users [23]. In the fog network, trust plays a bidirectional role. Firstly, the fog node sends a service request to IoT devices to check the device, requesting if it is authentic or not. Furthermore, the IoT device sends a validation request to the fog node to verify if the fog node is secured or not. Bidirectional data is based on the robust trust model to ensure whether the system is reliable or not. This trust model in cloud computing is directly connected to fog computing due to mobile nodes.

Some trust-based management models/reputation models are more beneficial in some service providers as well as e-commerce services. There are some issues at the time when computing trust models are designed. Firstly, how to achieve uniqueness, a new identity as well as accuracy. Secondly, how to face and treat accidental and internal incorrect behavior.

10.5.3 Attacks

The fog computing system is surrounded by various ransomware and malware attacks and without applied security, it's difficult to secure the fog nodes. There are some malicious attacks such as DoS (denial of service), DDoS (distributed denial of service), malware injection, side-channel attacks, authentication attacks, and man-in-the-middle attacks. These attacks are mostly on cloud computing but they also affect fog computing because fog computing is a smaller version of cloud computing. In predominance condition, devices are not connected to each other and authenticated, so they can directly attack DoS and this attack may be initiated when devices are connected to the IoT network for further processing. Another way to launch this attack is to generate a phishing address for to send a duplicate/fake request within the boundary of the IoT network [24, 25]. Traditional defense policies are not enough to secure the existing fog network because of the following challenges:

1. Size of the fog network.

2. Number of available fog nodes are large in number.

The main work is to overcome the processing speed, limited storage as well as high performance for thousands of fog nodes present in large-scale networks. A wide number of available fog nodes not only rely on the authentication, they also use third-party authentication called certificate authority. There is also a limitation of this authentication; it can increase filtering requests, which leads to demotivate the existence of nodes.

There are many ways to secure the data in cloud services such as encryption, configuration services, and debugging codes. The amount of data accessed can be monitored with the aid of user behavior profiling.

10.5.4 End User Privacy

Stolen end user privacy information is attracting the attention of researchers. There is a lack of data encryption and decryption which makes the IoT network vulnerable to attack. There is another privacy issue related to the location and usage pattern of generated data. Mainly, several IoT-based applications and devices are based on location, such as mobility and location-based applications. In the smart grids, smart meters are used to analyze usage patterns of clients electricity consumption such as how many people are living in a home and when they consume the electricity to turn on/off the lights. Ni [24] presented a new idea called fog-based vehicular crowdsensing (FVCS). In FVCS, mobile fog nodes work on a temporary basis to store and analyze all data, for providing internal services as well as creating a part of the central level cloud server. Internal services include traffic management, such as notifying users of traffic jams, and optimization of several parameters of vehicular networks.

10.5.5 Secure Communication between Fog Nodes

Security is the main issue and the predominant parameter for making a connection between two or more IoT devices. An IoT device only associates with a fog node when it needs to unload storage requests. In addition, the fog has only mutual interaction when it needs to manage the network. In the fog computing environment, if you want to secure a network, you first have to secure the following communications:

1. Mutual communication between fog nodes.

2. Mutual communication between the IoT node and fog node.

10.6 Conclusion

Over the last few years, IoT has captivated the market and created interest in its applications. The IoT has the ability to connect device to device, things to things, device to things and last but not least everything to everything. Due to traditional technology, such as centralized cloud servers. The IoT is trapped by boundaries and also faces some issues, such as high latency, limited storage and processing. To overcome these issues, fog computing was introduced, which worked as a key to unlock the potential of IoT. Fog computing is an extension of cloud computing but some features (distribution, homogeneity) that help to create it are unrelated to cloud computing. The fruitful synergy of IoT and fog computing will create a new future for different domains of IoT applications. In this chapter, we presented the role of fog computing in IoT applications and also outlined the security and privacy issues of IoT. Different domains of IoT applications that will be enhanced through fog are highlighted and future directions and issues that remain open for further research were also discussed.

REFERENCES

1. Bonomi, F., Milito, R., Zhu, J., & Addepalli, S. (2012, August). Fog computing and its role in the internet of things. In Proceedings of the first edition of the MCC workshop on Mobile cloud computing (pp. 13-16). ACM.

2. Vaquero, L. M., & Rodero-Merino, L. (2014). Finding your way in the fog: Towards a comprehensive definition of fog computing. *ACM SIGCOMM Computer Communication Review*, 44(5), 27-32.

3. Aazam, M., & Huh, E. N. (2014, August). Fog computing and smart gateway based communication for cloud of things. In 2014 International Conference on Future Internet of Things and Cloud (pp. 464-470). IEEE.

4. Yi, S., Li, C., & Li, Q. (2015, June). A survey of fog computing: concepts, applications and issues. In Proceedings of the 2015 workshop on mobile big data (pp. 37-42). ACM.

5. Stojmenovic, I., & Wen, S. (2014, September). The fog computing paradigm: Scenarios and security issues. In 2014 Federated Conference on Computer Science and Information Systems (pp. 1-8). IEEE.

6. Atzori, L., Iera, A.,& Morabito, G. (2010). The internet of things: A survey. *Computer networks*, 54(15), 2787-2805.

7. Yannuzzi, M., Milito, R., Serral-Gracia, R., Montero, D., & Nemirovsky, M. (2014, December). Key ingredients in an IoT recipe: Fog Computing, Cloud computing, and more Fog Computing. In 2014 IEEE 19th International Workshop on Computer Aided Modeling and Design of Communication Links and Networks (CAMAD) (pp. 325-329). IEEE..

8. Mahmud, R., Kotagiri, R., & Buyya, R. (2018). Fog computing: A taxonomy, survey and future directions. In Internet of everything (pp. 103-130). Springer, Singapore.

9. Iorga, M., Feldman, L., Barton, R., Martin, M. J., Goren, N. S., & Mahmoudi, C. (2018). Fog computing conceptual model (No. Special Publication (NIST SP)-500-325).

10. Bonomi, F., Milito, R., Zhu, J., & Addepalli, S. (2012, August). Fog computing and its role in the internet of things. In Proceedings of the first edition of the MCC workshop on Mobile cloud computing (pp. 13-16). ACM.

11. Atlam, H., Walters, R., & Wills, G. (2018). Fog computing and the internet of things: A review. *Big Data and Cognitive Computing*, 2(2), 10.

12. Chiang, M., & Zhang, T. (2016). Fog and IoT: An overview of research opportunities. *IEEE Internet of Things Journal*, 3(6), 854-864.

13. Hung, M. (2017). Leading the iot, gartner insights on how to lead in a connected world. Gartner Research, 1-29.

14. Manyika, J., Chui, M., Bisson, P., Woetzel, J., Dobbs, R., Bughin, J., & Aharon, D. (2015). Unlocking the Potential of the Internet of Things. McKinsey Global Institute.

15. Chiang, M., & Zhang, T. (2016). Fog and IoT: An overview of research opportunities. *IEEE Internet of Things Journal*, 3(6), 854-864.

16. Catarinucci, L., De Donno, D., Mainetti, L., Palano, L., Patrono, L., Stefanizzi, M. L., & Tarricone, L. (2015). An IoT-aware architecture for smart healthcare systems. *IEEE Internet of Things Journal*, 2(6), 515-526.

17. Botta, A., De Donato, W., Persico, V., & Pescap, A. (2016). Integration of cloud computing and internet of things: a survey. *Future generation computer systems*, 56, 684-700.

18. OpenFog Consortium. (2017). OpenFog reference architecture for fog computing. Architecture Working Group.

19. Carapinha, J., & Jimnez, J. (2009, August). Network virtualization: a view from the bottom. In Proceedings of the 1st ACM workshop on Virtualized infrastructure systems and architectures (pp. 73-80). ACM.

20. Gczy, P., Izumi, N., & Hasida, K. (2012). Cloudsourcing: managing cloud adoption. *Global Journal of Business Research*, 6(2), 57-70.

21. Fog Computing and the Internet of Things: Extend the Cloud to Where the Things Are https://www.cisco.com/c/dam/en_us/solutions/trends/iot/docs/computing-overview.pdf (Accessed on April 10, 2019)

22. Puri, V., Tromp, J. G., Leroy, N. C., Le Van, C., & Nguyen, N. G. (2018). Analysis of Telemedicine Technologies. Emerging Technologies for Health and Medicine: Virtual Reality, Augmented Reality, Artificial Intelligence, Internet of Things, Robotics, Industry 4.0, 153-161.

23. Elmisery, A. M., Rho, S., & Botvich, D. (2016). A fog based middleware for automated compliance with OECD privacy principles in internet of healthcare things. *IEEE Access*, 4, 8418-8441.

24. Ni, J., Zhang, A., Lin, X., & Shen, X. S. (2017). Security, privacy, and fairness in fog-based vehicular crowdsensing. *IEEE Communications Magazine*, 55(6), 146-152.

25. Le, D. N., Kumar, R., Nguyen, G. N., & Chatterjee, J. M. (2018). *Cloud Computing and Virtualization*. John Wiley & Sons.

PART III

SECURITY DESIGNS FOR SOLUTIONS AND APPLICATIONS

CHAPTER 11

THE ROLE OF INFORMATION-CENTRIC SECURITY IN THE MODERN ARENA OF INFORMATION TECHNOLOGY

Sushree Bibhuprada[1], Dac-Nhuong Le[2], B. Priyadarshini[1]

[1]Department of Computer Science and Information Technology, Institute of Technical Education and Research, Siksha 'O' Anusandhan University, India

[2] Haiphong University, Haiphong, Vietnam

Email: bimalabibhuprada@gmail.com, sushreepriyadarshini@soa.ac.in, nhuongld@dhhp.edu.vn

Abstract

Information-centric security is basically a paradigm employed for securing the information concerned (processed data) rather than the security of the networks or applications. In this context, database forms a main element of recent web-based apps and statistic-providing devices, as it eases and promotes the storage of application-related details that should be obtainable, procured and administered through the web. There is a growing concern about the risk exposure of these information management systems due to the recent rapid proliferation of various web-based information systems. Intrusion detection can be depicted as "the problem of detecting individuals who are using any of the devices without any type of permission (i.e., 'outsider threat') and those who possess beneficial allowance to the devices but are misusing their chances (i.e., 'insider threat')." In this chapter we discuss the various concepts such as confidentiality, integrity and availability; and provide brief introduction to intrusion detection systems (IDS) that dynamically checks the implementations taken in a provided environment, and determines whether these implementations are indicative of an intrusion or comprise a licit use of the environment. We thoroughly discuss how to identify sensitive data along with a brief discourse on usage of strong passwords and regular data backup.

Keywords: Intrusion detection system, confidentiality, integrity, availability

11.1   Introduction

The term data security [1-2] refers to protecting digital data preserved in a database from various evil forces as well as from the unwanted actions of unauthorized users, since data stands at the heart of any business. Basically, data refers to raw facts or figures that have some meaning. The processed data is regarded as information. In this regard, various things have to be considered when considering information security. They include: privacy, integrity, accessibility and responsibility. Basically, data privacy involves employing encryption or using data fragmentation along with encryption.

Data integrity is the term used to represent the accuracy coupled with reliability feature of data. Data integrity can be protected by using storage consolidation. Similarly, different ways exist for protecting data accessibility while preventing data loss; one approach is "replication." It affords recovery of data instantly in the occasion of any disaster. Similarly, protecting an organization's data is the responsibility of everybody connected to that organization. Besides, some of the sensitive important data includes: Social Security numbers, credit card numbers, driving license ID, personal information (e.g., college students, hospital patients, office employee and donor info), important proprietary research information, highly secured legal data, secured financial information, also proprietary information that should be kept secured and not be shared with the general population. This sensitive data should be protected.

Figure 11.1   The key components of information-centric security.

Information-centric security is predominantly a paradigm used for protecting the corresponding information rather than the security of the networks or applications. In this regard, the database is an essential component of new age web-based applications and information sites. Information is normally stored as data in the database management system, generally referred to as DBMS. Furthermore, there is a growing concern about the risk exposure of these information management systems owing to the current rapid proliferation of various web-based information systems. Hence, organizations need to carefully check access to the processed data concerned for both internal users and also outside executioner. Shield cracks, although intentionally done, can also happen accidentally, and are capable of causing a great deal of destruction to one customer or program; however, they also pose risks to all the details and data from any institute. So, based upon only prevention, security measures are not often enough to secure important data against the attacks [3]. It is the precaution against such threats that has made intrusion detection systems, also called IDSs, one of the most important components for tracking those resources and detecting any intrusive activity going on.

11.2   Complete Solution to Data Security

The total solution for database security should meet three requirements: confidentiality, integrity and availability, as shown in Figure 11.2. Each of them is discussed below.

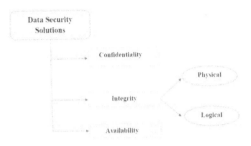

Figure 11.2   Data security solutions.

11.2.1   Confidentiality

Confidentiality refers to securing information against unauthorized and unplanned disclosure. It requires a set of rules generally executed through confidentiality agreements which limits access or puts restrictions on specific types of information. A confidentiality agreement (CA), or secrecy agreement (SA), is a legal contract between at least two parties that outlines confidential material, knowledge, or information that the parties wish to share with one another for certain purposes, but wish to restrict access to by third parties. There are various types of confidentiality agreements such as legal confidentiality, medical confidentiality, commercial confidentiality, banking confidentiality, etc.

11.2.2   Integrity

Integrity is about preventing unauthorized data modification. Data integrity is basically maintaining the continuance of and the commitment to the exactness and regularity of data over its complete life cycle, and is a hypercritical feature to the design, execution and use of any device which saves, operates or recovers information. The term "integrity" is wide-ranging in scope and may have wide-ranging distinct definitions depending on the particular situation, even under the same general umbrella of computing.

There are two types of integrity:

1. Physical Integrity (PI): It is about correctly saving and deleting the information itself. Challenges related to PI may include electromechanical failures, natural disasters, design-related flaws, erosion, blackouts and material fatigue; and also environmental menaces like dangerous chemical electromagnetic waves, very high temperature conditions, coercion and gravitational strength. Ways of assuring PI involve redundant hardware, an undisturbed power supply, some special types of RAID arrays, hardened chips through radiation, memory for error correction, utilization of a congregated file system, implementing file systems that engage block level checksums just like ZFS, storage arrays that evaluate parity calculations like exclusive OR or using a cryptographic hash function, and even keeping a watchdog timer on remarkable subsystems.

2. Logical Integrity (LI): It deals with how much a piece of data is correct and rational, provided any selected conditions. It involves subjects like "referential integrity" and

"entity integrity" in the proximate directory or else unerringly avoids the wrong detector statistic structures. Issues related to LI include confirming that the information "makes sense" in the provided total domain. Problems involve design flaws, program errors, and common personal faults. Popular ways to ensure rational integrity involves such things as inspection limitations, remote critical limitations, project declarations, and also keeping a running balance of a checking account. Both logical and physical integrity frequently share numerous general problems like design flaws and common fallacies.

11.2.3 Availability

Availability concerns the prevention of and recovery from software and hardware errors and malicious data access denials. There is also an intrusion detection system which helps with the difficulty of finding out about individuals who use devices without any type of permission (e.g., "outsider threat") and those who have the authority or clearance to use the devices but are misusing their benefits (e.g. "insider threats"). In these contexts, the intrusion detection system, also called IDS, can be considered as a software or hardware product that dynamically checks the operations performed within a given appropriate environment and decides if the operations are indicative of a hack or are a legitimate use of the system. It takes information from ongoing actions in a system, analyzes the information compared to security-related topics, and gives it to the administrator for further analysis. Subsequently, the decision is made to check the possibility that these activities can be taken as a sign of any intrusion. IDSs aim to detect every type of intrusion caused by users who attempt to gain benefits that don't belong to them and also by approved persons who misuse the benefits assigned to them.

11.3 Intrusion Detection and Security

An intrusion is defined as any set of actions that attempts to compromise the integrity, confidentiality, or availability of a source [1]. The intrusion detecting system, also called IDS, monitors web traffic and reports any dangerous or unusual activities. While irregularity recognition and reporting back is the main purpose, some IDSs are able to operate when dangerous activities or unusual traffic is found, and block traffic directed from any suspicious IP address.

11.3.1 Divergent Type of Intrusion Detection System

There are various types of intrusion detection systems (IDS), as shown in Figure 11.3. They have distinct purposes and detect suspicious activities using dissimilar types of procedures like the following:

- Network-based intrusion detecting systems (NIDS) are stationed at a deliberate position or positions within any network, from where they can check entering and outgoing traffic in all devices connected to the web network.

- Host-based intrusion detecting systems (HIDS), as shown in Figure 11.4, run almost every computer or gadget connected to the web network with direct entry into the internet and enterprise internal network. HIDS has an edge over NIDS in the way that

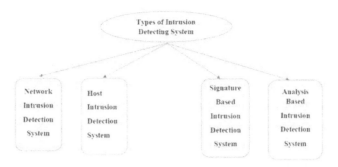

Figure 11.3   Types of intrusion detecting systems.

they might be capable of noticing unregistered network packages that originate from inside any corporation or destructive traffic that a NIDS has neglected to spot. HIDS is also suitable to find out about dangerous traffic that starts from the organizer itself when the provider has been contaminated with malware which is also trying to get into other gadgets.

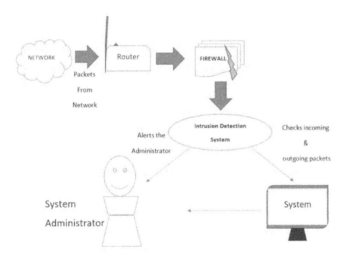

Figure 11.4   Host intrusion detecting systems (HIDS).

- Signature-based intrusion detecting systems (SIDS), as shown in Figure 11.5, check every package traveling through the web network and checks them against a database of signatures and looks for familiar warning signs of dangerous attacks, just like an antivirus software.

- Anomaly-based intrusion detecting systems (IDA) monitor network traffic using confirmed guidelines to determine what is usual for the web network regarding ports, pacts, bandwidth and other gadgets. These types of IDS notify executives of possibly dangerous activities.

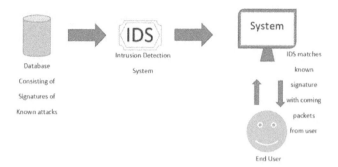

Figure 11.5   Signature-based intrusion detecting systems (SIDS).

Intrusion detecting systems have historically been divided into two categories: static and dynamic. A static IDS confirms suspicious activities to create awareness or records entries, but will do nothing about them. An active IDS (intrusion detection and prevention system) creates awareness and records entries, but can also be converted to take action, like closing access to IP addresses or blocking access to important reservoirs.

Snort is the most commonly suggested open-source, free and lightweight network intrusion detection system (NIDS) to detect emerging threats. Snort compilation could be done in almost all Unix or Linux OS, and another type is also obtainable for Windows.

11.3.2 Potentiality of Intrusion Detection Systems

Intrusion detection systems (IDSs) monitor traffic across the web network to find out when an attack is being conducted by any uncertified bodies. Security department personnel are tasked with fulfilling some or all of the following IDS requirements [4]:

- Checking the performance of firewalls, routers, key controlling servers and documents required by other safety personnel to discover and block cyberattacks and retrieve information after an attack.

- Giving executives a method to organize, tune and interpret applicable OS inspect trails and other types of records that are most common or very hard to discover or parse.

- Giving an easy handy interface so inefficient or even low-IQ agents can also help with governing the security system.

- Involving a large strike signature database to which data of the network could be compared.

- Detecting and outlining when the IDS finds out that information-containing documents have been changed.

- Creating a shock to notify that safety has been breached.

- Responding to the trespasser by blocking them or else closing the server.

An intrusion detection system could be applied as a program application attached to a user's hardware or else as a network security appliance; therefore, cloud-based intrusion detection systems also secure information and systems in cloud environment.

11.3.3 Advantage of Intrusion Detection Systems

Intrusion detection systems provide any institution with a lot of privileges, beginning with the potential to detect safety breaches. The IDS may be used to help analyze the number and kind of strikes, and institutions can utilize this data to alternate their safety systems or update to extra powerful controls. The IDS [5-9] could furthermore assist companies in detecting problems or errors with their network device arrangement. These points can then also be used to detect upcoming threats.

Intrusion detection systems may also assist the venture in attaining regulatory compliance. The IDS provide businesses larger and clearer detectability [1-5] covering their web network and make it trouble-free to attend to safety security rules and directives. Also, organizations may also utilize their IDS documents as part of the authentication to show they are converging some particular compliance necessities.

Intrusion detecting systems may additionally enhance or develop safety reactions. Since IDS sensors are able to discover network hosts and gadgets, they can further be used to check information within website hosting packages, and also detect the OSs of the facility being used [1]. Utilizing an IDS to delete this data can be more productive than physical enumeration of attached systems.

11.4 IPS vs. IDS

An intrusion prevention system, also called an IPS, is almost the same as an IDS, but only conflicts in the way that an IPS can be arranged for stopping likely risks. Just like IDS, an IPS can also be utilized to record, check and describe activities, but it can also be arranged to terminate risks without even the participation of any system executive. However, institutes must be careful with IPSs because they can also deny licit traffic if not tuned perfectly.

A very limited number of ways has been suggested in the last few years to identify intrusions in databases. Data mining techniques, network and hidden Markov model are commonly used in the subject area of database intrusion detection, which is briefly described in the current chapter. Every technique here aims to discover suspicious transactions, more precisely in databases, but one of the major difficulties in this field is to secure the database from the well-formed but dangerous transactions conjointly, narrowing the creation of "false alarms" that represent one of the central complications of existing database IDSs. True positives (TP) are a type of intrusion-based transactions intercepted by the IDS; and false positives (FP) are the genuine transactions considered intrusive ("false alarms"). It is found that the reason behind limiting of the performance of an IDS is not the capability to detect intrusive conduct accurately (TP) but its potential to decrease false alarms (FP). The most important motivation for this chapter is to solve this problem. The main focus of our chapter is to look at the security solution which will be able to detect anomalous user requests given to a DBMS while minimizing false alarms [10, 11].

A true positive is the outcome where the model correctly predicts the positive class, whereas a true negative is the outcome where the model correctly predicts the negative class. A false positive is the outcome where the model incorrectly predicts the positive class, whereas a false negative is the outcome where the model incorrectly predicts the negative class.

11.5   Relevant Methods to Increase Data Safety

The cybersecurity world is advancing very fast and, at the same time, developments in the field of technology have become notable for recommending ways to help cyber hackers or advanced cyber lawbreakers to play with data safety loopholes. The constantly rising graph of cybercrimes is a great threat to worldwide internet customers, business organizations and other institutes [12-14].

The best latest case of this increasing rate of those attacks is the ransomware virus also known as WannaCry. These were considered to be the largest attacks in recent years, infecting numerous internet users, firms and institutions all around the world. The question arises: "Why have both large and small businesses been affected and influenced by this great attack?" It as if the new e-world is beginning to watch and believe that safety aspects will not only come under the topic of safeguarding information, but actually in shielding data by securing the building blocks of firms.

There are a lot of methods institutions can use to secure their business from cyberattacks, which can be found in a Privacy End article, which highlights various estimates involving improved technologies, the latest software, experienced employees and pre-arranged preventative aspects.

11.5.1   Limit Data Access

Many of the businesses and institutions give special access of their important information to many insiders and employees. You need to think about who the people in your institution are who have permit rights to important customer information. Are you able to detect everyone's permit rights? Most organizational officers and workers are oblivious to the particulars of individual workers who have permission to access information and the reason for which they accesss it. This poses a big threat to the system, leading to data loss, hacking and theft.

This implies that it's essential for firms to limit the data permits. Organizations must set parameters on what workers do and don't need permits for, and also make sure they only have permits for what they need, and nothing more. All these restrictions may help institutions to control their information more effectively and make sure it is being protected from loss.

Accompanied by back-to-back eminent data infringements, many of which originated due to compromised advantageous permits and qualifications, it's important that businesses manage, command and surveil advantageous permits in their web circle to deal with that danger. Reported outcomes indicate many firms can't correctly control the threats associated with advantageous access. Member transgressions, whether destructive or accidental, have the ability to go unnoticed for a long time, causing disastrous harm to a firm.

11.5.2   Identification of Sensitive Data

For many firms, it is very important to remember where the most sensitive information and important commercial details are kept. This will prove that people have the correct details and utilize more materials to protect their most vital and important resources.

Even though the most important data of a company is at most only 5-10% of the company's entire data stored, a data trade-off of vital or important data might result in a great diminution of the name and income of a firm. For organizational integrity, we would be setting larger severe estimates on important vital data over other commercial information.

11.5.3   Pre-Planned Data Security Policy

When considering processes to reduce cyber threats, a major step is to create a bulk of security applications and data security policies. Implementation of this idea by any organization might assist remarkably in demanding the state and time of immediate reactions. With a plan and rules, one can instantly retaliate in order to diminish the harm caused by a deadly cyberattack.

With permit administration and powers, employee or worker permits could be identified easily and you will know which employee inside the institution probably might have been busted. Keeping in mind that a strategy and blueprint is only as good as its last emendation is very important. Industry directive, technology and best exercise is mostly changing.

Therefore, somebody has to own this scheme and procedure guide and always look at new ways of updating it to keep it pertinent.

11.5.4   Strong and Different Passwords for Every Department

Majorly important data in an organization should be locked away with very strong passwords. Making stronger passwords is essential to deal with a number of password hacking tools available on the market. It is vital to make sure that there are combinations of various characters involving numbers, alphabets, symbols and other capital letters.

However, utilizing exact passwords for accessing a variety of applications or websites is also a big threat. Once the password is found, hackers will try that password on almost all accounts one has.

So, institutions must keep unique special passwords for every worker and also for the various units. It can be simply done by a password managing software and verifying that each person hired has good data security education and password knowledge.

Whenever necessary, it is also suggested to use several multifactor authentications. Adding one more step to the password means one more move that hackers will have to deal with, therefore hacking is much more difficult and unlikely. Some examples of multiple authentication involve push notifications to cells, biometrics, smart cards and token authentication.

11.5.5   Regular Data Backup and Update

Daily security inspections and data backups are essential. For any unpredicted threat or data infringement, it's very important to have an institution back up their data. To run successful companies, one should keep the good practice of manual or automatic data backup on a daily/weekly basis.

Furthermore, the information must be kept safe through the latest applications and good quality antivirus software. Although, to do this, a company should have a workaholic and a professional IT unit. Make sure the company selects someone with the appropriate knowledge upon whom trust can be placed to do the work properly.

11.6   Conclusion

Today, in the e-world of high internet security threats it is essential for everyone to stay updated with the latest efficient data safety software and privacy improvements that are essential to shield and protect your greatest important resource, which is your information or data [13].

Data security is known as the way of keeping data safely protected from an unregistered approach and also authorized corrupted access. The central point of data safety is to ensure that information is guarded and safe from evil forces. Generally, data is kept in columns and rows in its original form inside databases and computers, and also over networks and other systems. Although some of this information may not be that important or essential, other parts may be private and highly significant. But an unaccredited pass to those personal data may cause various problems like leaking of personal information, corruption and privacy breaches.

So, the significance of data security comes into focus. Different types of digital privacy estimates must be used to prevent unapproved entry into URLs, databases or networks. There are a lot of processes to protect or ensure the safety of information, which is very essential, and some of them involve strong customer verification, backup remedy, encryption and document eraser. There are many effective global rules and directives that oversee data safety measures (*cyber security*). Data Protection Acts are enforced to confirm that private data is obtainable and available for only those whom it may concern.

REFERENCES

1. Le, D. N., Kumar, R., Mishra, B. K., Chatterjee, J. M., & Khari, M. (Eds.). (2019). *Cyber Security in Parallel and Distributed Computing: Concepts, Techniques, Applications and Case Studies*. John Wiley & Sons.

2. Huang, Z., Lai, J., Chen, W., Li, T., & Xiang, Y. (2019). Data security against receiver corruptions: SOA security for receivers from simulatable DEMs. *Information Sciences*, 471, 201-215.

3. Shenfield, A., Day, D., & Ayesh, A. (2018). Intelligent intrusion detection systems using artificial neural networks. *ICT Express*, 4(2), 95-99.

4. Catalano, A., Bruno, F. A., Galliano, C., Pisco, M., Persiano, G. V., Cutolo, A., & Cusano, A. (2017). An optical fiber intrusion detection system for railway security. *Sensors and Actuators A: Physical*, 253, 91-100.

5. Mohammadi, S., Mirvaziri, H., Ghazizadeh-Ahsaee, M., & Karimipour, H. (2019). Cyber intrusion detection by combined feature selection algorithm. Journal of information security and applications, 44, 80-88.

6. Baykara, M., & Das, R. (2018). A novel honeypot based security approach for real-time intrusion detection and prevention systems. *Journal of Information Security and Applications*, 41, 103-116.

7. Rowan, T. (2007). Intrusion prevention systems: superior security. *Network Security*, 2007(9), 11-15.

8. Patel, A., Taghavi, M., Bakhtiyari, K., & JuNior, J. C. (2013). An intrusion detection and prevention system in cloud computing: A systematic review. *Journal of network and computer applications*, 36(1), 25-41.

9. Wang, R. (2017). Research on data security technology based on cloud storage. Procedia engineering, 174, 1340-1355.

10. Le, D. N., Van, V. N., & Giang, T. T. T. (2016). A New Private Security Policy Approach for DDoS Attack Defense in NGNs. In Information Systems Design and Intelligent Applications (pp. 1-10). Springer, New Delhi.

11. Nour, B., Sharif, K., Li, F., & Wang, Y. (2019). Security and Privacy Challenges in Information Centric Wireless IoT Networks.

12. Le, D. N., Seth, B., & Dalal, S. (2018). A Hybrid Approach of Secret Sharing with Fragmentation and Encryption in Cloud Environment for Securing Outsourced Medical Database: A Revolutionary Approach. *Journal of Cyber Security and Mobility*, 7(4), 379-408.

13. Cha, S. C., & Yeh, K. H. (2018). A Data-Driven Security Risk Assessment Scheme for Personal Data Protection. *IEEE Access*, 6, 50510-50517.

14. https://searchsecurity.techtarget.com/definition/intrusion-detection-system

15. Hamdane, B., & El Fatmi, S. G. (2019). Information-Centric Networking, E-Government, and Security. In Security Frameworks in Contemporary Electronic Government (pp. 51-75). IGI Global.

CHAPTER 12

ENABLING MOBILE TECHNOLOGY FOR HEALTHCARE SERVICE IMPROVEMENTS

BHUMI DOBARIA, CHINTAN BHATT

U & P U. Patel Department of Computer Engineering, Charotar University of Science and Technology, Changa, Gujarat, India
Email: chintanbhatt.ce@charusat.ac.in

Abstract

The availability of low-cost mobile phones and the current broad coverage of GSM networks in developing countries presents a huge opportunity to provide services based on information and communications technologies (ICT). Mobile applications are a very developed market. So, people have access to mobile signals in their day-to-day lives. Very popular android applications are constructed for various domains in the market. These domains include healthcare, business, shopping, food delivery, etc., but the healthcare domain is not properly constructed for mobile application for those in rural areas. So, I tried to provide a time-saving solution for people to decrease the ratio of those with diseases like heart disease, cancer, diabetes and stress-related health problems. Also provided are functionalities like communication between patient and doctor, timely reminders to take medication or be vaccinated, and time-saving use of short messages and video phones.

Keywords: Mobile health, mHealth, healthcare system in India, telecommunication, development drameworks

12.1 Introduction

12.1.1 Healthcare System in India

India is the second largest populated country in the world with two thirds of the population living in rural areas. There has been an increase in the ratio of patients with chronic diseases. According to the World Health Organization (WHO), 2.5 million chronically ill patients die every year due to heart disease, diabetes and cancer [1, 2]. Throughout the years, India has made great strides in improving the overall health scenario.

In India, 29.7% of the total population is presently children under the age of 15 [3]. WHO[1] reports that 1.5 billion children die every year due to vaccine preventable diseases [3]. Due to the existing challenges in healthcare delivery, there is an urgent need to enact three-tier referral systems with information communication technology applications [4]. The use of telemedicine has been envisaged for providing healthcare services and enabling healthcare providers working at the primary level. But, implementation of telemedicine is still limited to only a few private and prestigious tertiary care public hospitals. Moreover, the cost of teleconsultation is too high to introduce in remote healthcare settings [5]. In view of unsuccessful implementation of telemedicine technology, a low-cost technologic alternative is the need of the hour. The application of mobile technology in the health sector has the complete potential to change the face of global health systems [6]. By 2009, 60% of people had access to a mobile cellular phone, and 100% of them had access to a mobile cellular phone by the end of 2018 (see Figure 12.1).

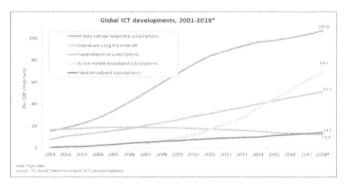

Figure 12.1   Ratio of mobile application users according ICT.

12.1.2 What is mHealth?

India provides a facility-based service to domiciliary care, in which chronically ill patients use telecare and mHealth. mHealth includes the use of telecommunication and multimedia technologies integrated with mobile and wireless healthcare delivery system, which is applied in chronic diseases like diabetes, obesity and cancer. Healthcare is improved by using mobile applications like mobile phones, short message reminders and video phones [7]. Moreover, primary and emergency care services are improved by using a patient's mobile reminders. Also, mobile applications have been created which improve the lives of chronically ill patients in rural areas. mHealth is in its early stages of development; however, it

[1] https://www.who.int/

has already started to transform healthcare delivery due to the success of its applications and programs that have been implemented in the developing world. Mobile devices which can be used in mHealth include laptops, tablets, mobile phones, smartphones, palmtops, notebooks and netbooks.

mHealth also combines mobile technologies with existing healthcare systems to provide healthcare delivery to consumers (see Figure 12.2).

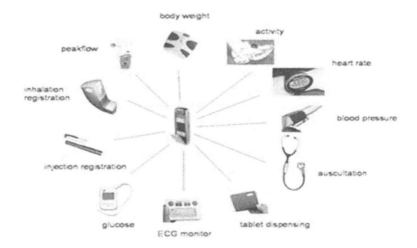

Figure 12.2   Schematic of mobile devices delivery of healthcare to consumers.

12.1.3   Worldwide mHealth Scenario

A 2011 global survey of 114 nations by WHO found that mHealth initiatives have been established in many countries but there is variation in adoption levels. Africa had the lowest rate of mHealth adoption while North America, South America and Southeast Asia showed the highest adoption level [8].

The most frequently reported types of mHealth initiatives globally were health call center/health care telephone help lines (59%), emergency toll-free telephone services (55%), emergencies (54%), and mobile telemedicine (49%). The least frequently reported initiatives were health surveys (26%), surveillance (26%), raising awareness (23%), and decision support systems (19%) [13]. A study by the United Nations Foundation and Vodafone Foundation has listed 51 mHealth programs that are operating in 26 developing countries all over the world. These programs and projects focus on six main areas: treatment and support services, data collection and remote monitoring services, disease surveillance and drug adherence services, health information systems and point-of-care services, and emergency medical services [9].

12.1.4   mHealth and Its Scope in India

India is the second largest mobile phone user country with over 900 million users in the world. It accounted for over 10% of the world's online population in 2011.

Therefore, the high penetration of mobile technology in India offers a positive promising scope for mHealth utilization in healthcare provision. The advancements in technology and communications in a healthcare scenario are also evident in India. An effort to discuss a few of the mHealth interventions in India is made henceforth.

- NIKSHAY:[2] The government of India introduced a mobile-based intervention called NIKSHAY in 2012. It is a web-enabled application, which facilitates monitoring of universal access to the data of tuberculosis (TB) patients by all concerned personnel. The innovative information technology (IT) application of NIKSHAY makes it possible for grassroot level healthcare providers to track every TB patient [10].

- Awareness generation is another prevalent mHealth domain in the country. The National Organ and Tissue Transplant Organization is spreading awareness regarding organ donation among the general population via SMS services.

- Maternal and Child Health: Most mHealth projects in India began their journey in 2008. India's Mother and Child Tracking System was the first of its kind where messages are sent to Janani Suraksha Yojana (maternal protection scheme) beneficiaries and accredited social health activist workers. This innovation helped to improve service delivery and meet the service needs of healthcare providers [11, 12].

12.2 System Design

The main purpose of the system is to improve healthcare for those in rural areas and also maintain a common patient record database. Using mobile devices and the internet, a user can gain access to the system and view detailed information contained therein anywhere and anytime. The communication between patient and doctor is improved using the system, which in turn benefits patients' health. Doctors can view patient record details along with previous medical records in order to provide the right patient diagnosis.

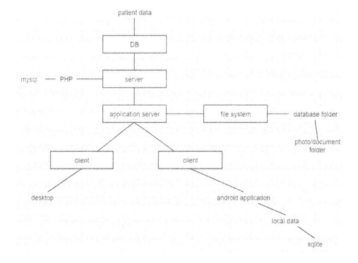

Figure 12.3 System design.

---

[2]https://nikshay.in/

12.2.1 Application Server

A mobile app server is mobile middleware that makes back-end systems accessible to disparate mobile applications to support mobile application development [13-20].

Client and server are connected through the internet using Java API for RESTful Web Services integrated with the application server. Many HTTP libraries, like Volley, Retrofit and Active Android, are also used. Desktop and Android application both send requests to the application server to store and receive data. Local data are stored using SQLite database in Android application, and PHP can work with MySQL database to store data.

These mobile apps have the following features:

- Data Routing: Data is packaged in smaller (REST) objects with some business logic to minimize demands on bandwidth and battery.

- Orchestration: Transactions and data integration across multiple sources.

- Authentication: Service secure connectivity to back-end systems is managed by the mobile middleware.

- Offline Support: Allows users to access and use data even though device is not connected.

- Security: Data encryption, device control, SSL, call logging.

12.2.2 File System

The file system controls how data is stored and retrieved. Without a file system, information placed in a storage medium would be one large body of data with no way to tell where one piece of information stops and the next begins.

The file system is mainly connected with application server. The file system stores patient photos and documents in different database folders and stores RESTful APIs inside a different folder.

12.2.3 Client

A client is a piece of computer hardware or software that accesses a service made available by a server.

Two types of clients are handled in this system:

1. The desktop client, which is a type of remote desktop client that provides an end user with access to a desktop or application through a web browser.

2. The Android application client, which can be used to view and make changes to data saved inside the local database.

12.3 Result Analysis

First scan the QR code with the chosen IP address, database name and password to continue. Then, login using the username and password (see Figure 12.4) .

```
({"ip":"192.168.1.21", "db":"genesis","pass":"root"})
```

Figure 12.4   Scan QR code and login.

Here, choose a photo or document option. Suppose you want to upload a photo, you would first select the photo button and then enter the patient's id.

Figure 12.5   Choose photo and search patient id.

Here, the name, gender and age of the patient which were obtained using the patient's id (see Figure 12.5 above) are displayed; and since the photo has already been uploaded the photo is also displayed. Otherwise, if the photo was not previously uploaded, choose the capture option (see Figure 12.6 below).

Figure 12.6   Display image and caputure image.

You can choose capture option, then capture photo using camera, then photo display on screen. Next, choose save button (see Figure 12.6), then photo will successfully upload (see Figure 12.7).

Figure 12.7   Captured image shown in ImageView and the uploading image.

The screen in Figure 12.8 gives a toast message that the photo was successfully uploaded.

Figure 12.8   Successfully uploaded image.

Otherwise, if you want to upload a document, choose the document option shown in the screenshot in Figure 12.9. Then search patient id and then press the submit button and go to next screen.

Figure 12.9   Choose document and search patient id.

Display patient name, age and gender of search patient id in the above screen. Here, the two options provided to direct document files are upload or otherwise capture a photo of the document using camera. Then, the upload.in option will direct upload file, so choose select file (see Figure 12.10). Among the many options provided are images, internal storage, downloads, photos, gallery in select file.

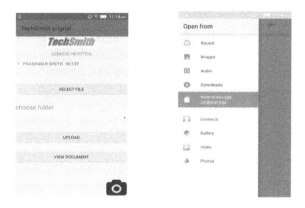

Figure 12.10 Display information and choose option in select file.

In the screen below (Figure 12.11), a file is selected and a folder is chosen. Choose the folder in which the document is uploaded. Suppose that Select 123.pdf name file and 01 OPD History folder are selected and then the upload button is chosen, then the file is then uploaded successfully in 01 OPD History folder. Here, a message is shown indicating that the file uploaded successfully.

Figure 12.11 Select folder and upload file.

The second option to provide capture document photo using camera (Figure 12.12).

Figure 12.12   Capture document photo using camera.

Otherwise, we will capture photo of document then upload, so capture photo after giving it a name then choose folder and upload (see Figure 12.13). Here, a toast message shows the upload was successful.

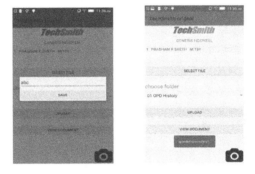

Figure 12.13   Give name of capture image and select folder and upload.

Then select view document. The screen shows which file is uploaded in which folder (Figure 12.14); open then view this file.

Figure 12.14   Show file and images in screen.

Here, photos uploaded in the photo folder are shown (Figure 12.14). Then select view document. The screen shows which file is uploaded in which folder; open view this file.

Figure 12.15   Show photo in folder.

Here, the document file and a photo of the document are uploaded in 01 OPD History folder (Figure 12.16).

Figure 12.16   Show document in folder.

12.4   Conclusion

The current study envisages the scope of mHealth in India. However, accessibility, utilization and effectiveness of mHealth interventions in Indian context need to be focused on in greater detail. There is a need for further systematic reviews to evaluate the existing interventions with special focus on their scope in developing nations such as India.

REFERENCES

1. Jersak, Luis Carlos, Adriana Cassia da Costa, and Daniel Antonio Callegari (2013), "A systematic review on mobile health care." Tech. Report 073, Faculdade de Informtica PUCRS-Brazil.

2. West, D. M. (2013). Improving health care through mobile medical devices and sensors. *Brookings Institution Policy Report*, 10, 1-13.

3. Eng, D. S., & Lee, J. M. (2013). The promise and peril of mobile health applications for diabetes and endocrinology. *Pediatric diabetes*, 14(4), 231-238.

4. Car, J., & Sheikh, A. (2003). Telephone consultations. *Bmj*, 326(7396), 966-969.

5. Kumar, B. P., & Ali, S. (2013). Telemedicine in primary health care: The road ahead. *International Journal of Preventive Medicine*, 4(3).

6. Kay, M., Santos, J., & Takane, M. (2011). mHealth: New horizons for health through mobile technologies. *World Health Organization*, 64(7), 66-71.

7. Rahar, U. S. (2011). Mobile based primary health care system for rural India. *International Journal of Nursing Education*, 3(1), 61.

8. Albabtain, A. F., AlMulhim, D. A., Yunus, F., & Househ, M. S. (2014). The role of mobile health in the developing world: a review of current knowledge and future trends. *JSHI*, 4(2), 10-5.

9. Annual report 2014-2015. Organization and Infrastructure. Ministry of Health and Family Welfare. Government of India. New Delhi. Available at http://mohfw.nic.in/WriteReadData/l892s/563256988745213546.pdf. Accessed 10 Dec 2016.

10. Garai, A., & Ganesan, R. (2010). Role of information and communication technologies in accelerating the adoption of healthy behaviors. *The Journal of Family Welfare*, Special Issue, 56, 109-118.

11. Le, D. N., Kumar, R., Mishra, B. K., Chatterjee, J. M., & Khari, M. (Eds.). (2019). *Cyber Security in Parallel and Distributed Computing: Concepts, Techniques, Applications and Case Studies*. John Wiley & Sons.

12. Leslie, I., Sherrington, S., Dicks, D., Gray, N., & Chang, T. T. (2011). Mobile Communications for Medical Care Mobile Communications for Medical Care: a study of current and future healthcare and health promotion applications, and their use in China and elsewhere (Final Report, April 2011). University of Cambridge and China Mobile, April 2011. University of Cambridge and China Mobile.

13. Kumar, S., Nilsen, W. J., Abernethy, A., Atienza, A., Patrick, K., Pavel, M., ... & Hedeker, D. (2013). Mobile health technology evaluation: the mHealth evidence workshop. *American journal of preventive medicine*, 45(2), 228-236.

14. Garai, A. (2011, October). Role of mHealth in rural health in India and opportunities for collaboration. In Background reading prepared for ICCP Technology Foresight Forum: Developments in Mobile Communication (Vol. 26).

15. Dadgar, M., Samhan, B., & Joshi, K. D. (2013). Mobile health information technology and patient care: A literature review and analysis.

16. Garai, A. (2011, October). Role of mHealth in rural health in India and opportunities for collaboration. In Background reading prepared for ICCP Technology Foresight Forum: Developments in Mobile Communication (Vol. 26).

17. Puar, V. H., Bhatt, C. M., Hoang, D. M., & Le, D. N. (2018). Communication in Internet of Things. In Information Systems Design and Intelligent Applications (pp. 272-281). Springer, Singapore.

18. Le, D. N., Van Le, C., Tromp, J. G., & Nguyen, G. N. (Eds.). (2018). Emerging Technologies for Health and Medicine: Virtual Reality, Augmented Reality, Artificial Intelligence, Internet of Things, Robotics, Industry 4.0. John Wiley & Sons.

19. Somula, R., Anilkumar, C., Venkatesh, B., Karrothu, A., Kumar, C. P., & Sasikala, R. (2019). Cloudlet services for healthcare applications in mobile cloud computing. In Proceedings of the 2nd International Conference on Data Engineering and Communication Technology (pp. 535-543). Springer, Singapore.

20. Sodhro, A. H., Luo, Z., Sangaiah, A. K., & Baik, S. W. (2019). Mobile edge computing based QoS optimization in medical healthcare applications. *International Journal of Information Management*, 45, 308-318.

CHAPTER 13

OPTIMIZATION OF ONTOLOGY-BASED CLINICAL PATHWAYS AND INCORPORATING DIFFERENTIAL PRIVACY IN THE HEALTHCARE SYSTEM

Soumya Banerjee[1], Rachid Benlamri[2], Samia Bouzefrane[3]

[1]Birla Institute of Technology, Mesra, India
[2]Lakehead University, Thunder Bay, Ontario, Canada
[3]CEDRIC, Conservatoire National des Arts et Métiers, Paris, France
 Email: soumyabanerjee@bitmesra.ac.in

Abstract

The inception of ontology-based clinical pathways significantly enhanced the benefits of healthcare, especially for chronic diseases, by envisaging the dynamic attributes of medical care and standardize treatment behavior in order to control and finally reduce the cost of healthcare. The system is expected to be more personalized and thus the heterogeneous data sources of clinical pathways also demand decent risk classification of sensitive data of patients. This chapter introduces a holistic approach to ensure such data protection by incorporating differential privacy of sensitive data in the healthcare system. The chapter presents a relevant algorithm for the proposed model. The functional model is described and performance comparison is given with respect to conventional clinical pathway (CP) model with optimization of state chart (optimal cluster of CP), and data privacy measure through machine learning is also elaborated.

Keywords: Clinical pathways, optimization, health services, differential privacy, machine learning

13.1 Introduction

With the increase of chronic diseases and an aging population, demand for healthcare services is rising worldwide, and many countries are financially challenged to cover adequate services to their citizens.

Therefore, it has become a notable challenge to ensure the dynamic attributes of medical care, standardize treatment behavior, control and finally reduce medical cost. Today, hospitals are asked to serve more and more patients, while maintaining the quality of healthcare with a restricted amount of resources, including staff and equipment. This situation causes many crucial problems, including over-crowded emergency departments, delayed treatment of urgent patients, long waiting time and decreasing satisfaction of both doctors and patients. Clinical pathway (CP) [1-3] is a group of treatment plans developed by medical experts according to specific evidence-based medical guidelines for a range of targets around patients, and these tasks have a specified time period and describe a specific disease diagnosis and treatment process, which can facilitate standardized medical treatment, reduce medical costs, and enhance patient satisfaction.

We formulate the problem of clinical pathways with ontological instances. The representation exhibits the practice-oriented knowledge inherent in CPs. Using the knowledge elements abstracted from different samples of CPs, several classes, slots and instances can be defined. The class hierarchy is linked by the class subsumption relation (primarily *is-a relationship*).

Following the convention, we consider the ontology of a clinical pathway model as a simple graph $G = (V, E)$. The concept is shown by a vertex v in the graph, while the relationship between concepts v_i and v_j is expressed by the edge $e = v_i v_j$ of it. The notion expresses the concept of clinical pathway state chart (CPSC), which is defined as a state chart, whose underlying graph is a bi-graph (*bi-partite graph*). Therefore, the principle of optimization with respect to multi-instance and multi-components of CPSC has also been observed.

However, the trend of clinical pathway is quite sensitive towards the data of healthcare and it mostly pivots on the private data analysis. In private data analysis, two settings may persist, e.g., interactive and non-interactive. In the interactive setting, where the database is held by a trusted server, users reciprocate queries about the data, and the suitable replies to the queries are modified to ensure the privacy of the database participants. In the non-interactive setting, the data owner either computes and publishes certain analytical facts on the data, or releases an anonymized version of the raw data. To achieve the privacy of healthcare data, we introduce an emerging concept of machine learning (known as differential privacy, DP) to measure the trust and similarity of healthcare data. Differential privacy [4] was first proposed by Dwork. Informally, if an algorithm can withstand the deviations of changes in terms of the given input, then it may be differentially private. The concept of a differential privacy protection model is conceived from a rudimentary observation: when the dataset D contains individual X, let ϕ be random query operation on D (such as count, sum, average, median and standard deviation or other range of queries); the results obtained are as $\phi(D)$. If the result of the query is still $\emptyset(D)$, when X's record is deleted, we conclude that X's privacy is protected from the differential attack. Differential privacy is to ensure that any operation on a single record (e.g., add, remove or modify a record) cannot impress on the penultimate result of the query. In other words, there are two adjacently similar sets of data (where only one record is different). In this context, the probability of obtaining the same result from the same query (which is operated on the two datasets) is quite identical to one. However, the interpretation of differential privacy can also be expressed as a specific technical strategy to facilitate the respectable information from the databases comprising personal information of people without revealing the personal identities of the individuals [5]. To formulate the structure of DP with machine learning perspectives, two primary noise mechanisms are introduced. They are Laplace mechanism (LM) and exponential mechanism (EM).

The essential components of DP are: magnitude of noise (expresses how much noise has to be deliberated to the results) and privacy budget (which is a scale of quantity of queries, which should be resolved in given data due to privacy restriction) [6]. Subsequently, there are adequate research works pertaining to the disclosure and protection of healthcare data with differential privacy [7]. Very recently, the statistical estimation in local level of privacy, has been emphasized with the concept of perturbation-calibration. This is further augmented by several iterative solutions of privacy [8]. However, the degree of privacy is changed as its core construction, and thus in symbolic control the incorporation of Levenshtein distance measure is introduced [9]. Apart from that, the hardcore machine learning and differential privacy can be synchronized as hybrid model of implementation [10, 11]. Even for authentic data generation, differential privacy has become responsible, and has already been used in testing and training for quality data generation [12].

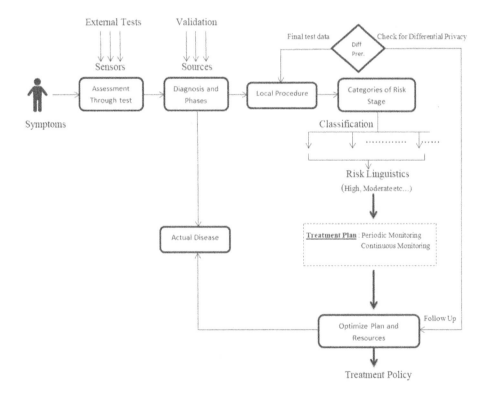

Figure 13.1   Conceptual optimized and data privacy layout of clinical pathways.

Considering this backdrop of clinical pathways, the importance of optimizing the resources and protecting the privacy of private healthcare data has become significantly important. The functional components in such model also have contributed towards the identification of ontological variables and formulation of suitable objective function for

CPSC and a noise parameter involved for trusted and integrated data source. To explore ontology, similarity measure and ontology mapping, irrespective of applications, Gao *et al.* proposed a wide range of research in computing of ontological similarity of singular value decomposition [13]. We also observe that clinical pathways have different bi-partite graph components, which can be optimized prior to building up a framework for a *clinical decision support system*. The scope of optimization inspires the initial model and its associated variables. Following the principle of integrity and privacy measure of healthcare data, differential privacy is proposed to ensure final protection of data of health stakeholders. The flow of working model of the proposal is given below (see Figure 13.1): for particular symptoms, the assessment and validation is incorporated through various health sensors. The application of wireless body area networks (WBANs) [2] has become a suitable measure to ensure continuous monitoring patient's physiological attributes, such as blood pressure and body temperature, with electrocardiograph (ECG) and electroencephalogram (EEG) [14-16]. The security aspects of health sensors are quite contemporary with respect to the IoT and sensors [17].

Once the local data processing from different sources of medical data is accomplished, then the aggregation and analysis of this sensitive health information can be done. As an outlier component of such feeding of sensor data and state and assessment data, differential privacy is introduced. Additionally, the treatment script of clinical pathways consists of risk linguistics (like classification of risk intensity for the symptoms of different diseases). The final decision of CP has the follow up and optimization action taken during the check procedure for differential privacy. The proposed layout is an augmentation for existing conventional clinical pathways with optimized state and guaranteed privacy of patients' information.

The remaining part of the chapter is organized as follows: Section 13.2 briefly describes the ontological application of CPs followed by the underlying mathematical model of optimization. Section 13.3 provides the list of parameters concerned with differential privacy and relevant algorithm for the proposed model. The functional model is described in Section 13.4 and performance comparison is given with respect to conventional CP model with optimization of state chart (optimal cluster of CP) and data privacy measure through machine learning in subsections. Finally, in Section 13.4, the gist of the contribution of the proposed model is formulated with the scope of future extension.

13.2   Ontological Structure of Clinical Pathways

Currently in healthcare organizations, a major trend is for the improvement of quality of care, while reducing costs, with the design and implementation of clinical pathways [18]. A clinical pathway (CP) can be defined as a structured and multidisciplinary care plan used to detail essential steps and timing in the care of patients with a specific clinical problem [19]. Research also demonstrated that the multi-agent simulation is possible for clinical pathway problem [20]. However, the many forms of clinical decision support system always solicit the scope and usage of ontological modeling combined with machine learning techniques [21]. This multidisciplinary industrial research project sets out to develop a hybrid clinical decision support mechanism (inspired by ontology and machine-learning-driven techniques) by combining evidence extrapolated from legacy patient data to facilitate cardiovascular preventative care [21]. Hence, the emphasis is put on the structure of ontology on CP. Clinical pathway ontology (CPO) is formally defined in OWL web ontology language (OWL) to provide common semantic foundation for meaningful representation and exchange of pathway-related knowledge. Clinical pathways normally include three major groups of temporal knowledge. The first group refers to a clinical-pathway-based care period (i.e., expected length of stay) and some time intervals within the period (e.g., the first day after surgery) used as temporal scopes for performing interventions. The second group is the temporal aspect, which is associated with a single intervention, that is, the start time, end time and duration. The third group consists of temporal relationships between two interventions and can be further classified into two other categories. The first one is known as relative temporal relation, which describes relative location relationships of two intervention executions on the same time axis. They can correspond to Allen's relations between two intervals [22] if the execution of an intervention is viewed as an interval. The second category is called the time interval relation that represents the comparison of a certain period of time with the interval between the start/end times of two interventions. For example, a test is executed within 24 hours after a treatment intervention.

Contribution: The major contribution of this chapter is bi-focal: firstly, the scope of indigenous process optimization could be essential in the process log of more complex clinical pathways (CP), envisaging different contexts and sources for collection of data (especially the sensors and associated IoTs). It evaluates an effective clustering for pareto-optimal states for any state of CP Pareto condition that is not mandatory: however, there might be opposite trends in states with respect to patients' attributes). Secondly, following the evaluation of effective cluster of state of CP, it introduces a privacy (DP) guarantee mechanism, which mathematically guarantees the trust.

DP does not expect any ground truth or past archival information and pre-assumptions of attackers. Here, DP is a privacy guard, which ensures trust and adds the deliberate noise after appropriate scaling to keep any observer in uncertain state for the CP. Hence, integrity of CP can be maintained. This chapter presents stochastic gradient descent (SGD) learning to minimize the objective function of final test instances of clinical pathways (optimal states for CP). Thus, the module is boosted with a machine learning routine and a few significant observations are made with post simulation results.

13.3 Proposed Model

A clinical pathway (CP) implies a generic framework to demonstrate the process of treating the patients in a hospital or its departments. Typical attributes of CPs are categorical with respect to a specific hospital or health institution and specialists [23]. However, in this chapter, CP is considered as the generic displacements of patients through either intra- or interdepartmental functionalities. The complexity of CP is proportional to the degree of propagation of the disease, existence of typical symptoms and strategy of treatment. Due to the patients' different symptoms and data acquisitions from different wearable and other sensors, various hospitals' structures and individual experience of a doctor, different patients are treated in different ways. Therefore, different CPs exist with respect to the broader amount of data diversification.

There are inherent optimization techniques to discover clinical pathway data. However, in spite of conventional data mining techniques (e.g., Alpha algorithm [14], Fuzzy Miner [25] and Heuristic Miner [26]), it is always possible to relate missing data in hospital records in terms of consistency and correctness. Therefore, certain supportive clustering processes are mandatory to represent the states of CP and their navigation. Recently, there are also substantial justifications concerning the volume of data in CPs and their associated processes [28].

In the next subsection, typical essential elements are presented to consolidate clustering model and optimization of process in the states of CP.

13.3.1 Elements of Optimization in CP

The elements of optimization consist of the following:

- Sequence of States: Suppose Z could be the collection of existing finite set of states in CP. In other words, states could be the ordered sequences of m, thus all the ordered sequences are part of Z, $m \in Z$.

- Subsequence of States: While rejecting some state elements, a new pre-ordered sequence of sub-states can be yielded.

- Alignment: Let $A_{lt} =< a_{lt_1}, a_{lt_2}, \ldots, a_{lt_m} >$, $a_{lt_2} \in Z$ be a template, which is a typical sequence of states. The template Z should be s specific w.r.t of the specific set of alignment X.

- Alignment Function: An alignment function, denoted $AF = AF(A_{lt}, X)$, relates a template $A_{lt} \in W$ and a set X to the value of non-aligned sequences with a parameter of X to be known as value of alignment.

- Length Function: A length function, denoted $L = L(T)$, connects a template $T \in W$ to its length.

Considering the status of L and V, which constitute the basis for multi-objective optimization problem:

$$min_{T \in \Omega} = \{AF(A_{lt}, X), L(A_{lt})\} \qquad (13.1)$$

However, in many instances, states of clinical pathways could have Pareto-optimal solutions, where the solution of any one of the states may fall in different cluster(s). Hence, categorically, optimization can be interpreted with identification of cluster sequences in different states of the same CP.

Generally, the k-means method is applied to reduce the degree of deviations under the pairwise sequence points (e.g., sequences) in the same cluster of CP. In the present case, points are sequences of different lengths and therefore any distance measure could be established to measure the pairwise sequence deviation(s), if any. The standard templates can be provided by physicians or hospital managers to align sequences of states inside a cluster. They are well-exposed to the details of patients' symptoms and the relevant medical data in the specific hospital during their stay. Hence, the result can distinguish the optimal and non-optimal pathways, and sequence or alignment of sequences can also be obtained.

13.3.2 Functional Model of Differential Privacy

The disclosure of health data has a number of characteristics that need to be considered in any practical mechanism used to preserve privacy. However, there are different types of data sources, with respect to heterogeneous data sources: At the patient level data, we identified four types of health data that are commonly used for data-driven analyses:

- Data directly related to a patient (diagnoses, administrative information, characteristics).

- Data concerned with care activity (medication, surgeries, medical imaging, biology tests, etc.).

- Data towards the care event (date, duration, severity, cost, outcome, etc.).

- Data related to the organization (appointments, human and material resources, number of beds, work schedule, etc.).

A comprehensive literature review of 50 articles related to the "application of data mining techniques in healthcare" is available [26]. They highlight the massive interest of existing works for classification tasks. The most representative healthcare application of classification is to determine the diagnosis of a patient based on his/her symptoms.

Here, a detailed discussion on the dataset can be provided. As previously mentioned, once the differential privacy mechanism is chosen, the noise scale is also calibrated. In this study, we utilize the Laplace mechanism as the building block of the scheme. Subsequently, the noise level can be deliberately changed to Gaussian noise.

Hence, the sensitivity of the aggregation function is the only parameter that can directly affect the noise scale (i.e., the accuracy of the result). Considering practical applications, there are many diversified health data, such as blood pressure, body temperature, heart rate, and so on. Typical size and data range may vary.

The clinical pathway consists of different bi-partite graph components in the form of state chart. Therefore, aggregation and analysis of medical data from heterogeneous sources require distributive approaches from source and recipients nodes. This approach also solicits instances of models. Differential privacy can be combined with machine learning methods.

We divide checking procedure of differential privacy into two major sections:

a) A Stochastic Gradient Decent (SGD) for a maximum likelihood to train the linear model for the relation of response function and features. In this case, SGD is used to minimize the objective function of final test instances of clinical pathways.

If we have a set of observations O, with w as a vector of weights, NCP (no. of clinical pathway data points), i is the ith observation.

$$O(w) = \frac{1}{NCP} \sum_{i=1}^{NCP} O_i(w) \tag{13.2}$$

b) Anticipating the deliberate noise of and risk in linguistics towards different levels, Laplace noise is introduced. The state chart of clinical pathway is distributed and hence a differential privacy with SGD for local noise (denoted as l for the N data points of CP) on the recipient side of the support system.

Hence, the following expression is given:

$$w^{t+1} = w^t - \eta \Delta O_{NCP_l}(w^t) + L(0, \frac{\Delta f}{\epsilon}) \tag{13.3}$$

η is the learning rate, scaling is done with Laplace distribution from 0 to $\frac{\Delta f}{\epsilon}$, here Δf is the sensitivity of medical information.

The functional model can be interpreted by the following high level description of algorithm 13.1:

Algorithm 13.1. High level description of differential privacy.

Input Parameters:

- Y: response value;

- $\breve{Y}$: predicted value;

- K: number of instances in the model;

- w: set of model weight;

- η: learning rate of changes added by the noise in information;

- ϵ: budget allocated for privacy;

- $L(\mu, s)$: Laplace distribution with mean μ and scale s.

Output: Average K instances for the medical records under process.
Begin

Normalize response Y and features F to [0.1]
   if $N_i > 0$ **then**
       Request vector weight w^t from the source point of CP
                    /*CP: Clinical Pathway*/
       Calculate average gradient;
       Update model $w^{t+1} = w^t - \eta \Delta O_{NCP_l}(w^t) + L(0, \frac{\Delta f}{\epsilon})$;
   return w^{t+1};
   initiate K instances
   for each requested instances of CP update t **do**
       Choose a random instance of CP as w^t;
       Pass the value of w^t to recipient;
       Accept modified w^{t+1} from the recipient;
       Replace a random instance w^{t+1} from local noise;
                /* modifications in medical records*/
   endfor
end

13.3.3 About the Data Visualization

For validation of results, there is a string-encoded pursuit to test the privacy and process optimization model. Interestingly, we deploy the dataset containing the intraocular pressure for 250 patients visiting an ocular disease clinic [29]. The dataset presented is in terms of intraocular pressure (IOP) ranges (known as Woolson dataset) with the differential privacy, applied at the minimum value of $e = 0.1$.

Conventionally, the approach of yielding the differential privacy is to create a tailored informational collection from an e-differentially private model for the information (typically from a differentially private histogram), or to augment the noise to compensate the estimations of the first records (most likely in mix with some earlier collected capacity of medical information from different sensors to decrease the measure of required changes). The proposed functional model has been developed to achieve this objective.

The data snap is given in Table 13.1 with intraocular pressure ranges, and for primary iteration, the cost of the initial privacy budget with $e = 0.1$. However, this data is addressed with machine-learning-driven DP.

Table 13.1   Intraocular pressure ranges with DP with a point of cost $e = \sim 0.121$ onwards.

Range	No. of Patients	No. of Patients with DP
08-09	01	~ 1.09
10-11	02	~ 0.34
12–13	17	~ 15.72
14-15	20	~ 18.68

13.3.4 Validation of Results

The event traces of process optimization in CP can be visualized with respect to different types of traces. Multiple underlying treatment patterns are also discussed in several studies [30, 31]. They are also the empirical elements of CP, e.g., number of patient traces, number of events, number of activity types n of comorbidity types (presence of one more additional disease with the primary disease), minimum length of stay (day) in the hospital, maximum length of stay and duration of present treatment plan. Therefore, a typical log has to be prepared and analyzed. This is shown as SER. SER is the ratio between the achieved summarization errors and the total event numbers in the log. The smaller SER indicates that more medical behaviors are covered by the derived summary, and better summarization quality is achieved

Considering the process optimization plan and clustering with the configuration of binary tree, the plot (see Figure 13.2) is linearly decreased with the increases of the number of input traces. The traces and tendency of the curve can be more precise, if more data for a specific disease are provided in addition to the ocular disease.

To demonstrate the efficiency of differential privacy under CP, the following use cases are considered (the assumption is the heterogeneous data sources from different sensors for medical records).

Case I: In the ideal case of information privacy in clinical pathway is the confirmation of privacy with follow-up process before finalizing the treatment policy. The ideal value could be ϵ.

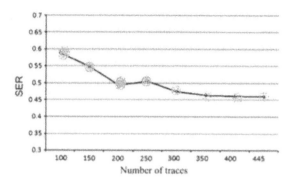

Figure 13.2 Optimized event trace from event log.

Case II: Considering the use case, when the recipient updated an existing model, it has the distributed model instances (like K as mentioned); however, it is unknown which instances (consisting of certain medical records) are augmented. Primarily, the value of dynamic instances are considered as $K = 2$: now we compute loss of privacy as ϵ:

$$exp(\epsilon) = \max_{R^1,R^2,P,P'} \frac{Pr[R^1,R^2|P]}{Pr[R^1,R^2|P']} \tag{13.4}$$

Hence, we consider a probability of modification in medical records over the random choice, after introducing the deliberate noise of Laplace followed by Gaussian. Therefore, properties of Laplace must demonstrate numerical differences when it is replaced by Gaussian noise in information content for validation through differential privacy.

Then, considering the instance value of $K = 2$,

$$exp(\epsilon) = \max_{R^1,R^2,P,P'} \frac{exp(-\frac{|R^1-R^2+\eta P|}{\frac{2\eta}{\epsilon}}) + exp(-\frac{|R^2-R^1+\eta P'|}{\frac{2\eta}{\epsilon}})}{exp(-\frac{|R^1-R^2+\eta P'|}{\frac{2\eta}{\epsilon}}) + exp(-\frac{|R^2-R^1+\eta P|}{\frac{2\eta}{\epsilon}})} \tag{13.5}$$

Numerically, a maximum value is obtained when $R^1 = R^2$ and $P' = -1$, $P = 0$ or $P' = 1$, $P = 0$.

Thus, $exp(\epsilon) = \frac{2}{2exp(-\frac{\epsilon}{2})}$ or modified $\epsilon = 0.5$ (previous value of ϵ).

Hence, initially, for $K = 2$, it is evident that expected privacy loss for unknown augmentation of medical record is 0.5 (previous value of privacy ϵ) + 0.5 (modified value of privacy ϵ) = 0.25 (value of ϵ as derived privacy).

Therefore, in the aggregation of the CP, the source point of CP must be modified.

Briefly, the high level description of aggregation is as follows. The justification for constructing a balanced binary tree for aggregation of information can also be explained towards the data collection points of CP.

Data collection for CP is across the different nodes and thus the source and recipient of changes are distinguished. Each recipient node (either the different patient's data) maintains a binary tree over stipulated time steps to track the changes of the corresponding states. The binary tree ensures that each change affects only $log_2 d$ nodes of the tree.

Percentage of stable and trusted CP, with return value (the number of CP's element being returned) equal to 3 and 5 for the dataset (Woolson dataset) and varying values of the privacy parameter ϵ. In both cases, high accuracy is achieved for a reasonable level of privacy (ϵ around 2). These results are averaged over 30 iterations.

Algorithm 13.2 High level description of information aggregation.

Input: for every t, report from the ith patient recipient.
Begin
      Create a balanced binary Tree T with d leaves;
      for $t \in [d]$ **do**
          for each level of tree divide t **do**
              Calculate T_{sum} for all the levels of patient report:
                $T_{sum}[level, t/2^{level-1}]$
              /* to collect all reports about all the changes from all levels and time t*/
          endfor
      endfor
end

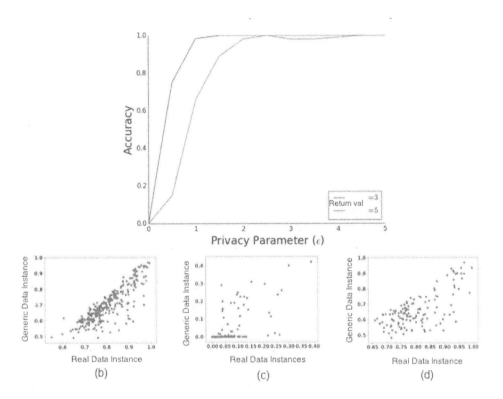

Figure 13.3   Accuracy with differential privacy value.

The highlight of the proposed algorithm demonstrates that, if no noise is added (Figure 13.3(a)), it implies the augmentation of medical records by adding one additional attribute, which may change the frequency of a certain disease in some extent. This change is especially significant when the number of people in the database is small or a group of people is changed. From Figure 13.3(b) and Figure 13.3(c) it is evident that deliberate noise was added. The observer is in a dilemma about augmenting additional attribute towards existing medical records, as the output becomes more uncertain and disperse (Figure 13.3(d) associated with a noise distribution). Thus, the generated data will hardly leak any patient's privacy information. This uncertainty will become broader when more noise is added, which indicates the higher value of ϵ from lower value to the highest value, irrespective of type of noise (e.g., Laplace or Gaussian).

13.4 Conclusion and Further Scope of Research

This chapter explored the scope of finding an optimal cluster (could be a Pareto-optimal) from state chart of clinical pathways. Following the optimal cluster of the state instance, a privacy protection mechanism (known as differential privacy) has been introduced, which is boosted by machine learning. Our proposal has been validated with a public data set. Until the chapter was written, no benchmark standard results were available towards finding an optimized state chart and privacy protected information. However, a few significant private or sensitive data, such as patient medical records, and the concentration of distribution may divulge critical patient information. During validation, it is observed that binary tree configuration can detect the optimal trace from medical log and, subsequently, two different use cases were discussed. The level of privacy budget (ϵ) is different for the two cases, which demonstrates the trusted CP cluster with respect to the accuracy. Finally, the dispersion of deliberate noise (with higher values ϵ) can also protect the medical information, once differential privacy ensures the privacy of data.

Health data sets are correlated and they possess natural constraints. Moreover, there are sufficient combinatorial processes. They could be in opposite trade-off. For example, one treatment would often precede another, or certain drugs can be prescribed in combination. There are certain correlations among drugs, and diagnoses (input from sensors), and between diagnostic center results and diagnoses itself, and even they may differ on the basis of the duration of the stay for the patients in hospital. In addition, the data collected from diversified and heterogeneous sensors also can improvise the effect of distortion in the medical data. Distortions to the data that produce results do not achieve the trusted data analysts in the data. This may act as barriers to the acceptability of the techniques, which are normally used to protect the privacy of the data. For example, if the distorted data demonstrates the two drugs that are known to interact in a damaging way to a patient's health, a drug that would never be prescribed with a particular treatment appears for the same patient, or a degree and dose that does not make a responsible treatment plan for a patient, then the analysts will cease to trust the data. In practice, this has created challenges for introducing mechanisms that add noise to data because it is not possible to guarantee that random and irrelevant data to yield appropriate output. We discovered that the health data also navigates through substantial ontology and this chapter initiates the idea to bridge the scope of optimized clusters and addition of the deliberate noise with privacy protection mechanism. Here, a boost to machine learning is given to propose a hybrid method of differential privacy. Differential privacy has been positioned as an emerging yet sound methodology, which can foster mathematical enhancement of the precision with respect to the privacy. The future work that could be explored is the alternative data release aspects with differential methods, such as embedded monitoring and broadcasting of e-health data [32-40].

Differential privacy could be the strongest privacy protection, which does not need any background information assumption of attackers. Therefore, more unsupervised approaches are expected. Hence, the improvement of the texture of hybridized architecture with the adjusted DP on the entire data mining system can be accomplished as a future extension of the work.

REFERENCES

1. Adeyemi, S., Demir, E., & Chaussalet, T. (2013). Towards an evidence-based decision making healthcare system management: Modelling patient pathways to improve clinical outcomes. *Decision Support Systems*, 55(1), 117-125.

2. Elghazel, H., Deslandres, V., Kallel, K., & Dussauchoy, A. (2007, October). Clinical pathway analysis using graph-based approach and markov models. In 2007 2nd International Conference on Digital Information Management (Vol. 1, pp. 279-284). IEEE.

3. Ciagli, E., Antonuzzo, L., Frosini, F., Cocchi, D., Regolini, J., Benassi, A., ... & Iadanza, E. (2017). Analysis and optimization of clinical pathway of a cancer patient in a University Hospital. In EMBEC & NBC 2017 (pp. 715-718). Springer, Singapore.

4. Dwork, C. (2011). Differential privacy. Encyclopedia of Cryptography and Security, 338-340.

5. Microsoft differential privacy for everyone. 2015. http://download.microsoft.com/.../ Differential_Privacy_for_Every one.pdf. Accessed 18 Dec 2017.

6. Machanavajjhala, A., He, X., & Hay, M. (2017, May). Differential privacy in the wild: A tutorial on current practices & open challenges. In Proceedings of the 2017 ACM International Conference on Management of Data (pp. 1727-1730). ACM.

7. Ye, Q., Hu, H., Meng, X., & Zheng, H. PrivKV: Key-Value Data Collection with Local Differential Privacy. In PrivKV: Key-Value Data Collection with Local Differential Privacy (p. 0). IEEE. DOI: 10.1109/SP.2019.00018

8. Jones, A., Leahy, K., & Hale, M. (2018). Towards Differential Privacy for Symbolic Systems. arXiv preprint arXiv:1809.08634.

9. Pihur, V., Korolova, A., Liu, F., Sankuratripati, S., Yung, M., Huang, D., & Zeng, R. (2018). Differentially-Private" Draw and Discard" Machine Learning. arXiv preprint arXiv:1807.04369.

10. Avent, B., Korolova, A., Zeber, D., Hovden, T., & Livshits, B. (2017). BLENDER: Enabling Local Search with a Hybrid Differential Privacy Model. In 26th USENIX Security Symposium (USENIX Security 17) (pp. 747-764).

11. Jordon, J., Yoon, J., & van der Schaar, M. (2018). PATE-GAN: Generating Synthetic Data with Differential Privacy Guarantees.

12. Le, D. N., Van Le, C., Tromp, J. G., & Nguyen, G. N. (Eds.). (2018). Emerging Technologies for Health and Medicine: Virtual Reality, Augmented Reality, Artificial Intelligence, Internet of Things, Robotics, Industry 4.0. John Wiley & Sons.

13. Gao, W., & Zhu, L. (2014). Gradient learning algorithms for ontology computing. *Computational Intelligence and Neuroscience*, 2014, 24.

14. Cavallari, R., Martelli, F., Rosini, R., Buratti, C., & Verdone, R. (2014). A survey on wireless body area networks: Technologies and design challenges. *IEEE Communications Surveys & Tutorials*, 16(3), 1635-1657.

15. Liu, B., Yan, Z., & Chen, C. W. (2013). MAC protocol in wireless body area networks for E-health: Challenges and a context-aware design. *IEEE Wireless Communications*, 20(4), 64-72.

16. De Bleser, L., Depreitere, R., WAELE, K. D., Vanhaecht, K., Vlayen, J., & Sermeus, W. (2006). Defining pathways. *Journal of nursing management*, 14(7), 553-563.

17. Dankar, F. K., & El Emam, K. (2013). Practicing differential privacy in health care: A review. *Trans. Data Privacy*, 6(1), 35-67.

18. Rotter, T., Kinsman, L., James, E. L., Machotta, A., Gothe, H., Willis, J., ... & Kugler, J. (2010). Clinical pathways: effects on professional practice, patient outcomes, length of stay and hospital costs. *Cochrane database of systematic reviews*, (3).

19. Song, L., & Guo, X. (2015, August). Research on Optimization of clinical Pathway Execution based on Multi-agent Simulation. In 2015 International Conference on Modeling, Simulation and Applied Mathematics. Atlantis Press.

20. Farooq, K., & Hussain, A. (2016). A novel ontology and machine learning driven hybrid cardiovascular clinical prognosis as a complex adaptive clinical system. *Complex Adaptive Systems Modeling*, 4(1), 12.

21. Allen, J. F. (1990). Maintaining knowledge about temporal intervals. In Readings in qualitative reasoning about physical systems (pp. 361-372). Morgan Kaufmann.

22. Bhatt, C., Dey, N., & Ashour, A. S. (Eds.). (2017). *Internet of things and big data technologies for next generation healthcare.*

23. Thuemmler, C., & Bai, C. (Eds.). (2017). *Health 4.0: How virtualization and big data are revolutionizing healthcare.* New York, NY: Springer.

24. Van der Aalst, W., Weijters, T., & Maruster, L. (2004). Workflow mining: Discovering process models from event logs. *IEEE Transactions on Knowledge and Data Engineering*, 16(9), 1128-1142.

25. Gnther, C. W., & Van Der Aalst, W. M. (2007, September). Fuzzy mining-adaptive process simplification based on multi-perspective metrics. In International conference on business process management (pp. 328-343). Springer, Berlin, Heidelberg.

26. Jothi, N., & Husain, W. (2015). Data mining in healthcare-a review. *Procedia Computer Science*, 72, 306-313.

27. Lee DG-Y (2008). Protecting patient data con mentality using differential privacy. Scholar Archive. chapter 3, 92.

28. Han, S., Zhao, S., Li, Q., Ju, C. H., & Zhou, W. (2016). PPM-HDA: privacy-preserving and multifunctional health data aggregation with fault tolerance. *IEEE Transactions on Information Forensics and Security*, 11(9), 1940-1955.

29. Huang, Z., Dong, W., Bath, P., Ji, L., & Duan, H. (2015). On mining latent treatment patterns from electronic medical records. *Data mining and knowledge discovery*, 29(4), 914-949.

30. Huang, Z., Lu, X., & Duan, H. (2013). Latent treatment pattern discovery for clinical processes. *Journal of medical systems*, 37(2), 9915.

31. Li, H., Dai, Y., & Lin, X. (2015, October). Efficient e-health data release with consistency guarantee under differential privacy. In 2015 17th International Conference on E-health Networking, Application & Services (HealthCom) (pp. 602-608). IEEE.

32. McSherry, F. D. (2009, June). Privacy integrated queries: an extensible platform for privacy-preserving data analysis. In Proceedings of the 2009 ACM SIGMOD International Conference on Management of data (pp. 19-30). ACM.

33. Le, D. N., Van Le, C., Tromp, J. G., & Nguyen, G. N. (Eds.). (2018). *Emerging Technologies for Health and Medicine: Virtual Reality, Augmented Reality, Artificial Intelligence, Internet of Things, Robotics, Industry 4.0.* John Wiley & Sons.

34. Li, N., Qardaji, W., Su, D., & Cao, J. (2012). Privbasis: Frequent itemset mining with differential privacy. Proceedings of the VLDB Endowment, 5(11), 1340-1351.

35. Grandi, F., Mandreoli, F., & Martoglia, R. (2019). Towards Patient-Centric Healthcare: Multi-Version Ontology-Based Personalization of Clinical Guidelines. In Semantic Web Science and Real-World Applications (pp. 273-301). IGI Global.

36. Shoaip, N., El-Sappagh, S., Barakat, S., & Elmogy, M. (2019). Ontology enhanced fuzzy clinical decision support system. In U-Healthcare Monitoring Systems (pp. 147-177). Academic Press.

37. Kasmire, K. E., Hoppa, E. C., Patel, P. P., Boch, K. N., Sacco, T., & Waynik, I. Y. (2019). Reducing Invasive Care for Low-risk Febrile Infants Through Implementation of a Clinical Pathway. Pediatrics, 143(3), e20181610.

38. De Medeiros, A. A., Weijters, A. J. M. M., & Van der Aalst, W. M. (2005, September). Genetic process mining: A basic approach and its challenges. In International Conference on Business Process Management (pp. 203-215). Springer, Berlin, Heidelberg.

39. Puar, V. H., Bhatt, C. M., Hoang, D. M., & Le, D. N. (2018). Communication in Internet of Things. In Information Systems Design and Intelligent Applications (pp. 272-281). Springer, Singapore.

40. Prodel, M. (2017). Process discovery, analysis and simulation of clinical pathways using health-care data (Doctoral dissertation, Universit de Lyon).

CHAPTER 14

ADVANCEMENTS AND APPLICATIONS IN FOG COMPUTING

Sumit Bansal[1], Mayank Aggarwal[2], Himanshu Aggarwal[1]

[1] Department of Computer Science and Engineering, Punjabi University, Patiala, India
[2] Department of Computer Science and Engineering, Gurukul Kangri University, Haridwar, India
 Email: research_sumit@yahoo.com, mayank@gkv.ac.in, himanshu@pbi.ac.in

Abstract
Cloud computing is the technology for on-demand distribution of services, like computation power, storage, applications, etc., by means of the Internet of Things (IoT), which is a set of interconnected things via the internet that has the ability to assess, act and communicate with the world. Fog computing is the modified version of the existing structure which promotes the data handling at the edges of the network instead of handling everything at the cloud level. It thereby reduces the large amount of data sent to the cloud by processing the collected data at fog devices. Fog computing is a limited researched area with wide applicability. For the application of fog computing in the existing infrastructure, edge devices are used to convert cloud computing into fog computing. An edge device is a smart self-controlled device with high computability which could be managed by the cloud decision makers. A few examples of edge devices are smart plugs, smart refrigerators, Libelium devices, smartphones, etc. For latency reduction via fog computing, actuators are used. Actuators are devices which can complete works mechanically without human intervention. Fog computing is also helped by smart detection, which is performed by internet connected devices known as ICOs. ICOs are devices which accumulate functional data with the help of various technologies and transfer it to other devices. Large-scale research is possible in the field of fog computing. Fog computing is useful because it helps to reduce the latency security threats. It reduces dependency on the cloud to process the data, as fog computing uses local networks which are more reliable. Fog computing can be used

in various future vision projects like smart homes, smart agriculture, smart transportation, smart waste management, smart rail, smart healthcare, etc.

Keywords: Internet of Things (IoT), ICO, edge device, actuator, Gateway, Fog nodes

14.1 Introduction

14.1.1 Cloud Computing

Cloud computing is the technology for on-demand distribution of services like computation power, storage, applications, etc., by means of a cloud platform via the internet with different payment methods [1, 2]. IBM introduced the concept of cloud computing, which gives ubiquitous access to the data and many other services with pay-per-use method. It provides computational power, storage, processors, development platforms, etc., for different scientific experiments, sports, medical sciences, education, business, agriculture, etc. The National Institute of Standards and Technology (NIST) termed cloud computing as a pattern of using and configuring resources as per the needs of the clients; and explained its architecture with five characteristics, three service models, and four deployment models, as shown in Figure 14.1.

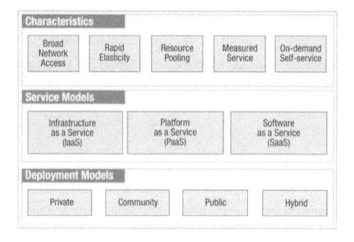

Figure 14.1 Visual model of cloud computing.

14.1.2 Internet of Things

The Internet of Things (IoT) is defined as the set of interconnected things that are connected via the internet and which has the ability to assess, act and communicate with the world [3, 4]. The main focus of IoT is to sense, understand, process and act, which makes daily life easier by making it convenient to use things in an effortless manner. It forms the basic infrastructure of any computing system as well as functions as the method of communication for the transportation of data. It can be used with the fog and other computing systems as well as can be applied for communication purposes because it can integrate both local as well as wide area networks. For example, a smart home could be fitted with a number of smart appliances connected to the internet. These appliances can be controlled from distant locations; from office, gym, even from other countries, etc.

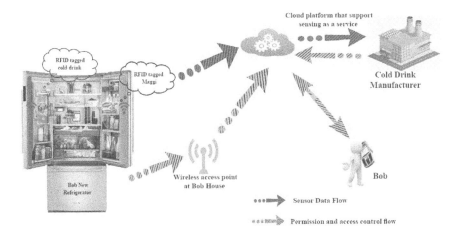

Figure 14.2   Smart devices connected to remote locations via IoT.

14.1.3 Fog Computing

Fog computing is a distributed or scattered computing infrastructure where data, computation power, storage and applications are divided into perhaps the most reasonable, well-organized place between the information source and the cloud. It is known as fog networking or fog computing or fogging. Fog computing promotes handling the data at the edges of a network instead of handling everything at the level of cloud as suggested by cloud computing; hence, fog computing is ideally an extension of cloud computing. This idea of processing the data at the level of edges or fog nodes is known as edge analytics. The target of fogging is to process data so that the amount of data to be sent to cloud could be reduced and efficiency could be enhanced for processing, analysis, and storage at cloud level [5-8].

In this computing system, the sensors located at the end user or client end of the communication collects the data according to the capacity provided to them and can even collect multiple types of data at the same time due to their increased capacity and smartness. These sensors then send this data to the fog device located near the sensor by use of a local network or communication methods or can process it themselves into the information on the basis of their computability. This data or information collected by the fog device then is processed further to compress and reduce the amount of data to be sent to the next level. This processed information is then sent to the cloud platform via the internet and is a lot less in amount and not nearly as good in quality because it is not the raw data which needs to be processed to generate the information. The cloud platform further processes or analyzes the collected data and takes the necessary action required to fulfill the task. These actions then revert back to the fog devices by means of the internet in the form of commands which are understood by the fog device due to the capability provided to them by means of computability power. After this, it forwards the commands to the action devices known as actuators for the mechanical action, if involved in the process, or to the sensors in the form of positive or negative response of the data collected and sent by them. It also can provide commands to stop or modify the functioning of the sensors. Hence, in this system the intermediate role is played by the fog devices, which reduce workload by load balancing of the cloud and have many more benefits in comparison to the previous computing systems like cloud computing.

Fog computing is a new field of research where only limited research has been done till date, and a large potential is hidden for further discovery of its benefits for humankind. Many scientists have tried to increase the availability of the research material by applying this technology to the simulation-based studies and analyzing the results obtained from them. These were then extrapolated to the real-life scenarios to decide whether they could be functional in a real-life situation or not [9]. Although there may be limitations to its uses due to its higher cost or other challenges due to the unavailability of adequate research in this field, it can be easily explored if proper planning and management is done for the research. It can play a huge and important role in the future in various fields due to its sustainable and stable infrastructure (see Figure 14.3).

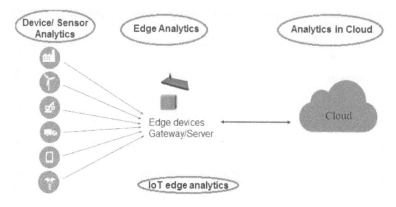

Figure 14.3   IoT edge analytics.

14.2   Fog Computing Architecture

14.2.1   Features of Fog Computing

Fog computing stores nearly all of the data near the edge of the network within the fog nodes provided in the fog infrastructure instead of transporting or sending all of the data to cloud, which reduces the storage problem faced at the level of the cloud platforms due to reckless transmission of raw data being sent to them. This storage crisis due to the raw data gets reduced and can be further reduced by introduction of intermediate level computability devices within the system [8-10].

Fog computing includes the use of local area networks and other local methods of communication instead of using main networks (e.g., internet) to send data to fog nodes or edge devices from the smart sensors, so they can keep working even in cases of failure of main networks with minimal loss of data and information. Furthermore, the important decisions could be taken at the level of the fog nodes only, which prevents huge financial losses and reduces the inconvenience caused to the consumers.

Instead of using cloud computing infrastructure, fog computing uses edge devices (e.g., leaf nodes) to process large amounts of data, which is sometimes referred to as "big data." This data is processed into information at the fog nodes or edge devices because of the computability residing within the edge devices. This processed information reduces the high amount of raw data into compact and useful information and solves the problems caused due to high data transmission.

An edge device is a self-controlled device having high computational ability. It differs from fog devices very little, which is due to the greater computability provided to the edge device compared to that of the fog device. It is not completely self-controlled but plays a major role in decision making in the absence of commands from the cloud platform. It is said that these devices are managed rather than controlled via cloud decision makers because of the computational ability available with them, which helps them analyze the processed information or even raw data. These devices get their responses and commands from the cloud decision makers, which reduce their work and increase their efficiency.

This computing has a unique feature of being located close to the end users or clients who are generating the requirements, which makes it understand their objectives better than the traditional computing systems which are usually located far away from the end users. This feature helps it recognize the context awareness of the user's demands and generates the request accordingly by keeping in mind the context of the task. Therefore, it increases the quality of service provided to the user in comparison to the traditional computing systems.

Latency reduction is a big favor done by fog computing, which also makes it superior to the traditional computing systems like cloud computing. It occurs in the fog computing due to the application of the fog devices in the system which makes processing easier and shorter and reduces the time consumed, resulting in an early and better response production which works in favor of excellent quality of service (QoS) being provided to the client. As compared to cloud or other computing systems, a large amount of time could be saved by application of the fog devices.

14.2.2   Architecture of Fog Computing

Fog computing denotes a form of infrastructure that employs few or many end-user edge devices to process a substantial amount of data storage (instead of storing the data directly in cloud storehouse), communication control (instead of sending to cloud), assortment, quantification and management (instead of commanding via network gateways) [11-13]. The fog computing architecture is shown in Figure 14.4.

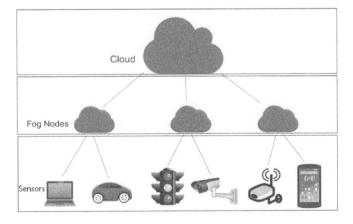

Figure 14.4   Fog computing architecture.

This computing system represents a notion that promotes and assists the transportation of data, storage of data, processing and analysis of leaves (i.e., edge nodes), hence reducing the workload on the cloud decision makers. But this doesn't imply that complete functioning and entire analysis is done on edges; instead, it encourages the use of fog nodes maximally possible within the restrictions of reality, so as to also keep a check on the cloud load. It also keeps a check on the power provided to the edge devices so they do not get enough computability to match that of cloud and its cost and other factors are kept under control. It also has the proximity to users to enhance better understanding of the client requirements and reply in the required manner as per the request specifications by getting known to the context awareness of the request. It works by collecting the available multiple nodes to work in a collaborative manner for building a good and efficient system adequate for an early and better response.

14.2.2.1 Sensors

The sensors located at the end user or client end of the communication collects the data according to the capacity provided to them and can even collect multiple types of data at the same time due to their increased capacity and smartness. Nowdays, smart sensors are being used which can follow multiple types of commands which a traditional sensors system could not follow. They could record more than one type of data, like fingerprint, motion detector and iris scanner, which can perform all three functions in one device and even send the data on demand rather than pushing data all the time to the next level of communication.

14.2.2.2 Fog Device

The sensors then send this data to the fog device located near the sensor by use of local network or communication methods or can process it themselves into the information on the basis of their computability. This data or information collected by the fog device is then processed further to compress and reduce the amount of data to be sent to the next level. Edge devices can also be used in the same context as that of the fog device, the only difference being the higher computability power in the edge device as compared to fog device.

14.2.2.3 Cloud Platform

The processed information is then sent to the cloud platform via use of the internet and is a lot less in amount and not nearly as good in quality because it is not the raw data which needs to be processed to generate the information. The cloud platform further processes or analyzes the collected data and takes the necessary action required to fulfill the task. These actions then revert back to the fog devices by means of the internet in the form of commands to fulfill the requests and the necessary tasks for them.

Fog networking is a two-layered structure which consists of two planes:

- *Control Plane*: Arrangement of network and its management is controlled by control plane.

- *Data Plane*: It is responsible for transferring the data from its origin to its destination.

14.2.3 Components of Fog Computing

14.2.3.1 Edge Devices

These are small devices which can perform functions of a fog node on an IoT platform and can even perform analysis at the edges in the fog computing setup because they have their own computability power, which is less than that of cloud but more than that of a fog node. The analysis done at the edge device is known as edge analytics [14]. Due to their higher computability, these devices can also take actions on their own in cases of emergencies, etc., when necessary. Some of the edge devices are smart power plugs, smartphones, smart watches, smart water bottles, smart refrigerators, Libelium sensors, etc. Examples of their application are shown in Figure 14.5 below.

Event Sensor Node   Smart Plug   Smart Watch   Smart Bottle   Smart Mobile   Smart Fridge   Smart A.C

Figure 14.5   Several different types of edge devices.

A smart watch can avoid sending unnecessary data to the cloud by withholding daily information and not pushing data all the time to cloud and can process the collected data within itself because of the low computing capability provided to the device. By this, the total data generation and communication to the cloud can be reduced because of the intermediate link provided in the fog computing infrastructure for an edge device.

Similar examples can be used in an infinite number of fields by use of fog computing structure, which would ease the burden on the clouds usually placed on the cloud computing structure.

14.2.3.2 *Actuators*

Actuators are the devices which actually perform the action when given a command by a source by various physical means like using mechanical and hydraulic methods, etc. These are the ground level devices which complete the tasks in reality. Actuators play a very important role in fog computing as well as in IoT because they can complete actions mechanically without human intervention; hence, they can reduce the risk to human beings because they are not controlled manually. Actuators can work with various sensors and fog devices and are used to complete automatic actions after receiving commands from the fog devices. An example describing their function is given below [15, 16].

In smart agriculture, portable sheds are made in which the crops can be turned over in cases of heavy rains to minimize the damage from it. These sheds are fitted with mechanical motors which can roll and unroll the shed when turned off and on respectively. These mechanical devices are the actuators which are connected to fog devices located nearby, which when rain is detected above a certain level gives commands to these actuators to unroll. This command could also be given by cloud platform directly or via fog devices after the analysis of the information sent from the fog device. These mechanical devices could also be given commands by cloud system by bypassing the fog device in cases of failure.

14.2.3.3 *Classification*

On the basis of direction of motion:

- Non-Linear Actuators

- Linear Actuators

On the basis of working mechanism:

- Piezoelectric Actuators

- Hydraulic Actuators

- Mechanical Actuators

- Pneumatic Actuators

14.3 Communication in Fog Computing

14.3.1 Communication Steps

For the proper functioning of fog computing, communication connections are required at various steps (see Figure 14.6) [17, 18], which are as follows:

- Internet Connected Objects (ICOs) are linked to Gateway Devices.

- Gateway Devices need to be linked to Cloud Platform.

Figure 14.6   Connectivity between ICOs, gateway device and cloud platform.

14.3.2 Discovery and Detection of ICOs

For establishing configuration and connection in an IoT platform, a few steps are to be followed:

- Corresponding fog gateway must be linked to ICOs. For this to happen, both devices must agree to a common linking protocol.

- Next, fog gateways get introduced to the ICOs by specific description given by them about themselves (e.g., sensor ID, etc.).

- Then, by using that information fog gateways configure themselves to the IoT platform.

- Then, after the configuration is done, IoT cloud platform prepares to receive data from the fog gateway and then sends back the relevant commands to the ICOs via fog gateways or directly.

A connection is established between an ICO and a gateway device via discovery or detection of one of the devices and the functioning open network in the other corresponding device, and is used as a basic method for building a fog computing network in the given real-life application (see Figure 14.7).

- 1st Method: In this method, Gateway devices are discoverable which are waiting passively for connection and are searched by the ICOs which remain open continuously to get detected.

Figure 14.7   ICO detection and discovery.

- 2nd Method: In this method, ICOs are discoverable which are waiting passively for connection and are searched by the Gateway devices which remain open continuously to recognize the corresponding counterparts.

Short-range communication protocols like Bluetooth or Wi-Fi connection may be used in both of the above methods of connectivity between ICOs and Gateway Device. Their usage provides an edge over long-distance networks because they can work even in the absence of internet connectivity and do not get interrupted with failure of long-distance connection. The functioning of the remaining network is ensured by its usage for communication, which is a feature in fog computing and not available in traditional computing systems.

14.3.3 Models of Communication

There are three models of communication (Figure 14.8), which are given below:

- Device to Device (D2D)

- Server to Server (S2S)

- Device to Server (D2S)

Figure 14.8   Models of communication.

The device-to-server method of communication is the most widely used model of communication in establishment of connection between the gateway device and cloud platform where the fog device acts as device and cloud platform acts as server. Other models of communication like server to server and device to device are used in other forms of communication in the fog computing and are used less in the gateway device and cloud platform connection.

14.3.4 Communication Protocols

Fog computing domain uses various communication protocols for connectivity between their components for data transfer such as Wi-Fi, Bluetooth, Bluetooth Smart, Zigbee, ANT, Z-Wave, 6LowPAN, Thread, Cellular (GSM/HSPA), WiMAX, RFID, NFC, etc.

14.3.5 Communication Protocol Requirements

There is absence of an accepted protocol which could be applied to smart city domains on a wide scale because it must support a variety of requirements [18-20]. Some of the requirements are mentioned below:

- Recording events every time they happen

- Sending information from one to many

- Small packets of data are to be dispatched in huge volumes

- Push information over unreliable networks

- High sensitivity to energy consumption

- Security and privacy

- High sensitivity to responsiveness

- Scalability

14.3.6 Methods of Data Collection

Data collection is the backbone of any computing system as it forms the basic requirement for any of the functions further performed. An efficient data collection system is a requirement for the proper functioning of the computing system. It can be in the form of raw data collection which is done by the sensors at the lowest level of the hierarchy of the computing system. The collected raw data can either be sent directly to the cloud platform as done in the cloud computing or it can first be in the form of information by the intermediate devices known as fog devices. This processed information can now be pushed forward for further analysis by a higher computability power device. Data collection can be done directly in the form of information instead of raw data by the use of smart sensors as used in the newest technology of fog computing [21-15].

A faulty data collection technique can result in huge misfortunes; hence, maintaining a good data collection technique is very much essential for the efficient functioning and correct response generation by the computing system. A few of the classifications of data collection are given below.

14.3.6.1 Based on Responsibility

On the basis of the responsibility of data collection, the data could be collected by gateway devices or fog devices from sensors via two main approaches:

Figure 14.9 Pull Technique (a) from internet connected object to gateway device; (b) from gateway device to cloud platform.

- Pull Approach: Using this technique, fog gateways collect data from ICOs by giving the command or requesting the ICO for the transfer of data over the network which is connecting them both (see Figure 14.9). Also, the same technique can be used by IoT cloud platforms to obtain data from fog gateways by giving commands to the fog devices to send data to them for further analysis. The pulling component of the connection provides the network for the data collection from its other counterpart. This can be done as an on-demand method or as a fixed time period approach.

- Push Approach: Using this technique the ICOs can forward data to fog gateways by forwarding the request to the gateway device for the transfer of data over the network which is connecting them both (see Figure 14.10). Also, the same technique can be used by fog gateways to forward data to cloud platform. The pushing component uses the network provided from the other counterpart and pushes data over.

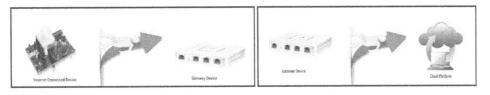

Figure 14.10   Push Technique (a) from internet connected object to gateway device; (b) from gateway device to cloud platform.

14.3.6.2 Based on Frequency
On the basis of the number of times data needs to be collected from the location, two main approaches are generally used [26-30]. These are based on the frequency of data collection fixed after a certain period of time to make it an efficient system of data collection. The two commonly used approaches are:

- Instant Approach (also referred to as Threshold Violation): In this approach, only when an event happens or gets triggered is the data transferred to the next destination decided by the hierarchy of the computing system. Sensors can also trigger an event by themselves (e.g., sensor detects a motion, temperature touching a certain number) for collection of data but is to be programmed beforehand to get triggered or to trigger it. This approach may be combined with any of the other data collection techniques, like push or pull techniques, or both can even be used simultaneously. However, when an event occurs automatically, then ICO can only send data via using push technique. Also, a fog gateway can get data or the collected information by questioning its ICOs about the event using the pull approach.

- Interval Approach (also referred to as Periodically): In this approach, the sensor is programmed beforehand to trigger an event after a certain period of time, or periodically, and when the event gets triggered by time set by the programming (Periodically), then data is sent to the next level of destination for further processing. This approach may be combined with any of the other data collection techniques, like push or pull techniques, or both can even be used simultaneously. For example, an ICO can be designed in such a way that it detects and forwards data after a specific time period (like 20 seconds) whereas, on the other hand, a fog gateway can be designed in such a way that it asks for information from the linked ICOs after the lapse of a specific time period (like 20 seconds).

14.4   Application or Programming Models

An application or programming model is the graphical or structural representation of the system which describes how a system will be executed in a real-life or simulator scenario. It basically represents how the architecture designed for the computing system will be executing its functions when applied to function in the application. DDF (distributed data flow) is the model which is used by the most programming models for the development of fog computing model [31-35]. The architecture of fog computing generally uses the two basic models given below.

14.4.1   Sense-Process-Actuate Model

In this model, a three-step approach is used for the completion of request via sense, process and actuate, as suggested by the name of the model. Data accumulated by the sensors is sent to a fog device located near the sensor using a local network or communication methods. After receiving the data, the fog device processes the data via the applications working on them, which is present due to the computability power provided to them in this hierarchy of computing system. The data is converted to information and then is analyzed in the fog device itself. After analysis, the decision for the command is taken by the fog device and these commands are then given to the actuators via the connecting local network between the fog device and actuator to complete the task because actuators are the devices that complete the function mechanically after taking commands.

This type of model is used in situations where the decision making does not require high computability power or analyzing capacity within the fog device and requests are fulfilled on a small scale. It can also be used in emergencies when there is not enough time to push the information to the cloud platform or wait for the result, and a result is required immediately. Similarly, in situations like failure of communication or transmission over long distance due to technical faults, this model can prevent reliability over the cloud platforms and can complete decision making on its own (see Figure 14.11).

Internet Connected Object   Gateway Device   Actuator

Figure 14.11   Sense-process-actuate model.

14.4.2   Stream Processing Model

In this model, a three or more-step approach (depending on number of intermediates between sensor and cloud platform) is used for the completion of a request via sense, process and forward (stream), as suggested by the name of the model (see Figure 14.12). Data accumulated by the sensors is sent to a fog device located near the sensor via local network or communication methods. After receiving the data, the fog device processes the data via the applications working on it, which is present due to the computability power provided to them in this hierarchy of computing system. The data is converted to information and then the data is sent from the fog devices to the cloud platforms. Data collected via the data streams sent by the fog devices is stored in cloud storehouses in the form of processed information which can be used by cloud decision makers for global analytics to be done in the future whenever necessary. This type of model is used where there is no necessity for immediate decision making. The data or the information is collected to complete the analysis for future planning [36-40]. This model is beneficial because of less data formation due to multilevel processing of data into information and compactness of stored data, which occupies much less space in the global cloud storehouses as compared to storage of large amounts of raw data in cloud computing infrastructure. It makes the system more efficient, and reduces the latency in analysis of data.

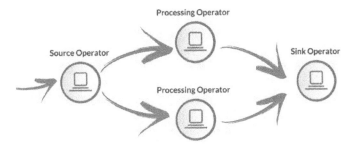

Figure 14.12   Stream processing model.

14.4.3   Benefits of Fog over Cloud Computing

Fog computing decreases the amount of so-called "big data" to a lesser amount of information by converting raw data into a compact form of information at the level of edge devices; whereas, at the same time, there is a large amount of data generation occurring in the cloud computing which is being sent to the cloud unprocessed in large volumes. This occurs due to the high computability power provided to the edge devices, which are capable of performing data analytics consisting of compressing data, deleting unnecessary data, etc. It also reduces data by filtering the unnecessary data out of the equation. Intelligent sensing is another way to reduce data which is performed on the basis of previous knowledge and intelligence collected by the device by the experience of the older working schemes. It manifests itself by sensing and collecting only useful data and discarding the additional wasteful data even at the level of sensors with the help of smart sensors [41-45].

Another benefit of fog computing is less latency, which makes it superior to the traditional computing systems like cloud computing. It occurs in fog computing due to the application of fog devices in the system, which makes processing easier and faster, resulting in early as well as better response production which improves the quality of service (QoS) provided to the client. As compared to cloud or other computing systems, a large amount of time can be saved by the application of fog devices.

Higher availability is also a feature seen in fog computing. It is due to the fact that fog computing reduces the overreliance of computing systems on the cloud platforms which differs from the cloud computing system where the system is entirely dependent on cloud decision makers. Also, connecting to cloud platform can be less reliable at times because of a number of different connectivity issues. So, even after the connection is lost with the cloud, the edge devices can perform analysis uninterruptedly at their level due to the fact that they are made self-reliable to perform small functions by giving computability power to them also.

Security is another benefit which is more precisely given by the fog computing over the cloud computing. Security can be ensured by encrypting the data at the source itself with the help of intelligent edge devices fitted within the sensors and cloud platform which prevent data leakage or theft during the course of transmission over to the cloud server, which is always the risk faced by the cloud computing system. Also, raw data is processed at the level of edge devices, which produces fewer security concerns due to the compactness of data in information systems, thereby not exposing the raw data to data thieves. Also, there will be fewer security threats based on the communication because of fewer data transfers.

As the edge devices are located near the end user, more information can be collected about the local setting and requirements, more precisely known as context awareness, which helps them understand their objectives better than the traditional computing systems which are usually located far away from the end users. This feature helps them recognize the context awareness of the user's demands and generate the request accordingly by keeping in mind the context of the task. Therefore, they increase the quality of service provided to the user in comparison to the traditional computing systems.

The concept of mobility can be applied to control a large number of ICOs with the help of only a few gateway devices. It would help in covering a large geographical area with only a few gateway devices. In this technique, fog gateway devices would be programmed beforehand to move along a predetermined path so as to cover all the allotted ICOs to the gateway device in the setting. Connections with the ICOs are periodically made via the use of connecting techniques discussed above for a limited period of time as the gateway device is moving. After the connection is made, data is transferred via various data collecting techniques to the gateway device. After data collection is over, the gateway device moves forward to the next ICO for the same process. In this way it can cover a large number of ICOs repeatedly during the course of the day, collecting data several times as compared to the system which can collect data from only a single ICO, as seen in other computing systems. This decreases the cost for the gateway devices as well as maximally utilizes the available resources to reduce the waste of resources.

14.4.4 Simulator Tool

Upon examining the architecture of fog computing and its benefits over cloud computing, a few limitations were detected regarding the application of fog computing in real-life scenarios.

For the purpose of accessing the infrastructure of fog computing before its application in a real-life scenario, a simulator tool is introduced [23] so as to check the competency of fog computing in the simulation before testing it in real-life scenarios. This simulator tool is known as iFogSim. A simulator tool is a device which allows usage and testing of a new system developed in controlled and manually generated environment before its actual usage at the final stage. It creates a similar environment to that of the real-life condition beforehand so that data could be collected about its functionality and can be analyzed properly to reduce future disastrous consequences in cases of system failure. The results generated in the simulation can be extrapolated to the real-life conditions and can also be analyzed for the limitations posed by the system in the simulation. That is why the simulator tool and simulation studies can be really beneficial in this field.

14.4.4.1 Functions of iFogSim

iFogSim[1] is a simulator software purposed to represent the miniature version of IoT (internet of things) and fog computing in the virtual environment for the assessment of influence of resource management methods on the basis of various parameters like latency, network congestion, energy usage and cost [44]. It simulates the components of fog computing like cloud data center, edge devices and network links to evaluate performance statistics. It was introduced as the sense-process-actuate model. iFogSim is evaluated on the basis of memory usage and simulation accomplishment time.

Also, there were a few case studies done to demonstrate working of IoT and fog environment models and to draw comparisons to that of the already existing systems and various resource management strategies to prepare a foolproof system before its actual application in real-life conditions.

iFogSim is cost effective because it is only a small-scale experiment and does not involve large-scale sampling. The outcomes of the simulation study can give ideas and approximate values about the real-time scenario but it has to be kept in mind that all the simulation studies and their results cannot be simply generalized at large-scale due to smaller sample size usage in the simulation. The problems faced during the actual implementation cannot be fully assessed on iFogSim due to lack of full extrapolation from the real systems.

14.4.4.2 Advantages and Disadvantages of iFogSim

The advantages of iFogSim are:

- The technical flaws in the concept of fog computing can be analyzed beforehand to avoid applying them to present computing infrastructure.

- Various fog computing infrastructures can be assessed on this tool to rule out their defects before their application in the real-time environment.

- As it is only a simulator tool, there is less risk involved in management of real-time data because the disadvantages of fog computing are not fully explored.

- Assessment of the values to be seen and problems to be faced in real-time application can be detected in advance.

The disadvantages of iFogSim are:

- The simulation studies and their results cannot simply be generalized over a large scale due to smaller sample size usage in the simulation.

- The problems which would be faced during the actual implementation cannot be fully assessed on the simulator tool.

- There is lack of full extrapolation from the real systems due to unavailability of higher technologies required for it.

14.5 Simulation-Based Experiments

In their research, Dsouza and Ahn used fog computing in healthcare to manage the data of patients to monitor their vital signs [15]. Fog computing can be used to manage the workload of doctors and reduce the human errors caused due to negligence or the work overload

---

[1] https://opensourceforu.com

of doctors. In this scenario, different patients' sensors are connected with the smart sensors. These sensors could sense all the data values (e.g., electromyography (EMG), blood pressure, electrocardiogram (EKG), glucose level, electroencephalogram (EEG) and respiration rate, etc.) of a patient within a single sensor.

A fog device is placed near the patient if sensors are present in a remote location or it could be placed in the office of the doctor to decrease response time, latency and network bandwidth.

Figure 14.13 shows the calculated value of network usage time for a different number of user requests launched by heart patients using both cloud- and fog-based environment. It shows that the value of network usage time is less in fog-based as compared to cloud-based environments because fog environment reduces the user requests coming towards cloud. Fog reduces 22.61-26.78% average network usage time as compared to cloud.

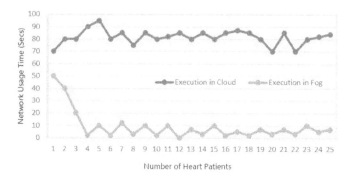

Figure 14.13   Network usage time vs. number of patients.

Figure 14.14 shows the comparison of latency for fog and cloud with a different number of user requests launched by heart patients. Fog performs better than cloud in terms of latency. Fog reduces 19.56-29.45% average latency as compared to cloud.

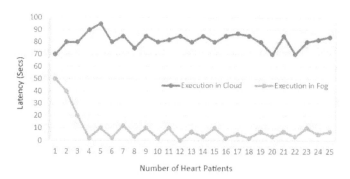

Figure 14.14   Latency time vs. number of patients.

Figure 14.15 describes the consumption of energy for fog and cloud environment used to process a different number of user requests launched by heart patients, showing that cloud consumes more energy than fog for the same number of user requests. The value of energy consumption in fog is 33.45% less than cloud at 33 number of user requests while 8.25% less than cloud at 20 number of user requests. Fog reduces 23.56% average energy consumption as compared to cloud.

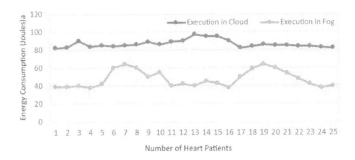

Figure 14.15   Energy consumption vs. number of heart patients.

Figure 14.16 presents the comparison of two different types of environments (cloud and fog computing) based on three parameters: network usage time, energy consumption and latency.

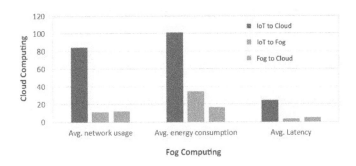

Figure 14.16   Comparison of performance parameters for two different environments.

Example 2: This simulation case study of a latency-sensitive online game is provided by Harshit Gupta *et al.* [43], namely a latency-sensitive online game.

Case Study: *A Latency-Sensitive Online Game*

In this case study the latency-critical application is a human vs. human game (EEG Tractor Beam game) in that it involves augmented brain-computer interaction. In order to play the EEG Tractor Beam game, a MINDO-4S wireless EEG headset needs to be worn by the client which is connected via Bluetooth to the gamer's smartphone. An Android game application is run on the user's smartphone. The smartphone application works on real-time processing of the EEG signals sensed by the EEG headset and the state of the user's brain is calculated with this.

On the mobile phone display, the game application displays all the players on a circle surrounding a destination object.

Each game player can exert an attractive force onto the target in proportion to his level of concentration. To win the game, the game player should try to pull the target toward himself by exercising concentration while depriving other players of their chances to grab the target.

For real-time data processing all the application should be hosted close to the data source, i.e., the smartphone itself. However, global coverage would not have been allowed in this deployment model, which typically requires deploying the application in the cloud. Such a mix of conflicting objectives makes this application a typical use-case for fog computing.

Application Model: The EEG Tractor Beam game consists of three major modules that perform processing: Client/Gamer, Coordinator/Cloud Platform and Concentration Calculator. AppModule is used in iFogSim to model the application modules. As depicted in Figure 14.17, there are data dependencies and modules that are modeled using AppEdge class in iFogSim. Finally, the rein loop of interest for EEG application is modeled in iFogSim using AppLoop class. The EEG signals application fed by a sensor EEG and an actuator DISPLAY displays the current game-scene to the gamer.

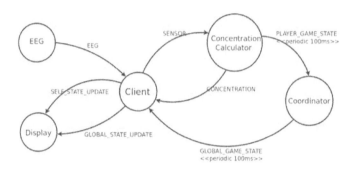

Figure 14.17 EEG game application prototype.

The above-mentioned function modules are as follows:

1. *Client/Gamer*: The Client/Gamer module interfaces with the sensor and accepts raw EEG signals. It reads the received signal data for any discrepancy and discards any seemingly inconsistent reading. For the consistent value of sensed signal, it sends the data variables to the Concentration Calculator module to receive the concentration level of the gamer from the signal. Upon receiving the concentration level, it shows it by sending the value to the actuator DISPLAY.

2. *Concentration Calculator/Fog Device*: The fog device module is responsible for determining the main brain-state of the user from the sensed EEG signal values and calculating the concentration level. After this the module informs the Gamer/Client module about the calculated concentration level so that the current state of the player could be updated.

3. *Coordinator/Cloud Platform*: Coordinator works at the global level and coordinates the game between multiple players that may be present at geographically distributed locations. The current state of the gamer is continuously sent to the Coordinator to update Client module of all connected users.

Table 14.1 describes the properties of tuples carried by edges between the modules in the application. For the Physical Network for the case study, they have considered a physical topology with four fog devices. Moreover, two different types of EEG headsets have been used. The physical topology of the case study is modeled in iFogSim via Sensor, Actuator classes, Fog Device and Physical Topology.

Table 14.1   Inter-module edges of the EEG game application.

TUPLE TYPE	N/W LENGTH	CPU LENGTH (MIPS)
CONCENTRATION	500	14
SENSOR	500	3500
EEG	500	2000 (A) / 2500 (B)
PLAYER GAME STATE	1000	1000
GLOBAL STATE UPDATE	500	1000
SELF STATE UPDATE	500	1000
GLOBAL GAME STATE	1000	1000

14.6   Scheduling

The distribution of memory bandwidth computer resources and processor time to the incoming threads is managed by a technique known as "scheduling." [25]

The user requests are to be lined up and processed in a proper and purposeful manner to get them fulfilled based on priority and limitations. The scheduling of the incoming requests is very much required due to the fact that it helps to segregate the requests on various bases determined by the applied algorithms. It helps to keep the work load of the various components of the system in check, which is known as "load balancing." For this purpose algorithms are designed which fulfill the criteria needed for the specific scheduling process to be followed in the application of computing system.

Process scheduling is the method of segregating the processes pending in the column. It forms the decision for the stoppage or running of a process by studying its priorities and limitations.

14.6.1   Classification of Scheduling

Preemptive Scheduling: In this type of scheduling, the ongoing process in the operating system is analyzed and is stopped in case a priority process gets in the way of operating system. The process with higher priority is given preference even over the ongoing process. For example, if a process within emergency completion comes up, it has to be completed first because of its necessity; hence, it can be completed in the preemptive scheduling.

Non-preemptive Scheduling: In this type of scheduling, the ongoing process automatically leaves the operating system voluntarily after completion occurs and the operating system becomes free to take over another process for completion. It does not segregate the processes on the basis of priority and does not fall for their completion preference. A process would only leave the system after its completion and no priority-based stoppage of an ongoing process is done in this type of scheduling.

14.6.2   Need for Scheduling

Response Time: Minimize the response time needed for the completion of the process so that there is no lag over the request completion. Also, it gives the estimated time period required for the starting and completion of process.

Minimize Job Delay: As the scheduling involves the lining up of processes in a particular sequence, it minimizes the delay faced in completion as compared to haphazard process taking and completion, which creates a lot of unnecessary load over the system resulting in unnecessary delays of the projects.

Completion Time: It gives the estimated time period required for the start and completion of the process and saves the requesting person from the unnecessary waste of time caused by being unaware of the completion time.

Idle Time Reduction: Idle time refers to the time wasted during the process of registering a request for completion, which is beyond the control of the user or the traditional systems. The process of scheduling streamlines the requests and hence decreases the idle time wasted in the request completion process.

Work-in-Process Inventory: Scheduling is necessary to form an inventory of ongoing processes, the processes pending and the completed processes because it manages the whole system efficiently and keeps the user informed of its number.

Machine Resources: As the resources at the disposal of the system are limited, they must be managed in an efficient manner. For generating maximum efficiency there cannot be a better alternative than scheduling because it prevents the waste of resources caused due to haphazard and improperly planned completion resources.

Meet Customer Due Dates: In this hectic world, everyone needs their work to be completed first and as soon as possible. If the system worked in a rash and unplanned manner, it would take a lot of time to complete even a single process, resulting in unnecessary delays and causing inconvenience to the customers. To meet the deadlines of the customers there must be a well-organized plan for the efficient functioning of the system, which is provided by the application of scheduling in the system.

14.6.3 Existing Scheduling Algorithms

Keeping in mind the demand for a scheduling application in the field of computing systems, there has been ongoing research into the development of algorithm design techniques for the process of scheduling. Till date, various algorithms have been designed according to the demands and needs created within the operating system and due to the increasing infrastructure of the computing software. The development of the simulator tool has lessened the need for the development of the algorithm for scheduling because it could be tested beforehand on the simulator tool before being applied in a real-life scenario and can generate feedback from the developed algorithm [28-33]. Based on the requirements various scheduling algorithms have been designed, a few of which are listed below:

- Min-min algorithm

- First come first serve algorithm

- Round robin algorithm

- Shortest job first algorithm

- Knapsack-based scheduling algorithm

- Trust-based scheduling algorithm

- Bees life algorithm (BLA)

- Cloudlet migration-based scheduling algorithm

- Task scheduling algorithm

14.7   Challenges in Fog Computing

Whenever a new process is developed, it is almost certain that new challenges will come along with it. This applies in the case of the development of fog computing in the era of cloud computing because of the various factors known and unknown that are responsible for them. But the usage of simulation studies and simulator tool has eased the process of finding those problems and also prevents future losses that may occur due to its direct usage in a real-life scenario. A few of the identified challenges in this field are discussed below.

14.7.1   Connectivity Challenges

Due to the increased connectivity requirements in fog computing due to usage of intermediate devices, there is increased need for communication between various levels of hierarchy of the system and also use of local networks; it is very evident that problems will also arise in the same system due to it.

- In the discovery of ICO by the gateway device by the ICO or vice versa, each ICO has a very limited time period to get connected to the gateway device so as to forward the data. The discovery of the device needs to be done efficiently and in a time-bound manner so that a gateway device does not pass the range before it and can get connected. Hence, the challenge lies within finding the common ground between them in order to achieve easier and earlier connectivity as soon as possible so that there is sufficient time for the data transmission between them.

- In similar cases of connectivity there is a need for availability of the open network during the entire communication as well as non-communication period, which will result in the waste of a lot of energy. Either gateway devices or ICOs needs to keep the connectivity method "ON" all the time. So, there is a need for development of that technology which could provide the correct time and location to both connecting objects so as to conserve a lot of energy wasted by it, which will make the process more efficient and cost-effective.

14.7.2   Context Awareness

Since fog computing uses the fog devices which are located near the end user, they need to be more aware of the situations going on near them, which is classified as the context awareness. This is possible only when the devices fitted are intelligent enough for the assessement.

- Fog gateway needs to be intelligent in order to be context-aware so as to be able to modify itself automatically, and fast enough to decode the data provided by sensors semantically in order to meet the context of the request and the specific requirements of the condition based on their capabilities. This is possible only when the knowledge collected by the global data analysis is applied along with coordination with the local knowledge. The increase of the intelligence of the device poses a big challenge in the fog computing application.

- Also, smart devices should be able to balance their work load. This can be done by maintaining coordination with other gateways and ICOs. It helps to reduce resource wastage. For this to occur under actual conditions, required techniques must be developed for the interconnectivity of the various devices within the system. This is called "cooperation and opportunistic sensing."

14.7.3   Data Handling

Although there is reduced data formation in the fog computing, processing and handling of data is occurring in more places (including fog devices). So, there is need for the proper handling of data at all the sites. Sometimes the expansion of the system is necessary, in which newer devices are inserted in the system temporarily for the backup, etc. So, there must be a provision in the infrastructure for easy insertion or removal of the higher computability devices in it.

- The challenge of data handling lies in the development of module-based data analytical components which when required can be attached to fog gateway on a temporary basis for the purpose of controlling the system remotely or for some other purpose in a similar situation. There is a need for the development of devices that can be remotely inserted as the gateway devices in the existing system, which have restricted computational abilities and can be removed when the purpose is fulfilled.

- Gateway devices are designed in such a way that resource restrictions are also placed on them but this could work against them in cases where the process cannot be completed with the available amount of resources with the device, due to which various data analysis processes cannot work on them and be completed on time, which needs to be sorted out, as this poses a challenge to the smooth working of fog computing.

14.7.4   Security

Although non-functional, security is an essential aspect of smart applications of fog computing. It is the basic necessity of any working system that data generated and transported by the system do not get leaked [35]. So, it is a foremost challenge to maintain the integrity of the system with utmost security and privacy.

- ICO to ICO: To rule out outside ICO interference, ICOs can use link layer-based encryption techniques. Each network will possess a common key which would be already known to the ICOs and each would have to submit its key for recognition. It would prevent the forceful entry of the external device in the system without permission of the system.

- ICO to Gateway: This type of communication can be secured with the application of an encryption-based networking and application layer. The encryption key would be known to gateway devices corresponding to each ICO device. With the use of the encryption key, fog gateways can verify the ICO. Also, a sequence number and random internal seed could be used to verify data security. This is the best type of security that could be developed for the security between the gateway device and the ICO.

- ICO to Cloud: To support such connection, the encryption keys can be stored directly in cloud without storing them in gateway device. Although it is a rarer form of security needed fog computing, a need could arise for bypassing the conventional system in various situations. Then, this type of security will ensure that no other cloud decision maker could access the ICOs of the other cloud without their permission.

- Gateway to Cloud: This type of communication is commonly needed for security in fog computing infrastructure because fog devices report directly to the cloud decision makers. This type of communication connection can be secured by the use of HTTPS (hypertext transfer protocol over SSL/TLS). It would prevent connection of a fog device with the other cloud platform and also would prevent the forceful entry of the fog device into the system, as these could pass on wrong information to the cloud decision makers, resulting in the generation of false commands in the system.

- Cloud to ICOs or Gateways: Although these are much less used methods for the surety of the security between different components of the fog computing, these types of connections between different devices can be secured by public-key cryptosystems. These can play a unique role in the security of the devices as well as the system.

14.7.5 Privacy

Another major issue in fog computing is privacy. Privacy issues arise when there is unnecessary collection of raw data from the source of the data production. Because where there is collection of raw data there could be transmission of unwanted data which may be the private property of the user. Privacy violations can result in huge ethical and legal concerns about the integrity of the system, leading to huge financial as well as non-measurable losses. To prevent the privacy violations, system developers and cloud decision makers must ensure that only a essential and sufficient amount of data is collected for the completion of the request forwarded to the system by the client. Also, constant monitoring of the process of collection of the data is required for ensuring zero privacy violations. This will not only prevent legal issues and complications but also will prevent ethical problems created by the privacy violations.

14.7.6 Pluggable Architecture

If the existing cloud computing system was to be replaced by a newer system like fog computing, it would take a lot of time to completely exchange the existing system with the new system. Moreover, all scenarios cannot be resolved by eliminating cloud computing and using fog computing alone, therefore, the system must be made in such a way that it must have a pluggable architecture. Pluggability between the different systems will allow easy switching from cloud computing to fog computing and vice versa. It will also increase the efficiency and capability of the infrastructure to complete a task due to the availability of multiple working systems.

14.7.7 Sustainability

As the population and its needs continue to grow day by day, the developer of any system must keep in mind that the system must be self-expanding or able to expand without compromising quality of service; that is, it should have a sustainable architecture. The structure of fog computing must be a sustainable one so as to meet the increasing demands within whatever limited resources the system has. It must also ensure that it does not become outdated in a small period of time because it will affect its cost-effectiveness. So, sustainability is a huge challenge posed by the development of fog computing. The strategy of systematization could be used for its development, for which knowledge of behavior and consumption patterns is essential.

14.7.8 Network and Storage

As discussed earlier, due to the increased connectivity requirements in fog computing due to usage of intermediate devices, there is increased need for communication between various levels of the hierarchy of the system and also use of local networks. It is very evident that problems will also arise in the same system due to increased connectivity.

- In fog computing, problems of connectivity and storage are likely to be faced. In communication, it is essential to connect all the devices with each other, which would likely cause bandwidth problems and network constraints.

- Also, the ICOs and fog devices have to store local data at their level in fog computing, which will result in storage issues due to memory constraints put on them due to their limited features.

14.8 Use Case Scenarios

In this section, a few of the different use case scenarios of application of fog computing in real-life scenarios are described to show its widespread applicability in various fields. The main objective is to use these scenarios to extract major functional requirements and characteristics of fog computing platforms.

14.8.1 Smart Home

Smart home use case scenario shows how home appliances and other devices fitted in the home could be controlled from within the home or even remote locations. This has been made possible by the application of fog computing in the decision-making process of the various steps in smart home control.

Smart Sensors: The smart home is known as such because it is fitted with smart sensors within different rooms in the home such as kitchens, etc. These smart sensors are capable of performing various types of data collection within a single device.

This device is capable of hearing and recognizing the voices of the owner and other residents via a voice recognizer. It can also detect motion occurring within different places in the house via motion detectors fitted in the same device. It can also detect motion during the night by the use of an infrared detector.

There are sensors fitted at the front gate for fingerprint and iris scanning along with other sensors to read the unique features of the residents of the house.

These sensors collect data triggered only by an event like voice command, motion of the person during day and night, fingerprint scanning, looking into an iris scanner, etc., which prevents unnecessary data collection by the sensors, thereby averting the problem of privacy violation.

Edge Devices: There is an edge device fitted in the house which collects the data from all the sensors. There can be multiple devices depending on the area and number of sensors in the house. Edge devices have higher computability in the architecture of fog computing. They can assess the voice command, motion detection data, fingerprint data, iris scanner data, etc.

Actuators: In a smart home all appliances used on a daily basis, like fans, lights, television, refrigerator, speakers, etc., are fitted with actuators. These actuators are capable of performing the function of turning the home appliance "ON" when given a command from the edge device.

After processing the data, it functions in the house via the two types of models described below:

- Sense-Process-Actuate Model: When the resident of a home gives a voice command to turn on a fan or a light, etc., or motion is detected in a room, or other types of data are collected, the smart sensor sends this data to the edge device fitted in the home. This device assesses and analyzes the data given to it and converts it into information. It then analyzes the information according to what the person is trying/commanding to do. After understanding the context of the request provided by the user, the device then forms a command for the completion of the request. The command formed by the device is then sent to the appropriate actuator for the actual performance of the task. The actuator receives the command given to it, like start the fan, turn on the light, etc., by the edge device. It acts upon the appliance concerned and turns it on or off as described in the command. If connected to a cloud platform, the edge device then also forwards this information to the same for future use or analysis and records the performed task for future use.

- Stream-Processing Model: This model could be used in the smart home for controlling the appliances and entry to the house from a remote location. The smart sensors used in the home are the same as those mentioned in the above example. The front door of the house is fitted with the iris and fingerprint scanners.

Sensors are connected to the edge device and the device is further connected to the cloud platform. The cloud platform could be assessed by a smart device like a smartphone or a smart watch. If any movement or iris or fingerprint id is attempted by a person whose data is not connected with the edge device, the data collected by the device is sent to the edge device which compresses the data into information and sends it to the cloud. The cloud assesses the information on the basis of previous knowledge.

If the information can be recognized as a known person or object it can send a notification to the smartphone connected with it and wait for the response of the owner for the necessary action such as whether a gate should be opened or not. If it could not recognize the person, it can still send the notification to the owner and wait for the response.

If the person tries the entry multiple times, which exceeds the limit set by the owner, and and the owner does not reply, then the cloud prepares a command for the edge device for the action. The edge device reads the command and then forwards it to the actuator concerned for the action. The actuator will ring the theft alarm fitted at the gate and turns on the anti-theft measures, which will prevent forceful entry into the home.

If the owner reads the notification, then he/she can control the further steps with his/her smartphone. The owner can manually give a command to the cloud for the anti-theft measures in case of nonrecognition. The owner can give the command for opening the door in case he/she recognizes the person. Similarly, the owner could also control the functioning of the various appliances fitted in the house by giving a command to the cloud, which would forward it to the edge device for execution via actuators.

All this could be done from anywhere in the world because the cloud platform is connected to the smartphone via the internet. Remote control of the entire home can be enabled with just a few simple commands issued by the smart device of the owner without actually coming to the home or a location nearby.

This type of case scenario has been imagined and put forward for the applicability of smart devices and the fog computing system in the working of the smart home and smart functions within the home.

14.8.2 Smart Rail

In the smart rail use case scenario, the signal lights of trains and also track changes could be done using fog computing at the level of lights. Fog computing can also be used in the railway network to reduce the workload of railway workers as well as to reduce railway accidents.

Sensors: In this scenario the signal lights and tracks are fitted with the smart sensors. These sensors could detect the motion of a train (whether it is moving, stopped, accelerating, decelerating, etc.), distance of the train from the lights, check for the trains on both sides of the lights and also on parallel tracks.

Edge Device: It is placed near the lights if present at a remote location or it could be placed in the office at the railway platform. It has some computability power and judgement for emergency situations, etc. It is connected to all the lights nearby or programmed with it. These could be multiple in number according to the number of lights or the distance between the lights, etc.

Actuators: These are the devices which could take the commands from the edge device and perform the mechanical function to complete the task. These are fitted at the tracks and can change the tracks or can join/disjoin/rejoin the tracks according to the command given by the edge device.

After processing the data, it functions in the house via the two types of models described below:

- Sense-Process-Actuate Model: Smart sensors will detect the motion of the train and other features already mentioned above and collects the data. This data is sent to the edge device fitted near the lights or in the office at the railway platform. The edge device collects the data and processes it into information. The information formed is analyzed within the edge device due to its computability power. It considers the possibility of accident or other cases requiring the movement on the tracks. Once the requirement is recognized, it forms a command to be sent to the actuator. The command is sent to the actuator concerned, which is fitted on the tracks. These actuators understand the command and then move the tracks in the direction requested by the device command with the use of mechanical methods. This prevents the manual turning or changing of tracks, which causes thousands of accidents every year in railways. The edge device then sends the information of the request to the cloud for further analysis.

- Stream-Processing Model: This model of fog computing can be used in rail for controlling rail operations from remote locations. The sensors are fitted as described in the above example. These sensors are smart and can record various data values from different parameters. These send the data to the edge device fitted near them. The edge device collects the data and processes it in the information. This edge device is also connected to the cloud platform where all of the information is sent. The cloud further analyzes the information and compares it with the programmed schedule of the trains predesigned by the workers. After comparing the timing of the train and other parameters, if it matches with them and the track is empty according to the schedule then it prepares a command for the action to be taken. The command is sent to the device. The device understands the command and forwards it to the actuators concerned. The actuators receive the commands and act by changing the track of the train if requested and change the color of the signal lights per the command.

This cloud platform is also connected to a smart device, like a laptop or computer of the concerned official, and will send a notification in case a command requires human input. The concerned official can appropriately assess the condition and give the command to the cloud platform over the connected internet network.

All this could be done from anywhere in the world because the cloud platform is connected to the smartphone via the internet. Remote control of the entire rail can be enabled with just a few simple commands via the smart device of the official concerned, without actually coming to the location.

14.8.3 Smart Healthcare

In the use case scenario of smart healthcare, fog computing could be used to manage the data of patients to monitor their vital signs [4]. It can be used to manage the workload of doctors and reduce the human errors caused due to negligence or the work overload on doctors.

Sensors: In this scenario, patients' sensors are connected with the smart sensors. These sensors could sense all the data values (e.g., electromyography (EMG), blood pressure, electrocardiogram (EKG), glucose level, electroencephalogram (EEG) and respiration rate, etc.) of a patient within a single sensor. All of this data is combined in one device.

Edge Device: It is placed near the patient if sensors are present on a remote location or it could be placed in the office of the doctor. It has some computability power and judgement for emergency situations, etc. It is connected to all the sensors near it or programmed with it. These could be multiple in number depending on the number of sensors connected to the patients.

Actuators: These are the devices which take the commands from the edge device and perform the mechanical function to complete the task. For example, an oxygen tank can be fitted with sensors which can be turned on or off according to the command given by the edge device. Similarly, various other functions can also be performed by the actuator according to the requirement.

After processing the data, it functions in healthcare applications via the two types of models described below:

- Sense-Process-Actuate Model: Smart sensors will detect different values of the patient's body and other features already mentioned above and collect the data. This data is sent to the edge device fitted near the patient or in the doctor's office. The edge device collects the data and processes it in the information. The information formed is analyzed within the edge device due to its computability power. It considers the possibility of emergency or other cases. Once recognized as the requirement, it forms a command to be sent to the actuator. The command is sent to the actuator concerned, which is fitted on the oxygen tank or other equipment. These actuators understand the command and then turn "ON" the ball of an oxygen tank by the device command with the use of mechanical methods. This prevents any mishaps from occurring due to the negligence of personal care attendants, which can affect the life of the patient. The edge device then sends the information of the request to the cloud for further analysis.

- Stream-Processing Model: This model of fog computing can be used in smart healthcare for controlling the parameters of patients even from remote locations. The sensors are fitted as described in the above example. These sensors are smart and can record various data values from different parameters and then send the data to the edge device fitted near them. The edge device collects the data and processes it in the information. This edge device is also connected to the cloud platform where all of the information is sent. The cloud further analyzes the information and compares it with the programmed schedule of the patients predesigned by the doctor. After comparing it with the schedule of the patient, the command is sent to the device. The device understands the command and forwards it to the actuators concerned. The actuators receive the commands and act by turning on the oxygen tank.

This cloud platform is also connected to the smart device, like the laptop or computer of the doctor, and will send a notification in case a command requires human input. The doctor concerned can appropriately assess the condition and send the command to the cloud platform over the connected internet network.

All this could be done from anywhere in the world because the cloud platform is connected to the smartphone via the internet. Remote control of smart healthcare is enabled with just a few simple commands done via the smart device of the doctor without actually coming to the location.

14.8.4 Smart Agriculture

In this use case scenario, fog computing could be used to assess the quality and constant monitoring of growth parameters of crops. It could also be used for saving crops from the damage caused by various natural phenomena like heavy rains, strong winds, etc.

Sensors: In this scenario, the sensors are fitted near the crops or in the sky above the crops. These are smart enough for recording a large number of parameters from the crops and their surroundings. These can record rainfall, crop growth, sunlight, soil parameters, humidity, temperature, etc. They can collect the data at regular intervals as well as continuously, depending on the requirement.

Edge Device: This is a high computability device fitted near the smart sensors in places like farm sheds. These possess some computability power and judgement for emergencies like excess rainfall, etc. It is connected to all the smart sensors nearby or programmed with them. These could be multiple in number according to the number of sensors or the distance between them.

Actuators: These are the devices which can take the commands from the edge device and perform the mechanical function to complete the task. These are connected to the mechanical devices which can cover the crops with retractable sheds by unrolling after the command received from the edge device.

After processing the data, they function on the farm via the two types of models described below:

- Sense-Process-Actuate Model: Smart sensors detect the parameters from the crops and their surroundings. They can record rainfall, crop growth, sunlight, soil parameters, humidity, temperature, etc. This collected data is sent to the edge device fitted near the smart sensors in places like farm sheds. The edge device collects the data and processes it in the information. The information formed is analyzed within the edge device due to its computability power provided in the framework of fog computing. It considers the possibility of damage to the crops due to heavy rainfall, strong winds, etc. Once the requirement for the action is recognized, it forms a command to be sent to the actuator. The command is sent to the actuator concerned, which is fitted to the mechanical devices near the crops. These actuators understand the command and then cover the crops with the retractable sheds by unrolling them with the use of mechanical techniques.

- Stream-Processing Model: This model of fog computing can be used in agriculture for continuous monitoring of crops from remote locations. The sensors are fitted as described in the above example. These sensors are smart and can record various data values from different parameters like rainfall, crop growth, sunlight, soil parameters, humidity, temperature, etc. They can collect the data at regular intervals as well as continuously, depending on the requirement. These send the data to the edge device fitted near them. The edge device collects the data and processes it in the information. This edge device is also connected to the cloud platform where all of the information is sent. The cloud further analyzes the information and compares it with the weather forecast and previous year's growth charts of the crops and with the normal values of the other parameters. This can help in judging the requirements of the soil or the crops and can be sent to the farmer on a smart device, like a smartphone, etc., to which the cloud platform is connected. Then the farmer can make a decision on the requirements put forward and command the cloud platform to complete the demands or wait a certain amount of time.

Smart agriculture can be done anywhere in the world because the cloud platform is connected to the smartphone via the internet. Remote control of the entire agricultural process can be enabled with just a few simple commands via the smart device of the owner without having to actually come to the farm or a nearby location.

14.8.5 Future Applications

A few examples of future fog computing applications are:

- Smart Agriculture
- Smart Home
- Smart Waste Management
- Smart Water Management
- Smart Cities
- Smart Healthcare
- Smart Vehicles
- Smart Building
- Smart Educational Institutes
- Smart Power Grid
- Smart Rail
- Smart Greenhouse Gases Control
- Smart Retail Store Automation
- Smart Manufacturing

14.9 Emerging Trends

As cloud computing is getting older and becoming outdated, fog computing is growing day by day. Limited research has been ongoing in this field, which is prompting research with great potential in the area [42].

Dew computing, which first appeared in 2015, is the latest ongoing field of research. It is the next level of development in this field. It consists of keeping the computing structure and functioning at the user level, which is one level ahead of fog computing, where the computing structure is kept beside the user in edge devices or fog devices. It was developed as an analogy to cloud, fog and dew, as these three are located on various levels in nature, with cloud being the farthest from the earth, dew being at the level of earth and fog coming in between them. Similarly, cloud computing, which has been getting older, is the farthest computing system from the user, whereas dew computing, which is the newest, is situated at the level of the end user, while fog computing comes in between them.

Dew computing focuses on the idea of getting the computing system down to the user level. It is developed in such a way to provide the computing functions of the smart devices at the user level. The functions can be performed at the user level and can be sent to the cloud when necessary. After connecting to the cloud platform via the internet it can synchronize all the information performed at the user level to the cloud for keeping the cloud platform updated and also updates the system of the user with the recent updates sent by the cloud.

As all the functions can be performed at the user level there is no requirement for the internet or connectivity to be available all the time to the cloud platform and reduces the dependence on the cloud for the completion of the requests. After the task has been completed it can synchronize all its information to the cloud when the connectivity becomes available and suitable.

This computing technique has made the user free from the requirement of internet connectivity and dependence on the internet providers. It has been possible due to the uses of extremely smart devices like smartphones and smart laptops because they can keep the required infrastructure within them without taking up a large amount of space or cost.

New algorithms for dew computing have been devised because there is limited usage of the existing algorithms in the upcoming computing systems.

14.10 Conclusion

Due to the rapid growth of the fog computing network, the scope of work in this field is wide-ranging. The ongoing work and research in this field attests to the large potential in this area.

As the demands of the user and server are rising, the existing structure and algorithms have failed to fulfill the requirements of the system, generating the need for development of the fog computing.

Although the development of the fog computing system is currently in the initial stage and has not yet gone through an extensive growth phase, in the near future it will be seen as a very useful computing technique because of its wide-ranging features and benefits over cloud computing. There are many challenges noted in it but these are part and parcel of the development of any new technology.

The development of simulator tools and simulation studies as well as newer algorithms has initiated the technological advancement of fog computing. After the review of the existing scheduling algorithms, there is still a large amount of information remaining to be discovered in this field of research.

As the population and its needs grow day by day the development of any system must be done by keeping in mind that the system must be able to self-expand or be expanded without compromising the quality of service provided by the system; that is, it should have a sustainable architecture. The structure of fog computing must be a sustainable one so as to meet the increasing demands using whatever limited resources the system has. As the existing system is cloud computing, if it was replaced by a newer system like fog computing it would take a lot of time to completely exchange the existing system with the new system. Moreover, since all scenarios cannot be resolved by use of fog computing alone the system must be made in such a way that it must have a pluggable architecture.

The presentation of use case scenarios along with the human imagination can put wheels on the advancement of fog computing and it can travel at warp speed if pointed in the right direction.

Till now only a few of the applications of fog computing have been identified because of limited availability of data on its potential and the way it works. But it can grow to an infinite number of applications in coming years as the technology for its application in a real-life scenario will continue to advance.

In the future, if the focus shifts to the formation and development of an algorithm for newer requirements of the system, then it could help to develop a better system to address user demands and provide better quality of service.

REFERENCES

1. Le, D. N., Kumar, R., Nguyen, G. N., & Chatterjee, J. M. (2018). *Cloud Computing and Virtualization*. John Wiley & Sons.

2. Arya, D, & Dave, M. (2017). Advanced Informatics for Computing Research Conference paper, National Institute of Technology Kurukshetra, India, Volume 712 issue 3, https://doi.org/10.1007/978-981-10-5780-9 (Accessed on: 02-09-2018)

3. Chiang, M, & Zhang, T. (2016). Fog and IoT: An Overview of Research Opportunities. IEEE Internet of Things Journal, volume 3, issue 6, pp 854-864, ISSN: 2327-4662. https://doi.org/10.1109/ JIOT.2016.2584538 (Accessed on: 05-09-2018)

4. Gill, S.S., Arya, R.C., Wander, G.S. and Buyya, R., (2019). Fog-based Smart Healthcare as a Big Data and Cloud Service for Heart Patients using IoT., In International Conference on Intelligent Data Communication Technologies and Internet of Things, pp. 1376-1383. Springer.

5. Bhatt. Chintan, & Bhensdadia. C.K. (2017). Fog Computing: Applications, Concepts, and Issues, *International Journal of Grid and High Performance Computing (IJGHPC)*, volume 9, issue 4. (Accessed on: 02.1.2019)

6. Bittencourt, L. F. (2017). Mobility-Aware Application Scheduling in Fog Computing Cloud Computing, *IEEE*, Volume 4, Issue 2, ISSN: 2325-6095, DOI: 10.1109/MCC.2017.27 (Accessed on: 05-09-2018)

7. Agarwal, S, Yadav, S, & Yadav, A. K. (2016). An Efficient Architecture and Algorithm for Resource Provisioning in Fog Computing. *International Journal of Information Engineering and Electronic Business*, volume 8, issue 1, pp 48-61, https://doi.org/10.5815/ijieeb.2016.01.06 (Accessed on: 02-09-2018)

8. Cisco Systems. (2016). Fog Computing and the Internet of Things: Extend the Cloud to Where the Things Are. www.wisco.wom, https://doi.org/10.1109/HotWeb.2015.22 (Accessed on: 26-09-2018)

9. Choudhari, T., Moh, M., & Moh, T. S. (2018). Prioritized task scheduling in fog computing., In Proceedings of the ACMSE-2018 Conference., pp 22. (Accessed on: 12-08-2018)

10. Cover, C. (2016). Fog Computing: Helping the Internet of Things Realize, *IEEE*, volume 49, issue 8, pp 112 - 116, ISSN: 0018-9162, DOI: 10.1109/MC.2016.245 (Accessed on: 18-09-2018)

11. Gupta, M. (2017). Fog Computing Pushing Intelligence to the Edge, IJSTE - *International Journal of Science Technology & Engineering*, Volume 3, Issue 08, pp 42-46, ISSN (online): 2349-784X, https://pdfs.semanticscholar.org/dfda/1b0137384c4edb7 ac2e4c4b3dd9b6bfb38cf.pdf. (Accessed on: 18-10-2018)

12. Dsouza, C, & Ahn, G. (2014). Policy-Driven Security Management for Fog Computing: Preliminary Framework and A Case Study, IEEE 15th International Conference on, pp 16-23, ISBN: 978-1-4799-5880-1, DOI: 10.1109/IRI.2014.7051866 (Accessed on: 06-10-2018)

13. Buyya, R, Srirama, S.N, Casale, G, Calheiros, R, Simmhan, Y, Varghese, B, Gelenbe, E, Javadi, B, Vaquero, L.M, Netto, M.A. and Toosi, A.N, (2017). A Manifesto for Future Generation Cloud Computing: Research Directions for the Next Decade, pp 1-43. http://arxiv.org/abs/1711.09123 (Accessed on: 12-09-2018)

14. D, S, & Nichols, G. (2017), "Cutting Edge: IT's Guide to Edge Data Centers", https://internetofthingsagenda.techtarget.com/resources/Internet-of-Things-IoT-Cloud (Accessed on: 14-07-2018)

15. FOG Computing. (2016), https://doi.org/10.4010/2016.634 (Accessed on: 12-08-2018)

16. Dastjerdi, A. V, & Buyya, R. (2016). Fog Computing: Helping the Internet of Things Realize its Potential, *IEEE*, volume 49 issue 8, pp 112 -116, ISSN: 0018-9162, DOI: 10.1109/MC.2016.245 (Accessed on: 21-09-2018)

17. Bhatt M. Chintan, & Peddoju, S.K. (2016). *Cloud Computing Systems and Applications in Healthcare*. IGI Global. (Accessed on: 04.1.2019)

18. Puar, V. H., Bhatt, C. M., Hoang, D. M., & Le, D. N. (2018). Communication in Internet of Things. In Information Systems Design and Intelligent Applications (pp. 272-281). Springer, Singapore.

19. Heya, T. A, Arefin, S. E, Hossain, M. A, & Chakrabarty, (2018). Comparative analysis of computation models for IoT: Distributed fog vs. Conventional cloud. 4th International Conference on Advances in Electrical Engineering, ICAEE, pp 760-765. https://doi.org/10.1109/ICAEE.2017.8255456 (Accessed on: 24-10-2018)

20. Khalid, A., & Shahbaz, M. (2017). Service Architecture Models For Fog Computing: A Remedy for Latency Issues in Data Access from Clouds. KSII Transactions on Internet and Information Systems (TIIS), volume 11 issue 5, pp 2310-2345. https://doi.org/10.3837/tiis.2017.05.001 (Accessed on: 14-08-2018)

21. Ni, L, Zhang, J, Jiang, C, Yan, C, & Yu, K. (2017). Resource Allocation Strategy in Fog Computing Based on Priced Timed Petri Nets, *IEEE*, volume 4 issue 5, pp 1216-1228, ISSN: 2327-4662, https://doi.org/10.1109/JIOT.2017.2709814 (Accessed on: 4-10-2018)

22. Ningning, S, Chao, G, Xingshuo, A. N, Qiang, Z, (2016), Fog computing dynamic load balancing mechanism based on graph repartitioning , *IEEE*, volume 13 issue 3, pp 156-164,ISSN: 1673-5447, DOI: 10.1109/CC.2016.7445510 (Accessed on: 4-10-2018)

23. Oueis, J, Strinati, E. C, & Barbarossa, S. (2015). The Fog Balancing: Load Distribution for Small Cell Cloud Computing. IEEE 81st Vehicular Technology Conference (VTC Spring),pp 1-6, ISSN: 1550-2252, https://doi.org/10.1109/VTCSpring.2015.7146129 (Accessed on: 10-10-2018)

24. Panwar, N., Negi, S., Rauthan, M. S., Aggarwal, M., & Jain, P. (2018). An Enhanced Scheduling Approach With Cloudlet Migrations For Resource Intensive Applications. *Journal of Engineering Science and Technology*, volume 13 issue 8, pp 2299-2317.

25. Poola, D., Ramamohanarao, K., & Buyya, R. (2014). Fault-tolerant workflow scheduling using spot instances on clouds. *Procedia Computer Science*, volume 29, pp 523-533. https://doi.org/10.1016/j.procs.2014.05.047 (Accessed on: 08-09-2018)

26. Patil, P. V. (2015). FOG Computing, ISSN: 2572-4908, https://www.igi global.com/journal/international-journal-fog-computing/175202 (Accessed on: 14-09-2018.)

27. Perera, C, Qin, Y, Estrella, J. C, Reiff-Marganiec, S, & Vasilakos, A. V. (2017). Fog Computing for Sustainable Smart Cities: A Survey, *Journal ACM Computing Surveys*, Volume 50 Issue 3, pp 32-35, https://doi.org/10.1145/2818869.2818889 (Accessed on: 15-09-2018)

28. Pham, X. (2016). Towards task scheduling in a cloud-fog computing system, 18th Asia-Pacific Network Operations and Management Symposium (APNOMS), IEEE, pp 1-4, ISBN: 978-4-88552-304-5, DOI: 10.1109/APNOMS.2016.7737240 (Accessed on: 17-09-2018)

29. Rahbari, D., & Nickray, M. (2017). Scheduling of fog networks with optimized knapsack by symbiotic organisms search. In Open Innovations Association (FRUCT), IEEE 21st Conference., pp. 278-283. DOI: 10.23919/FRUCT.2017.8250193., (Accessed on: 23-09-2018)

30. Rahbari, D., & Nickray, M. (2017). Scheduling of fog networks with optimized knapsack by symbiotic organisms search. In Open Innovations Association (FRUCT), 1st Conference of (pp. 278-283). IEEE.

31. Rodriguez, M. A., & Buyya, R. (2015). A responsive knapsack-based algorithm for resource provisioning and scheduling of scientific workflows in clouds. In Parallel Processing (ICPP), IEEE 44th International Conference., pp. 839-848. DOI: 10.1109/ICPP.2015.93., (Accessed on: 26-10-2018).

32. Sun, Y., Lin, F., & Xu, H. (2018). Multi-objective Optimization of Resource Scheduling in Fog Computing Using an Improved NSGA-II., *Wireless Personal Communications*, pp 1-17. DOI: https://doi.org/10.1007/s11277-017-5200-5 (Accessed on: 16-10-2018).

33. S, Nichols, G, Pham, X, Yi, S, Li, C, Li, Q, Nikolopoulos, D. S. (2016). Scalable Distributed Computing Hierarchy: Cloud, Fog and Dew Computing, Open Journal of Cloud Computing (OJCC), Volume7 issue 7, pp 48-61. https://doi.org/10.5815/ijitcs.2016.04.01 (Accessed on: 02-09-2018)

34. Slabicki, M, & Grochla, K. (2016). Performance Evaluation of CoAP, SNMP and NETCONF Protocols in Fog Computing Architecture, (May). *IEEE*, pp 1315-1319, ISSN: 2374-9709, https://doi.org/10.1109/NOMS.2016.7503010 (Accessed on: 14-07-2018)

35. Stojmenovic, I, & Wen, S. (2014). The Fog Computing Paradigm: Scenarios and Security Issues, *IEEE*, pp 1-8, ISBN: 978-83-60810-58-3, https://doi.org/10.15439/2014F503 (Accessed on: 14-09-2018)

36. Stolfo, S. J, Salem, M. Ben, & Keromytis, A. D. (2012). Fog computing: Mitigating insider data theft attacks in the cloud., CS Security and Privacy Workshops, Proceedings - IEEE, pp 125-128, ISBN: 978-1-4673-2157-0, https://doi.org/10.1109/SPW.2012.19 (Accessed on: 06-07-2018)

37. Sun, Y, Dang, T, & Zhou, J. (2016). User scheduling and cluster formation in fog computing-based radio access networks. IEEE, International Conference on Ubiquitous Wireless Broadband (ICUWB), pp 1-4, ISBN: 978-1-5090-1317-3, https://doi.org/10.1109/ICUWB.2016.7790393 (Accessed on: 04-08-2018)

38. Varghese, B, Wang, N, & Nikolopoulos, D. S. (2017). Feasibility of Fog Computing, Cornell University Library, https://arxiv.org/abs/1701.05451 (Accessed on: 02-09-2018)

39. Verma, M. (2016). Real-Time Efficient Scheduling Algorithm for Load Balancing in Fog Computing Environment, *I.J. Information Technology and Computer Science*, Volume 8 issue 4, pp 1-10, https://doi.org/10.5815/ijitcs.2016.04.01 (Accessed on: 14-07-2018)

40. Yi, S, Hao, Z, Qin, Z, & Li, Q. (2016). Fog computing: Platform and applications. Proceedings - 3rd Workshop on Hot Topics in Web Systems and Technologies, pp 73-78. ISBN: 978-1-4673-9688-2, https://doi.org/10.1109/HotWeb.2015.22 (Accessed on: 17-08-2018)

41. Yi, S, Li, C, & Li, Q. (2015). A Survey of Fog Computing: Concepts, Applications and Issues. 2015 Workshop on Mobile Big Data, pp 37-42, ISBN: 978-1-4503-3524-9, https://doi.org/10.1145/2757384.2757397 (Accessed on: 20-08-2018)

42. You, W, & Learn, W. (2015). Fog Computing and the Internet of Things: Extend the Cloud to Where the Things Are, pp 1-6, http://www.cisco.com/c/dam/enus/solutions/trends/iot/ docs/-computingoverview.pdf (Accessed on: 13-09-2018)

43. Le, D. N., Kumar, R., Mishra, B. K., Chatterjee, J. M., & Khari, M. (Eds.). (2019). *Cyber Security in Parallel and Distributed Computing: Concepts, Techniques, Applications and Case Studies*. John Wiley & Sons.

44. Gupta, H., Vahid Dastjerdi, A., Ghosh, S. K., & Buyya, R. (2017). iFogSim: A toolkit for modeling and simulation of resource management techniques in the Internet of Things, Edge and Fog computing environments. *Software: Practice and Experience*, 47(9), 1275-1296.

45. Bitam, S., Zeadally, S., & Mellouk, A. (2018). Fog computing job scheduling optimization based on bees swarm. *Enterprise Information Systems*, volume 12, issue 4, pp 373-397 (Accessed on: 14.09.2018)

CHAPTER 15

TAXONOMY OF CYBER-PHYSICAL SOCIAL SYSTEMS IN INTELLIGENT TRANSPORTATION

Dhiraj, Anil Saini

Central Electronics Engineering Research Institue, India
Email: dhiraj@ceeri.res.in, anil@ceeri.res.in

Abstract

Cyber-physical system (CPS) results from the combination of physical processes with communication and computation. The purpose of this integration is to add more value and intelligence to social life. The CPS and in particular CPSS, i.e., cyber-physical social systems, are still in their adolescent stage, and therefore various challenges and developments still need to be addressed. The majority of the present-day designed physical systems and their cyber modules are used by human beings in social and natural environments. Techniques, such as big data for social transportation, provide the necessary methods and opportunities for solving transportation problems. The data generated in CPS and rapid growth in usage of social networks offer near real-time human-sensing capabilities as a complementary information source. In this chapter, a detailed framework of CPSS in intelligent transportation is explained that characterizes the different methods and approaches required for the application of CPSS in smart transportation. The framework not only highlights the different novel technologies utilized in CPSS for transportation in general but also presents the different challenges which need further research. It is anticipated that the framework and is explanation will be highly useful for further development of cyber-physical-social systems for intelligent transportation.

Keywords: Cyber-physical-social systems (CPSS), intelligent transportation system (ITS), social intelligence, internet of things, social transportation, data analytics

15.1 Introduction

The present-day evolution in the form of cyber-physical-social systems (CPSS) is the outcome of the technological developments in cyber-physical systems (CPS) and cyber-social systems (CSS) [1-3]. With the social and technical development, the physical systems from fields such as infrastructure, manufacturing, healthcare, energy, and transportation are controlled by cyber systems with the help of novel technologies such as big data, cloud computing, social network and intelligent systems [4-6]. In general, the CPSs do not wholly estimate the impact from humans and their societies, which are diverse, non-heuristic-based and complex in nature. So, to make CPSs more human-centric, feedback from social factors needs to be incorporated to optimize their control and management [7-9]. The evolution of the internet of things (IoT) plays a crucial role in the convergence of the physical and cyber worlds by ensuring safe and energy-efficient transmission between them [10]. As shown in Figure 15.1, the physical environment is monitored by fixed sensor network installations such as wireless sensor networks for the environment and smart home monitoring [11-14] and sensor deployments for air quality monitoring. The heavy cost involved in fixed installation of sensor networks and the fact that they cover less area led to mobile sensing initiatives which involve sensors mounted on mobile phones or other computing devices and public transportation vehicles [14, 15].

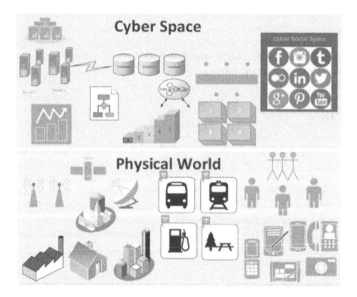

Figure 15.1 Major constituents of cyberspace and physical world.

The increasing usage of sensor-enabled smartphones and tight interactions between them and their users make them more suitable tools to sense and inform about the surrounding environment. The huge number of such active sensors provides localized information such as noise, temperature and CO_2 levels [16], traffic conditions [17], etc. This collected data can then be aggregated and analyzed by the processes in the cyber world.

Similarly, a large number of people also share information in near real-time about city-related events, such as crime and accident reporting [18, 19], and natural calamities, such as forest fires, earthquakes and tsunamis [20], on social networking platforms, which means that they can act as a reliable source of city dynamics. This technological revolution which considers human and social dynamics to be an integral part of CPS is termed CPSS [6]. The huge amount of data obtained by sensing physical phenomena by distributed sensor networks that is contributed by city residents through their sensor-enabled mobile phones and on social networking websites provides large-scale intelligence mining possibilities to assist in ensuring intelligent services in urban environments [21]. The physical world data collected using different types of sensors is largely dependent on its surrounding environment and external conditions such as physical location, time and situation. So, such factors need to be taken into consideration to extract the relevant inference from the processed data. A number of studies have been undertaken related to CPS and CPSS from different perspectives, such as some focus on different types of architectural explorations of CPSS, system-level design methods of CPSS [22, 23], and smart city implementation, while considering different computational models and run-time environments [24]. This chapter, however, presents a framework-based approach to the design of a CPSS targeting intelligent transportation and presents its major constituent design blocks, such as machine intelligence, communication and control, various data sources and its resulting applications, particularly targeting physical transportation systems and social transportation systems.

The remainder of the chapter is organized as follows: Section 15.2 presents a general overview of CPS, CPSS and its usage in intelligent transportation. Section 15.3 introduces the proposed CPSS conceptual framework entailing the different layers that are essential from a transport-centric perspective and compares the reviewed works with the defined criteria. Challenges and promising research areas are discussed in Section 15.4, with conclusions drawn in Section 15.5.

15.2 General Overview of CPSS in Intelligent Transportation

15.2.1 What is CPS?

A cyber-physical-system (CPS) is composed of a physical system and its cyber systems which are tightly integrated at all scales and levels. It is designed to provide a wide range of innovative applications and services. In today's modern world they are finding their presence in all types of physical systems and are making the systems smarter, energy-efficient and comfortable, e.g., intelligent transportation, intelligent/assisted living, smart healthcare, intelligent manufacturing, smart farming, etc. The CPS has now become ubiquitous in everyday life and its applications are continuously increasing. The potential benefits of CPS are manifold in nature, e.g., precision with repeatability, ability to work in real-time, can be trained to work intelligently, and ability to collect and process heterogeneous types of data from a variety of sensors [1-3].

15.2.2 Transition from CPS to CPSS

The social complexity of CPS has now become unignorable in presently designed CPS. In fact, it is now playing a decisive role at all the stages of CPS. As the designed CPSs are mostly used by humans in their social and natural environments, the social system must be of the same importance as their CPS counterpart. The collective composition of cyber, physical and social system as shown in Figure 15.2, composes an entity called cyber-physical-social system (CPSS) [25].

It is nowadays considered essential to include humans in intelligent transportation-based system design and various researchers have proposed three important aspects in designing CPS: physical system controlled by physics of transportation system like traffic flow, latency, behavior; cyber system controlled by distributed computing and communications; and the social system which is solely governed by the human organization and behavioral decision-making. Wu *et al.* explore the social informatics and its relation with smart transportation-based CPS [8]. Formally, the CPSS is a kind of system composed of a physical system and its social system including humans and the cyberworld that interconnects them.

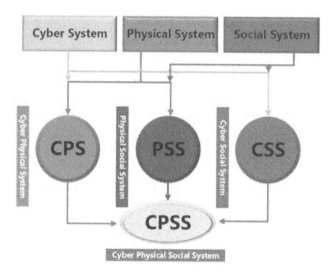

Figure 15.2 Evolution of cyber-physical-social systems (CPSS).

15.2.3 CPSS in Transportation

Urban transport is a typical example of cyber-physical social system. It relates to the two main properties of intelligent transportation, i.e., engineering the complexity of elements and social attributes of complexity elements. The engineering complexity elements of traffic involve transportation infrastructure components such as vehicles, roads, bridges, waterways, and parks, traffic control systems and other control factors. The traffic social complexity involves elements which participate themselves such as pedestrians, drivers and passengers, environment, culture, and management. The CPSS for intelligent transportation has a realistic demand in modern society and can solve basic transport-related scientific issues such as traffic behavior analysis and control.

15.3 Conceptual Framework of CPSS in Transportation

Our proposed CPS framework for a transportation system is focused on intelligent data processing of social-centric elements involved in building a system called Cyber-Physical-Social System for Transportation System. The elements of CPSS implementation are recognized to include the sensor and actuator networks that sense and interact with the physical world and social world.

For a social-oriented perspective of CPSS implementation in intelligent transportation, the emphasis needs to be on the social data source, collection, and machine learning algorithms in order to obtain intelligence from data. In addition to this, we recognize that the communication elements are the important part of a CPSS framework. Use of sensor network (e.g., wired/wireless networks for data transfer) is part of the enabling technologies (3G, 4G or WiFi networks) in the case of mobile/smartphone data source.

Following the identification of the requirements, the layers for the proposed CPSS framework can be identified as consisting of four layers: Data sources, communication and control, machine intelligence/intelligent data processing, and applications, as shown in Figure 15.3.

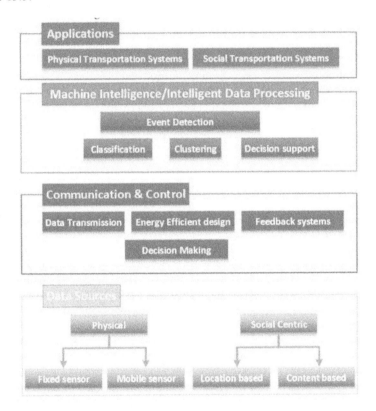

Figure 15.3 Framework of cyber-physical-social systems.

1. *Data Sources*: This layer consists of gathering the data from various data sources, including data from both physical and social world. The data collection mechanism covers a wide range, including data upload and retrieval from sensor gateways, cloud platforms, vehicle, smartphones, and users. Social-centric data involves citizens explicitly uploading data from sensor-rich mobile phones as well as from online social networks such as Twitter, Facebook, and LinkedIn.

2. *Machine Intelligence/Intelligent Data Processing*: This layer details the various machine-learning-based, semantic-based or logic-based data processing methods that are employed in the state of the art to derive information from the physical sensor network, social sensing data, and social networks. Data processing is usually supported by the

machine learning techniques, available to discover data correlation and dependence, cross-space collaboration, classification, clustering, etc.

3. *Semantic Analysis and Management*: Researchers have discovered a number of methods that involve the generation of semantics rules using an ontological approach. The Wi-City-Plus [26] smart city system employs rules expressed in fuzzy logic to determine the minimum average customer satisfaction for an event service using social network data. The ontology of CPSS framework is presented in this work, with data from both private and public databases of city interest, and data from participatory sensing. Star City [27] is a system that supports semantic traffic analytics and reasoning for the city. Star City, which integrates (human and machine-based) sensor data using a variety of formats, velocities, and volumes, has been designed to provide insight into historical and real-time traffic conditions, all supporting efficient urban planning.

4. *Classification and Clustering*: The classification and clustering techniques are commonly used methods of machine learning. Applying these techniques to CPSS for transportation system will add intelligence and ability to learn with the system. Some of the methods used by these available technologies are based on state-of-the-art techniques for text analysis and pattern classification. These technologies and techniques have been analyzed, tuned, adapted, and integrated in order to build the intelligent system. Le *et al.* [28] presented an experimental study, which has been performed for determining the most effective among different state-of-the-art approaches for text classification. In particular, the authors proposed an intelligent system, based on text mining and machine learning algorithms for real-time detection of traffic events from Twitter stream analysis.

5. *Event Detection*: Event detection and alert indications play an important role in intelligent transport system. Researchers have proposed various techniques for event detection targeting both socio-cultural or traffic event extraction from physical and social data. Smirnov *et al.* [29] presented an approach to context-driven composition of a service network for transportation safety tasks. The approach relies on new possibilities offered by modern technologies such as GPS, sensor networks, cloud computing, and cyber-physical human systems. Le *et al.* [28] proposed a mobile crowd sensing technology to support dynamic route choices for drivers to avoid congestion. The system first detects the event by analyzing the traffic data through mobile crowd sensing to raise an alarm or detect a congestion event and provide the less crowded route. A noise detection and prediction model is proposed in [29]. In this, the authors use multiple regression modeling to build the functional relationship between noise and multiple independent parameters. For developing the models, the authors initially considered all previously mentioned independent variables for the regression analysis.

6. *Decision Support*: Decision support system is another important component of intelligent transport system. Researchers have proposed various decision support systems for traffic signaling, traffic monitoring, bus travel time predictions, etc. The research work in [30, 31] discussed the travel time estimation and prediction for planning and operation of bus transport system. The accurate travel time prediction is an important requirement in most of the intelligent transport system (ITS) applications. Therefore, the authors proposed the solution for predicting travel time of buses under Indian traffic conditions which was developed using Kalman filtering with no automated data

collection techniques. Pandey and Subbiah presented a comprehensive survey on the Social Internet of Vehicles and proposed a novel social recommendation model that could establish links between social networking and social internet of vehicles (SIoV) for reliable exchange of information and intelligent analysis of the information to draw authentic conclusions for making the right assessment [32, 33].

7. *Communication Layer*: This layer responds to the queries like how the sensor network is connected, what medium to use to send and receive the data from various data sources, and what communication technologies should be used [34-37].

8. *Application*: This layer consists of the different kinds of applications that are enabled by CPSS. The applications use various detectors which collect traffic information from various vehicles, infrastructures, and environments. The data sources may be static in nature with a fixed scope and the other is dynamic, such as detectors installed on vehicles. The hosting vehicles usually connect with each other to form vehicular networks and communicate through wireless sensor networks such as Wave/802.11p and ZigBee/802.15.4. The collected traffic information from heterogeneous sensors is analyzed using data mining algorithms and the traffic situations can be monitored and visualized in detail. [38-45]

Table 15.1 provides a summary of the surveyed works and describes the methods applied for each of the CPSS frameworks. In addition to the data-specific elements and intelligence used in these works, Table 15.1 also lists the system components encountered in the reviewed works. The review includes both national (India) as well and international studies on the cyber-physical-social system for intelligent transport system.

Table 15.1 Summary of taxonomy of CPSS-dependent intelligent transportation systems.

References	System Components	Data Source	Machine Intelligence/ Data Processing	Communication and Control	Application
Real-Time Urban Monitoring [26]	Communication Layer, monitoring layer, data collection	Mobile phone and vehicle real-time location data	Image Processing, geographic interpolation,3-D visualization of traffic,	3G/4G/GSM Network	Real-time traffic monitoring, tourist management, decision making for Urban planning.
Context-Aware Service Composition [27]	knowledge logistics, Context-aware Model,	sensors, Web-sites, databases, mobile phones	Self-contextualization, context-based decisions	GPS, Sensor Networks	Context-driven transport safety system, emergency situation response
STAR-CITY [28]	Data Modeling, Data Transportation	Weather conditions, bus data streams, sensor data, social media feeds, static city map.	Semantics-aware traffic analytics and reasoning, Stream auto-Correlation and association rules for prediction.	-	Prediction of traffic conditions, traffic diagnostic
City Pulse [29]	Large Scale Data processing Module, Decision support module, Application module,	Real-time IoT sensor data, Social Media data streams,	Intelligent data aggregation, Event Detection, Contextual Filtering, Semantic modeling Reasoning	IoT Communication protocols,	Travel planner parking monitoring
In-vehicle noise prediction for Mumbai [30]	Acoustic data collection Noise modeling	Acoustic data from Various transport modes such as train, car, buses	Multiple regression modeling	3G/4G/GSM Network	Vehicle noise pollution monitoring
Travel time modeling Bangalore city [31]	Data Collection Travel time modeling	Vehicles, Local Buses.	Kalman Filter model to predict travel time.	-	Travel time prediction, Traffic congestion control
Rastey Rishtey, India [32]	Data Collection Android App	GPS data from Smartphones, Social network	Crowdsourcing GPS traces	3G/4G/GSM Network	GPS trace analysis
Social Networking and Big Data Analytics for Internet of Vehicles	Social Networking Big Data Modeling	Social Networking data on Internet of Vehicles	Big Data Analytics	3G/4G/GSM Network, WSN	Reliable and trustworthy recommendation system for IoV
Mobile Crowd Sensing for Traffic Prediction[34]	Data Collection Framework Cloud Computing Platform	Smartphones, sensor-equipped vehicles, vehicles social network	Cloud-assisted Mobile Crowdsourcing for Traffic Traffic Prediction	3G/4G/GSM Network	Traffic prediction and congestion Alleviation.
Real-Time Detection of Traffic [35]	Twitter APIs Pre-Processing Model Classification Model	Twitter Streams	SVM Classification	3G/4G/GSM Network	Real-Time traffic event monitoring and detection

15.4 Research Challenges

The previously designed CPSS lacks the modeling, analysis, and verifications of their components. So, we are unable to validate them with enough level of confidence. The major constraints and challenges of CPSs are:

- Lack of formal mathematical models to specify their behavior imposed by various controls of deployed systems.

- Establishment of feedback-based control systems are still missing.

- Real-time system level abstractions demand new distributed computing and communication methods.

- Feasibility of resilient and robustness in system design due to uncertainty in the environment and errors in physical devices is still a challenge to be met.

15.5 Discussion and Conclusion

The CPS-based industry commonly known as Industry 4.0 has brought new insights into manufacturing. Similarly, the transportation based on CPS and in particular CPSS has led to fruitful achievements in both research and its applications. The CPSS-based transportation systems are based on the implementation of software-defined transportation systems and their management using societal feedback. Using the feedback from social signals, CPSS-based transportation can completely control and manage the traffic in both physical and cyber spaces. The control of transportation will provide a methodology for faster implementation of novel methods and techniques in communication, management, and control of transportation. The CPSS-based framework for smart transportation for both physical and social transportation systems has been proposed and numerous applications have been compared based on the factors defined in the framework for intelligent transportation. We will research further about the CPSS and continue to practice its applications in manufacturing, healthcare, agriculture, and transportation.

In this chapter, we reviewed the CPSS and proposed a framework targeting the CPSS from the intelligent transportation perspective. We studied and presented some reported approaches and commercial solutions which propose new ways of combining social data with sensor deployments. The contributing features of this study target the passively submitted data from social networks, which is analyzed using machine learning or intelligent data mining approaches for cross-space, multimodal data streams. Smart transportation requires an infrastructure that can handle a large volume of data in near real-time for most of the cases. So, innovative techniques for data processing capable of handling a large volume of data from heterogeneous transport situations are required. Combining the sensor data with social streams results in a powerful tool to analyze the transport environment and how people interact with it, leading to a new set of applications. The information gathered from the reported work in the literature reports the involvement of social factors in smart transportation and provides meaning to patterns analyzed from the different sensor data streams obtained from mobile and fixed sensors. The probable future direction can be extracting statistical patterns from various traffic sources, which can then be numerically correlated with non-relational sensor data inputs.

REFERENCES

1. Zeng, J., Yang, L. T., Lin, M., Ning, H., & Ma, J. (2016). A survey: Cyber-physical-social systems and their system-level design methodology. *Future Generation Computer Systems*.

2. Ning, H., Liu, H., Ma, J., Yang, L. T., & Huang, R. (2016). Cybermatics: Cyber-physical-social-thinking hyperspace based science and technology. *Future generation computer systems*, 56, 504-522.

3. Zhuge, H. (2014). Cyber-Physical Society- The science and engineering for future society. *Future Generation Computer Systems*, 32, 180-186.

4. Cyber-physical system: from Wikipedia, the free encyclopedia. http://en.wikipedia.org/wiki/Cyber-physical system, October 15, 2017.

5. US National Science Foundation. Cyber-Physical Systems (CPS), NSF 08611 [Online], available: http://www.nsf.gov/pubs/2008/nsf08611/ nsf08611.htm, October 15, 2017.

6. Wang, F. Y. (2010). The emergence of intelligent enterprises: From CPS to CPSS. IEEE Intelligent Systems, 25(4), 85-88.

7. Smirnov, A., Kashevnik, A., Shilov, N., Makklya, A., & Gusikhin, O. (2013, November). Context-aware service composition in cyber physical human system for transportation safety. In 2013 13th International Conference on ITS Telecommunications (ITST) (pp. 139-144). IEEE.

8. Wu, P. L., Raguraman, D., Sha, L., Berlin, R. B., & Goldman, J. M. (2014, August). A treatment validation protocol for cyber-physical-human medical systems. In 2014 40th EUROMICRO Conference on Software Engineering and Advanced Applications (pp. 183-190). IEEE.

9. Gelenbe, E., Gorbil, G., & Wu, F. J. (2012, July). Emergency cyber-physical-human systems. In 2012 21st International Conference on Computer Communications and Networks (ICCCN) (pp. 1-7). IEEE.

10. Conti, M., Passarella, A., & Das, S. K. (2017). The Internet of People (IoP): A new wave in pervasive mobile computing. *Pervasive and Mobile Computing*, 41, 1-27.

11. Othman, M. F., & Shazali, K. (2012). Wireless sensor network applications: A study in environment monitoring system. *Procedia Engineering*, 41, 1204-1210.

12. Posnicek, T., Kellner, K., & Brandl, M. (2014). Wireless sensor network for environmental monitoring with 3g connectivity. *Procedia Engineering*, 87, 524-527.

13. Ye, D., Gong, D., & Wang, W. (2009, December). Application of wireless sensor networks in environmental monitoring. In 2009 2nd International Conference on Power Electronics and Intelligent Transportation System (PEITS) (Vol. 1, pp. 205-208). IEEE.

14. Smirnov, A., Kashevnik, A., & Ponomarev, A. (2015). Multi-level self-organization in cyber-physical-social systems: smart home cleaning scenario. *Procedia Cirp*, 30, 329-334.

15. Sanchez, L., Muoz, L., Galache, J. A., Sotres, P., Santana, J. R., Gutierrez, V., ... & Pfisterer, D. (2014). SmartSantander: IoT experimentation over a smart city testbed. *Computer Networks*, 61, 217-238.

16. Kang, L., Poslad, S., Wang, W., Li, X., Zhang, Y., & Wang, C. (2016, September). A public transport bus as a flexible mobile smart environment sensing platform for IoT. In 2016 12th International Conference on Intelligent Environments (IE) (pp. 1-8). IEEE.

17. Jin, J., Gubbi, J., Marusic, S., & Palaniswami, M. (2014). An information framework for creating a smart city through internet of things. IEEE Internet of Things journal, 1(2), 112-121.

18. Guo, W., Zhang, Y., & Li, L. (2015). The integration of CPS, CPSS, and ITS: A focus on data. *Tsinghua Science and Technology*, 20(4), 327-335.

19. Anantharam, P., Barnaghi, P., Thirunarayan, K., & Sheth, A. (2015). Extracting city traffic events from social streams. *ACM Transactions on Intelligent Systems and Technology (TIST)*, 6(4), 43.

20. Zhou, Y., De, S., & Moessner, K. (2016). Real world city event extraction from Twitter data streams. *Procedia computer science*, 98, 443-448.

21. Sakaki, T., Okazaki, M., & Matsuo, Y. (2010, April). Earthquake shakes Twitter users: real-time event detection by social sensors. In Proceedings of the 19th international conference on World wide web (pp. 851-860). ACM.

22. Guo, B., Wang, Z., Yu, Z., Wang, Y., Yen, N. Y., Huang, R., & Zhou, X. (2015). Mobile crowd sensing and computing: The review of an emerging human-powered sensing paradigm. *ACM Computing Surveys (CSUR)*, 48(1), 7.

23. Hehenberger, P., Vogel-Heuser, B., Bradley, D., Eynard, B., Tomiyama, T., & Achiche, S. (2016). Design, modelling, simulation and integration of cyber physical systems: Methods and applications. *Computers in Industry*, 82, 273-289.

24. Salim, F., & Haque, U. (2015). Urban computing in the wild: A survey on large scale participation and citizen engagement with ubiquitous computing, cyber physical systems, and Internet of Things. *International Journal of Human-Computer Studies*, 81, 31-48.

25. Qiao, C., Sadek, A. W., Hulme, K., & Wu, S. (2010). Addressing design and human factors challenges in cyber-transportation systems with an integrated traffic-driving-networking simulator. In Workshop, October (Vol. 28, p. 29).

26. Calabrese, F., Colonna, M., Lovisolo, P., Parata, D., & Ratti, C. (2011). Real-time urban monitoring using cell phones: A case study in Rome. *IEEE Transactions on Intelligent Transportation Systems*, 12(1), 141-151.

27. Lcu, F., Tallevi-Diotallevi, S., Hayes, J., Tucker, R., Bicer, V., Sbodio, M., & Tommasi, P. (2014). Smart traffic analytics in the semantic web with STAR-CITY: Scenarios, system and lessons learned in Dublin City. Web Semantics: Science, Services and Agents on the World Wide Web, 27, 26-33.

28. Le, D. N., Kumar, R., Mishra, B. K., Chatterjee, J. M., & Khari, M. (Eds.). (2019). *Cyber Security in Parallel and Distributed Computing: Concepts, Techniques, Applications and Case Studies*. John Wiley & Sons.

29. Konbattulwar, V., Velaga, N. R., Jain, S., & Sharmila, R. B. (2016). Development of in-vehicle noise prediction models for Mumbai Metropolitan Region, India. *Journal of Traffic and Transportation Engineering* (English Edition), 3(4), 380-387.

30. Deeshma, M., & Verma, A. (2015). Travel time modeling for bus transport system in Bangalore city. *Transportation Letters*, 7(1), 47-56.

31. Puiu, D., Barnaghi, P., Tnjes, R., Kmper, D., Ali, M. I., Mileo, A., ... & Gao, F. (2016). Citypulse: Large scale data analytics framework for smart cities. *IEEE Access*, 4, 1086-1108.

32. Sen, R. (2014, January). RasteyRishtey: A social incentive system to crowdsource road traffic information in developing regions. In 2014 Seventh International Conference on Mobile Computing and Ubiquitous Networking (ICMU) (pp. 171-176). IEEE.

33. Pandey, M. K., & Subbiah, K. (2016, December). Social networking and big data analytics assisted reliable recommendation system model for internet of vehicles. In International Conference on Internet of Vehicles (pp. 149-163). Springer, Cham.

34. Wan, J., Liu, J., Shao, Z., Vasilakos, A., Imran, M., & Zhou, K. (2016). Mobile crowd sensing for traffic prediction in internet of vehicles. *Sensors*, 16(1), 88.

35. Rajkumar, R., Lee, I., Sha, L., & Stankovic, J. (2010, June). Cyber-physical systems: the next computing revolution. In Design Automation Conference (pp. 731-736). IEEE.

36. Paul, M., Sanyal, G., Samanta, D., Nguyen, G. N., & Le, D. N. (2018). Admission control algorithm based on the effective bandwidth in vehicle-to-infrastructure communication. *IET Communications*, 12(6), 704-711.

37. Le, D. N., Kumar, R., Nguyen, G. N., & Chatterjee, J. M. (2018). *Cloud Computing and Virtualization*. John Wiley & Sons.

38. D'Andrea, E., Ducange, P., Lazzerini, B., & Marcelloni, F. (2015). Real-time detection of traffic from twitter stream analysis. *IEEE transactions on intelligent transportation systems*, 16(4), 2269-2283.

39. Garca-Romeo, D., Valero, M., Medrano, N., Calvo, B., & Celma, S. (2015). A high performance LIA-based interface for battery powered sensing devices. *Sensors*, 15(10), 25260-25276.

40. Hancke, G., Silva, B., & Hancke Jr, G. (2013). The role of advanced sensing in smart cities. *Sensors*, 13(1), 393-425.

41. Ilic, M. D., Xie, L., Khan, U. A., & Moura, J. M. (2008, July). Modeling future cyber-physical energy systems. In 2008 IEEE Power and Energy Society General Meeting-Conversion and Delivery of Electrical Energy in the 21st Century (pp. 1-9). IEEE.

42. Karsai, G., & Sztipanovits, J. (2008, October). Model-integrated development of cyber-physical systems. In IFIP International Workshop on Software Technolgies for Embedded and Ubiquitous Systems (pp. 46-54). Springer, Berlin, Heidelberg.

43. Lee, E. A. (2008, May). Cyber physical systems: Design challenges. In 2008 11th IEEE International Symposium on Object and Component-Oriented Real-Time Distributed Computing (ISORC) (pp. 363-369). IEEE.

44. Lee, E. A., & Seshia, S. A. (2016). *Introduction to embedded systems: A cyber-physical systems approach*. Mit Press.

45. Neema, H., Lattmann, Z., Meijer, P., Klingler, J., Neema, S., Bapty, T., ... & Karsai, G. (2014). Design space exploration and manipulation for cyber physical systems. In Workshop on Design Space Exploration of Cyber-Physical Systems (IDEAL').

CHAPTER 16

CYBERSPACE FOR SMART PARENTING WITH SENSORS

Alok Ranjan Prusty

Ministry of Skill Development and Entrepreneurship, Government of India, India
Email: dralokrprusty@gmail.com

Abstract

In today's highly competitive world, individuals are caught up in their work almost all of the time. In earlier times, parents, and especially mothers, took special care of their toddlers as they could be at home all the time. However, now this scenario has changed, and even mothers work both in and outside of the home for the sake of their families. The nuclear family these days doesn't leave anyone behind to take care of the toddlers after maternity leave. Hence, this leaves two options; either a day care center or an in-home caregiver. However, do the parents go to work hassle free? If this is the question, then the answer is no; because in the back of their minds they always worry about how their children are doing and constantly keep checking on them. In the professional world, keeping a constant check by calls becomes very difficult. Therefore, this chapter discusses smart ways to keep a check on the toddlers when away from them by using machine-to-machine (M2M) communication with sensors. Comparatively speaking, this helps working parents to be aware of the child's activities by sending processed data from the sensors to the parent. This chapter can be useful for research scholars, industries and all working parents. The project discussed in this chapter can be devised and modified further to solve the problem of keeping track of toddlers and a fully developed system with customized properties will help in designing a low-cost device for smart ways of parenting.

Keywords: Sensors, parenting, cloud, network, low power, M2M

16.1   Background

Over the decades, parenting has become more challenging because everyone is caught up in their work. Years ago the concept of parenting was different, with mothers staying at home to take care of the toddlers. Even if the mother was working, the rest of the family was around to take care of the children. This generation of parents are working and either hire a nanny or leave the child at a day care center. This problem can be alleviated if technology is used in the proper way. The idea of connected devices and sensor networks technology can be very helpful in collecting, processing and communicating data. In this chapter a detailed description is given of the recent developments in parenting applications; followed by a project to help readers, students and scholars have a better understanding of smart ways to parent; thereby helping the modern generation of parents take care of their children when they are not physically, but virtually, present. The condition of the child can be tracked down through the networked devices. The rest of the chapter is organized as follows: Section 16.2 begins with a discussion of the key concepts of the internet of things (IoT) used in this project, followed by steps taken and the working principle to implement this project in Section 16.3. Section 16.4 shows the results and analysis, followed by the conclusion in Section 16.5.

16.2   Internet of Things

In the present era, the use of technological skills and knowledge to improve the quality of life (QoL) is becoming a universal trend. One of the most important technological advancements is best known as the Internet of Things (IoT) [1]. The internet of things system [2] refers to the network of physical objects that is the set of devices and systems that are interconnected with sensors and actuators through wire or wireless medium, allowing and collecting information and managing physical items in the setup [1]. According to the Institute of Electrical and Electronics Engineers (IEEE), sensors can be defined as an electronic device that produces electrical, optical, or digital data derived from a physical condition or event. Data created from sensors is subsequently transformed, by one or more devices, and turned into information (output) which is useful in analysis, based on which decision making is carried out by "intelligent" devices or individuals (people) under the IoT setup [3]. IoT has a heterogeneous network, having IP and non-IP devices connected through IP Gateways. A huge amount of data will be generated by the sensors. Data analytics may be used to create intelligence, which may be further used for various operational and planning activities [4]. IoT applications include, but are not limited to, smart cars, wearable devices [5], human implanted devices, home automation systems [6], and smartphones, which are increasingly being used to measure the world around them. Similarly, wireless sensor networks (WSN) [7, 8] are special types of ad-hoc network which contain very tiny sensors that can be partially used as an IoT technology that is able to measure various parameters in disasters, like earthquakes, landslides, extreme weather, floods, tides and many more, for early prediction and rescue [9, 10]. The IoT will revolutionize and change the way all businesses, governments, and consumers interact with the physical world. This level of disruption will have a significant impact on the world in improving the quality of life [4]. Interestingly, the Cisco Research Center has revealed that in present-day society the number of internet-connected devices is greater than the number of people on Earth [11]; hence, the internet of things is considered a priority when it comes to solving different problem domains.

16.2.1 Machine to Machine

The IoT ecosystem may have M2M devices, gateways, M2M communication technologies, big data and process management, IoT platform, user interface (web, mobile, HMI) and end-to-end security. M2M refers to the technologies that allow wired or wireless system to communicate with devices of same ability. M2M uses a device (sensor, meter, etc.) to capture an "event" (motion, meter reading, temperature, etc.), which is relayed through a network (wireless, wired or hybrid) to an application (software program), that translates the captured event into meaningful information [4].

M2M has five basic components: 1) M2M Device, which is a device that is able to reply to a request for data present within that device [12]; 2) M2M Area Network, which offers interconnectivity among M2M devices and M2M gateways; 3) M2M Gateway, which has M2M capabilities to make sure M2M devices interwork at different hierarchical levels of M2M communication networks; 4) M2M Communication Networks, which provide the communications between the M2M gateway(s) and M2M application [13]; and 5) M2M Applications. These components are in charge of sensing, varied device access, information processing and applications and processing in comprehensive IoT design in different sectors like healthcare, smart robots, cyber transportation systems (CTS), manufacturing systems, smart home technologies, and smart grids [13]. A few more examples of M2M are in the field of industrial maintenance where it is essential to keep an eye on the temperature variation and vibrations of industrial motors in order to sense any irregular functions. Similarly, smart cars are the best way to not only reduce accidents but also save valuable time, reduce the stress of driving, etc. Another widely operated example is smart grid, an electrical grid which is intended to optimize the efficiency of power transmission and quality of service to the end-user. In this network, devices are mostly connected with sensors that repeatedly send the data related to power consumption to the central server that identifies the consumption pattern and amount of power transmission. Other sectors like healthcare, tourism, smart home, agriculture and many others have successfully implemented M2M and more research and development is going on in this field.

16.2.2 Smart Wearables

Wearables are devices incorporated into items which can be easily worn on the body. These devices mostly track information in real time. They have different tiny sensors on board that receive data in order to synchronize with mobile devices or computers. Presently, the smartphone market has given a boost to wearable electronics. Wearables appear in several different forms, targeting different accessories and clothing that people wear. Though small in size, they continuously sense, collect, and upload various physiological data [14] to improve quality of life. According to a report [15] by the International Data Corporation (IDC), the overall wearables market is expected to grow from 113.2 million shipments in 2017 to 222.3 million in 2021, with a compound annual growth rate (CAGR) of 18.4%, which will include intelligent clothing like step-counting shoes, smart jackets and smart earwear like fitness tracking wireless headphones, smart watches, wrist bands, smart glasses, smart jewelry, electronic garments, and so on [15, 16]. Recently, Levi's clothing company collaborated with Google to manufacture smart jackets that sync with a smartphone, assisting the user to play music on their phones, get call notifications and receive map directions with a single tap on the jacket [17]. Wu *et al.* described the implementation of a hybrid wearable sensor network system with wireless body area network (WBAN) for short-range wireless communication and a low power wide area network (LPWAN) for long-distance data transmission [18]. The nearby body sensors collect the environmental and physiological data and transmit it to local servers for processing through the IoT gateway node, which if further transmitted to remote servers sometimes called cloud server, to provide different, more intense IoT applications. In the past few years, a large variety of wearables have hit the market. There are two key aspects to the IoT in connection to wearable device development, which are the devices themselves and the server side architecture that supports them [19].

16.2.3 Smart Parenting

As we are entering a wearable era and new technology is being developed every day, some of these gadgets actually could be useful to monitor several behaviors of your kids in order to keep an eye on them. The inspiration for smart wearables for kids arose from the growing need for safety for little children in current times, as there could be scenarios of the child getting lost or harmed in large, crowded areas and many others [19]. Al-Mazloum et al. proposed a GPS- and SMS-based child tracking system using a smartphone [20]. The parent tracks the location of the child through a real-time map. The parent app sends a SMS to find the location of the child through his/her phone. Information like location coordinate and time will be sent to the parent through SMS, and based on that information the location is displayed on the map. Jain et al. proposed an Android-based tracking application [21]. If the parent needs to know the location of the child, the parent sends a message to the child; this message contains a secret code, which is automatically detected by the mobile device and sent to the users location without turning on the GPS. Jatti et al. proposed a programmable device that is programmed to continuously monitor distinguishing parameters in terms of relationship between stress and skin resistance, stress and body temperature, and the system will take action when any unsafe situation presents itself [22]. It does so by detecting the change in the monitored signals, following which appropriate action is taken by means of sending notifications to designated individuals. A child tracking system is extensively used everywhere to assure parents that their wards are safe and their child is happy at his/her place [23, 24]. Quick response to a child's need and their constant monitoring, up to the age of 18 months, is a prerequisite and essential in parenting. A little carelessness on the part of parents can cost a lot [25, 26].

There have been a lot of deaths as well as accidents reported in the Middle East, as well as around the world, such as children falling off balconies, playing with guns, putting their hands into live sockets, falling into buckets filled with water and so on. These kinds of misfortunes could be avoided if there was something to continuously monitor the activities of the child [27]. These kinds of events and possibilities motivate us to develop a Child Care System, also called smart parenting, where an automated device serves as a parenting aid for parents who are finding it difficult to attend to their children for any reason such as cooking, household chores, office work and others. However, it cannot be a replacement for the parents, but rather supports them [28, 29]. Currently, many popular baby monitoring systems have been developed that allow parents to monitor their child through motion and sound. As of now, parenting or baby care systems are mostly helpful in situations where the baby is confined to its crib or when the baby is asleep; that is, at early stages of development. Many studies are being conducted to develop devices by which the parent can constantly look at the baby monitor in order to know what their child is doing [30]. NICU (neonatal intensive care unit) is a device for children who are able to crawl or walk; thus, helping parents keep track of them. NICU has been designed as a device which can be an assistant to the parent, following the child and automatically alerting the parent so that the child does not wander off to unsafe areas around the house [25]. In [31] the author has covered various topics such as tracking and monitoring of baby or people with special needs, including making a mobile application to keep track of various parameters like temperature, lighting condition, humidity and others.

16.2.4 Accelerometer Sensor

An accelerometer is an electromechanical device that records acceleration forces. These forces may be static, like the constant force of gravity, or dynamic, to sense motion [32]. The three-axis accelerometer widely used in many complex applications can determine the movement in a three-dimensional space. They are worn to find the movement of a person and to find the stress level at different positions as well [32]. Accelerometer-based wearables are very useful in keeping information about personal activities and their energy depletion in many applications such as medical and rehabilitation, movement recognition, older adults, sports, positioning, and others. Cai *et al.* discussed an application for muscular movement recognition and physiological signals to detect disorders like Parkinson's disease and others [33]. Gesture and movement recognition is a widely researched field concerning devices based on wearable accelerometers [29, 34-40]. Urmat and Yaln proposed and implemented an embedded system to assess the pedestrian walking position [41]. Oliver *et al.* explored the utility of accelerometers for determining sitting time in office workers [42].

16.2.5 Pulse Sensor

A pulse sensor fits over a fingertip and uses the quantity of infrared light reflected by the blood circulating inside. During the normal functioning of the body, the heart pumps blood, hence pressure rises sharply; accordingly the quantity of infrared light from the emitter gets reflected back to the detector. This method uses both transmittance and reflectance principles. It is a non-invasive, precise and cost-effective way to measure pulse rate or heart rate [43]. These sensors track a person's heart rate three minutes out of n hours; with the help of heart rate variability (HRV) [44]. The main method that most of these devices require to detect stress is the HRV, which is important for investigating parasympathetic and sympathetic functions of the autonomous nervous system [45]. Parasympathetic function is responsible when the body is at rest, and sympathetic function is in charge when the body responds to stressors [46].

16.3 Project

This project discusses the concept of using a smart way to keep a check on toddlers when away. This can be done by the use of the internet of things (IoT) and allied technologies with sensors using Arduino, gyro sensors, accelerometers, GSR sensors and others. The activities of the toddler and, in turn, the extracted data, pop a notification to the parents, saying they are needed. The different sensors are used for different purposes such as to detect if the child falls off something, or it will detect the heartbeat to notify the parent without making any actual decision or judgement on what happened. This helps the parent to be aware of the approximate activities of the child. The sensors are connected to Arduino, which in turn is connected to the cloud. The data from the sensors sent to the cloud and the processed data will then be sent to the user/parent through email. Thus, the user gets an approximate account of the activities of their young ones [47-50].

As mentioned in [31], the fall detection wearable can be used to monitor whether the user of the same is safe or has fallen down. This particularly can be used for infants, elderly people or for those with a medical condition. The threshold or orientation of the accelerometer is set and when the accelerometer falls and the heartbeat sensor detects something unusual, the system sends a message to the respective person. The Arduino Nano board, with a very low operating voltage, is used along with an ATmega328P processor [26].

The details are described with specifications in Table 16.1.

Table 16.1   Component specifications and use.

Sl. No	Component Used	Specification	Use
1	Arduino Nano	• Micro Controller ATmega328 operating voltage 5V • I/P Voltage 7-12V • Digital I/O pins 14 • Analog i/p pins 8 • Flash Memory 32kb • Clock Speed 16MHz.	Small compact device used for taking inputs and turn into output with the help of code.
2	Pulse Sensor	• Operating voltage: 3.3V – 5V • Current: 4mA • Indicator LED	Used to sense the heartbeat when placed on fingertip or back of earlobe or any capillary tissue.
3	Accelerometer	• 3-axis sensing. • Very low power. • Operating Voltage- 1.8V to 3.6V • 10,000 shock survival • Precise in size (4 mm ×4 mm ×1.45 mm)	This component is used to detect the change in orientation from the saved state so as to detect if the user has fallen.

The device's main aim is to notify the parent if the child is safe or in any kind of trouble. There are many possible ways to ensure the safety of the child. The device operates when it senses the heartbeat of the child. Furthermore, it keeps tracking the heartbeat, i.e., the pulse rate, of the child continuously. The tracking of the pulse rate helps the remotely present parent or guardian to ensure that their child is in safe hands or in normal condition. A change in the pulse rate other than the required rate will indicate an abnormal situation. The parent will be notified of any change. This notification is sent to the parent in a very simple way. The device is connected to an android application called Blynk at the time of installation. Blynk is a dynamic platform which can run on Android and iOS, which runs over the internet to control Arduino and other such devices. Blynk helps the device to get online irrespective of the type of internet connection and thus the internet of things is implemented. It has a very interactive interface which can be easily used. The data from the remote hardware device can be displayed and stored using this platform. The major components of the platform are the application, library and server. The Blynk cloud is an open source and can be used to create a private local server. The connection is as simple as clicking a button and the connection is done with the remote device [28]. The work of the device doesn't end here. The parent/guardian should be aware that their child is safe and sound, and this device allows them to properly check on the child. The use of an accelerometer in the device will notify the parent if the child falls down.

The block diagram of the project is shown in Figure 16.1. This device keeps track of the above-mentioned activities and then notifies the parent when the situation becomes abnormal. The working mechanism of the device is discussed in detail in the following section.

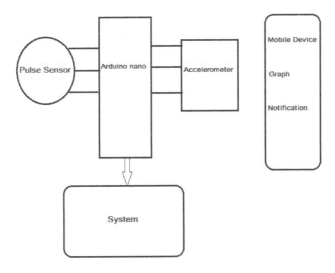

Figure 16.1   Block diagram of the project.

16.4   Steps and Working Principle

The project follows the steps as discussed in the following section. An Arduino board has been used in this project (Figure 16.2). For the detection of the heartbeat a pulse sensor has been connected and for fall detection the setup has been connected to a low power accelerometer.

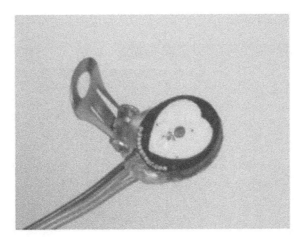

Figure 16.2   Pulse sensor.

The pulse sensor's S point is connected to the analog A_0 pin of Arduino, + is connected to the 5V pin and − is connected to the GND pin of the Arduino. The pulse sensor can sense the pulse from fingertip or back of the ear. The accelerometer is a very sensitive low power device. It detects if the child falls down and notifies the parent through the mobile application. The VCC of the accelerometer is connected to a very low 3.3V. The Ref or Aref pin of Arduino to 3.3 V has been connected because it has connected Vcc of accelerometer to 3.3V. The GND is connected to the board's GND. The x_out, y_out and z_out pins are connected to A_1, A_2, and A_6 pins of the board. The orientation of the accelerometer is maintained to mark the fall if caused.

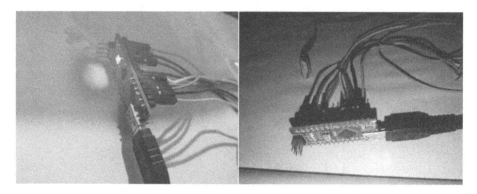

Figure 16.3   Aurdino Nano setup with sensors.

The pulse sensor (Figure 16.3) and the accelerometer are connected to the Arduino board which in turn is connected to the system. The coding has been done for the same and uploaded to the board. The data collected is sent to the cloud via the Blynk application. One can track the data on the application and the notification when required.

16.5   Result and Analysis

The experiment is performed (as shown in Figure 16.4) as per the method described in the distinguishing sections above.

Figure 16.4   IoT experiment.

The pulse sensor's action was tested by keeping the sensor on the tip of the finger. It takes a few seconds to read the heartbeats per second properly. The generated data is represented in the graph. The orientation of the accelerometer is maintained. When the accelerometer is given a jerk, it doesn't notify the parent/guardian that the child/baby has fallen, maintaining its peculiarity. Only when the orientation changes and accelerometer flips down completely from its original position, is the parent/guardian notified that "Your baby has just FALLEN".

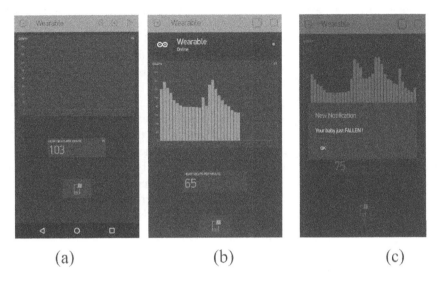

(a)   (b)   (c)

Figure 16.5   Experiment results on smartphone.

Figure 16.5 shows the different results as described. The above figure shows the layout of the data to be displayed. The first section will display the graph by recording the heartbeat rate of the ward. The second section displays the heartbeats per minute. And the last section displays the notification when a fall is detected.

(a) This figure displays the layout where the data is to be displayed. The play button on top right corner starts the retrieval of data when the device is online.

(b) This figure shows that the device is online. It also shows the graph as per the heartbeat sensed by the sensor.

(c) This figure shows the notification when the baby falls, i.e., the accelerometer falls or its orientation changes.

The device can be tested on any infant and will show the desired result. This device can further be implemented as a wearable by making it precise. It can also be modified to be used on the elderly. Although there are many concepts on child tracking [39, 40] and fall detection of elderly people [23], this project provides a whole new concept. Stated in the paper by Lee *et al.* [29], Owlet Baby Monitor is a device which is used to monitor a baby via a wearable (half open sock) and also a video camera. This device helps maintain insights into the regular activities of the baby. However, there have been complaints about the discomfort and muscular reactions of a few babies while using the monitor. But the designed device will also detect if the child falls down or not. It notifies the parent/guardian of the event via the mobile application. This is not only usable for working parents but also for housewives to track the baby's activity when they are busy doing any work at home and away from baby. Due to the use of low cost and low power components in this project the size and battery requirements will be minimized in different applications if used.

16.6 Conclusions

This chapter has shed light on the use of the internet of things (IoT) and machine-to-machine (M2M) communication in connection with wearables for smart parenting, which will be helpful for readers and researchers who develop applications and smart devices that will be helpful for all the working parents to keep track of their toddlers. The project has been designed in a way to detect if the child's pulse rate is normal. In addition to that, it will also detect and notify in case the child falls down. By instrumenting the Arduino Nano, accelerometer and pulse sensor together the device is coded to function. This project has been tested for its basic function. This device will be really helpful to all the working parents to keep a check on their young ones. The safety of the child is every parent's first concern, no matter whom they are left with. This device helps ensure that the ward is in proper hands. With further implementation the design can be modified to have additional features as well as made into a compact one to be one precise wearable. Although this device is used for watching children, it also applies to elderly people or patients. A fully developed system with customized properties will help in designing a low cost device for smart ways to parent.

REFERENCES

1. Yaqoob, I., Hashem, I. A. T., Ahmed, A., Kazmi, S. A., & Hong, C. S. (2019). Internet of things forensics: Recent advances, taxonomy, requirements, and open challenges. *Future Generation Computer Systems*, 92, 265-275.

2. Dorsemaine, B., Gaulier, J. P., Wary, J. P., Kheir, N., & Urien, P. (2015, September). Internet of things: a definition & taxonomy. In 2015 9th International Conference on Next Generation Mobile Applications, Services and Technologies (pp. 72-77). IEEE.

3. https://datafloq.com/read/5-components-iot-implementation-challenges/1860] retrieved on dt. 16/01/2019

4. [http://tec.gov.in/pdf/M2M/Communication%20Technologies%20in%20IoT%20domain.pdf] Technical paper retrieved on dt. 16/01/2019

5. Moustafa, H., Kenn, H., Sayrafian, K., Scanlon, W., & Zhang, Y. (2015). Mobile wearable communications [Guest Editorial]. *IEEE Wireless Communications*, 22(1), 10-11.

6. Nasrin, S., & Radcliffe, P. J. (2014, November). Novel protocol enables DIY home automation. In 2014 Australasian Telecommunication Networks and Applications Conference (ATNAC) (pp. 212-216). IEEE.

7. Prusty, A. R., Sethi, S., & Nayak, A. K. (2016). A hybrid multi-hop mobility assisted heterogeneous energy efficient cluster routing protocol for wireless ad hoc sensor networks. *Journal of High Speed Networks*, 22(4), 265-280.

8. Nayyar, A., Puri, V., & Le, D. N. (2019). Comprehensive analysis of routing protocols surrounding underwater sensor networks (UWSNs). In *Data Management, Analytics and Innovation* (pp. 435-450). Springer, Singapore.

9. Prusty, A. R., & Mohanty, A. (2019). Prospect of Low Power Sensor Network Technology in Disaster Management for Sustainable Future. In *Emergency and Disaster Management: Concepts, Methodologies, Tools, and Applications* (pp. 834-856). IGI Global.. doi:10.4018/978-1-5225-3194-4.ch007

10. Silva, F. A. (2014). Industrial wireless sensor networks: applications, protocols, and standards [book news]. *IEEE Industrial Electronics Magazine*, 8(4), 67-68.

11. Evans, D. (2012). The Internet of Things how the next evolution of the internet is changing everything (april 2011). White Paper by Cisco Internet Business Solutions Group (IBSG).

12. Chen, M., Wan, J., & Li, F. (2012). Machine-to-machine communications: Architectures, standards and applications. *Ksii transactions on internet & information systems*, 6(2).

13. Shah, S. H., & Yaqoob, I. (2016, August). A survey: Internet of Things (IOT) technologies, applications and challenges. In 2016 IEEE Smart Energy Grid Engineering (SEGE) (pp. 381-385). IEEE.

14. Sahoo, R., & Sethi, S. (2015). Remotely functional-analysis of mental stress based on gsr sensor physiological data in wireless environment. In Information Systems Design and Intelligent Applications (pp. 569-577). Springer, New Delhi. DOI: https://doi.org/10.1007/978-81-322-2247-7_58

15. https://www.idc.com/getdoc.jsp?containerId=prUS43408517] retrieved on dt 18/01/2019

16. Seneviratne, S., Hu, Y., Nguyen, T., Lan, G., Khalifa, S., Thilakarathna, K., ... & Seneviratne, A. (2017). A survey of wearable devices and challenges. *IEEE Communications Surveys & Tutorials*, 19(4), 2573-2620. DOI: 10.1109/COMST.2017.2731979

17. https://www.ness.com/smart-wearables-the-present-and-the-future/] report on dt. 16/08/2018 retrieved on dt 18/01/2019

18. Wu, F., Wu, T., & Yuce, M. (2019). An Internet-of-Things (IoT) Network System for Connected Safety and Health Monitoring Applications. *Sensors*, 19(1), 21.

19. Moodbidri, A., & Shahnasser, H. (2017, January). Child safety wearable device. In 2017 International Conference on Information Networking (ICOIN) (pp. 438-444). IEEE.

20. Al-Mazloum, A., Omer, E., & Abdullah, M. F. A. (2013). GPS and SMS-based child tracking system using smart phone. *Int. J. Electr. Comput. Electron. Commun.* Eng, 7(2), 171-174.

21. Jain, A., Mudgil, P., Dabla, R., & Satapathy, K. (2014). Android Based Tracking Application-DOPE HUNT. *International Journal of Soft Computing and Engineering (IJSCE)*, 4(14), 38-41.

22. Jatti, A., Kannan, M., Alisha, R. M., Vijayalakshmi, P., & Sinha, S. (2016, May). Design and development of an IOT based wearable device for the safety and security of women and girl children. In 2016 IEEE International Conference on Recent Trends in Electronics, Information & Communication Technology (RTEICT) (pp. 1108-1112). IEEE. DOI: 10.1109/RTEICT.2016.7808003.

23. G.R. Patil, Subham Kumar Sharma, Vikas Kumar Lathar & VipulTiwari, Arduino Based Fall Detection and Tracking of Elderly, *Imperial Journal of Interdisciplinary Research (IJIR)*, Vol-2, Issue-7, 2016, ISSN: 2454-1362.

24. Satish, M., Nandlal, C., & Sandip, G. (2015). Child Tracking System using Android phones. *International Journal of Advanced Research in Computer Engineering & Technology (IJARCET)*, 4(4).

25. Joshi, N. S., Kamat, R. K., & Gaikwad, P. K. (2013). Development of wireless monitoring system for neonatal intensive care unit. *International Journal of Advanced Computer Research*, 3(3), 106.

26. https://www.arduino.cc/en/Products/Compare, [retrieved on 29.09.2017]

27. RAJ, P. S., & ANURADHA, V. (2014). Design and Implementation of Children Tracking System using ARM7 on Android Mobile Terminals. *International Journal of Scientific Engineering and Technology Research*, ISSN: 2319-8885.

28. Doshi, H. S., Shah, M. S., & Shaikh, U. S. A. (2017). Internet Of Things (Iot): Integration Of Blynk For Domestic Usability. *Vishwakarma Journal of Engineering Research*, 1(4).

29. Lee, J. M., Newman, M. W., Gebremariam, A., Choi, P., Lewis, D., Nordgren, W., ... & Hannemann, C. (2017). Real-world use and self-reported health outcomes of a patient-designed do-it-yourself mobile technology system for diabetes: lessons for mobile health. *Diabetes technology & therapeutics*, 19(4), 209-219.

30. Garcia, J. E., & Torres, R. A. (2013, April). Telehealth mobile system. In 2013 Pan American Health Care Exchanges (PAHCE) (pp. 1-5). IEEE.

31. Shuo, C. (2015, May). Fall detection system using arduino fio. In Proceedings of the IRC Conference on Science, Engineering and Technology, Singapore (Vol. 13).

32. Thapliyal, H., Khalus, V., & Labrado, C. (2017). Stress detection and management: A survey of wearable smart health devices. *IEEE Consumer Electronics Magazine*, 6(4), 64-69.

33. Cai, F., Yi, C., Liu, S., Wang, Y., Liu, L., Liu, X., ... & Wang, L. (2016). Ultrasensitive, passive and wearable sensors for monitoring human muscle motion and physiological signals. *Biosensors and Bioelectronics*, 77, 907-913.

34. Nguyen, M., Fan, L., & Shahabi, C. (2015, November). Activity recognition using wrist-worn sensors for human performance evaluation. In 2015 IEEE International Conference on Data Mining Workshop (ICDMW) (pp. 164-169). IEEE.

35. San-Segundo, R., Lorenzo-Trueba, J., Martnez-Gonzlez, B., & Pardo, J. M. (2016). Segmenting human activities based on HMMs using smartphone inertial sensors. *Pervasive and Mobile Computing*, 30, 84-96.

36. Park, J. S., Robinovitch, S., & Kim, W. S. (2016). A wireless wristband accelerometer for monitoring of rubber band exercises. *IEEE Sensors Journal*, 16(5), 1143-1150.

37. Sheehan, K. J., Greene, B. R., Cunningham, C., Crosby, L., & Kenny, R. A. (2014). Early identification of declining balance in higher functioning older adults, an inertial sensor based method. Gait & posture, 39(4), 1034-1039.

38. Van Lummel, R. C., Ainsworth, E., Lindemann, U., Zijlstra, W., Chiari, L., Van Campen, P., & Hausdorff, J. M. (2013). Automated approach for quantifying the repeated sit-to-stand using one body fixed sensor in young and older adults. Gait & posture, 38(1), 153-156.

39. Pawade, R. H., & Gaikwad, A. N. (2015). Android Based Children Tracking System. *International Journal of Science, Engineering and Technology Research (IJSETR)*, 4(6), 2088-2092.

40. Delahoz, Y., & Labrador, M. (2014). Survey on fall detection and fall prevention using wearable and external sensors. *Sensors*, 14(10), 19806-19842. doi:10.3390/s141019806

41. Urmat, S., & Yaln, M. E. (2015, November). Design and implementation of an ARM based embedded system for pedestrian dead reckoning. In 2015 9th International Conference on Electrical and Electronics Engineering (ELECO) (pp. 885-889). IEEE.

42. Oliver, M., Schofield, G. M., Badland, H. M., & Shepherd, J. (2010). Utility of accelerometer thresholds for classifying sitting in office workers. *Preventive medicine*, 51(5), 357-360.

43. Mallick, B., & Patro, A. K. (2016). Heart rate monitoring system using finger tip through arduino and processing software. *International Journal of Science, Engineering and Technology Research (IJSETR)*, 5(1), 84-89.

44. [https://www.kickstarter.com/projects/839690415/the-wellbe-the-worlds-first-stress-therapy-bracele] retrieved on dt. 21-01-2019

45. Ghamari, M., Soltanpur, C., Cabrera, S., Romero, R., Martinek, R., & Nazeran, H. (2016, August). Design and prototyping of a wristband-type wireless photoplethysmographic device

for heart rate variability signal analysis. In 2016 38th Annual International Conference of the IEEE Engineering in Medicine and Biology Society (EMBC) (pp. 4967-4970). IEEE.

46. [http://www.liveoakacupuncture.com/ ans-analysis/] retrieved on dt. 21-01-2019

47. Azimi, I., Rahmani, A. M., Liljeberg, P., & Tenhunen, H. (2017). Internet of things for remote elderly monitoring: a study from user-centered perspective. *Journal of Ambient Intelligence and Humanized Computing*, 8(2), 273-289. DOI: 10.1007/s12652-016-0387-y

48. Mahmud, M. S., Wang, H., Esfar-E-Alam, A. M., & Fang, H. (2017). A wireless health monitoring system using mobile phone accessories. *IEEE Internet of Things Journal*, 4(6), 2009-2018.

49. Le, D. N., Kumar, R., Mishra, B. K., Chatterjee, J. M., & Khari, M. (Eds.). (2019). *Cyber Security in Parallel and Distributed Computing: Concepts, Techniques, Applications and Case Studies*. John Wiley & Sons.

50. Ray, P. P. (2018). A survey on Internet of Things architectures. *Journal of King Saud University-Computer and Information Sciences*, 30(3), 291-319.

9 781119 592266